PERUVIAN LIVES
ACROSS BORDERS

Peruvian Lives across Borders

Power, Exclusion, and Home

M. CRISTINA ALCALDE

Urbana, Chicago, and Springfield

© 2018 by the Board of Trustees
of the University of Illinois
All rights reserved
1 2 3 4 5 C P 5 4 3 2 1
♾ This book is printed on acid-free paper.

Library of Congress Cataloging-in-Publication Data
Names: Alcalde, M. Cristina, author.
Title: Peruvian lives across borders : power, exclusion, and home / M. Cristina Alcalde.
Description: Urbana : University of Illinois Press, [2018] | Includes bibliographical references and index.
Identifiers: LCCN 2017056068| ISBN 9780252041846 (hardback) | ISBN 9780252083464 (paperback)
Subjects: LCSH: Peruvians—Foreign countries. | Return migration--Peru. | Group identity—Peru. | Peru—Emigration and immigration—Social aspects. | BISAC: HISTORY / Latin America / South America. | SOCIAL SCIENCE / Women's Studies. | SOCIAL SCIENCE / Emigration & Immigration.
Classification: LCC JV7511 .A33 2018 | DDC 305.868/85—dc23 LC record available at https://lccn.loc.gov/2017056068

A mi familia, who provide me
with my sense of home . . .

CONTENTS

Acknowledgments ix

Introduction: Transnational Lives: Home, Privilege, and Exclusion 1

Chapter 1: Privilege, Racialization, and Exclusionary Cosmopolitanism in Transnational Trajectories 34

Chapter 2: Gendering Return: From Middle-Class Señoras to Migrants without Domestic Help, and Back 68

Chapter 3: Gendering Everyday Violence and *Seguridad* across Spaces 91

Chapter 4: Heteronormativity, Homophobia, and Home 118

Chapter 5: The Taste of Home: Nostalgia, Pride, and the Limits of Inclusion 142

Conclusion: Persistent Hierarchies and Transnational Lives 165

Notes 173

Bibliography 185

Index 207

ACKNOWLEDGMENTS

Research specifically for this book began just a few years ago, but the topics themselves and my research and interest in Peru and migration have a much longer history. It is impossible to list all the people, places, opportunities, and forms of support that have made this book possible, but here I attempt to include at least some of these.

My parents, Pilar Vargas and Xavier Alcalde, would tell me as a child who complained about moving around so much that I would one day be thankful for all these moves and the new homes and new people the moves involved. All these years later I still can't say I'm mostly thankful for the moves, but I recognize with much more certainty that my experiencing different ways of seeing the world early on made possible my finding anthropology a good fit in college and later deciding to focus on topics that eventually led to this book. My mother, father, brother, and sister (Pilar, Xavier, Gonzalo, and Gabriela) were my first and constant home amid movement across borders, and I am incredibly thankful that they are my family. Although I did not interview my parents for this book, they remain the most important return migrants in my life.

As a parent myself, I am also very thankful to my children, Santiago and Emilio, for being part of their lives and for keeping me grounded. I am very fortunate to have my smart, caring, generous and supportive spouse, Joe O'Neil, as a partner in this rich, complicated journey together. Gonzalo, Gabriela, Rob, Nico, Lucas, Paula, and Dan also remind me of how important transnational ties are, and I am grateful to have them all as family and in my life.

Contacting and asking people to meet with you for research can be a difficult, tricky process. Meeting someone who wants to know more about your life for their research can also be challenging and requires setting aside time that could be spent on other important things. I am profoundly grateful to every person who met and spoke with me in Lima, Munich, Toronto, and different cities in the United States for their time and graciousness and for sharing their experiences with me. I am also very grateful to everyone who completed the online survey.

At the University of Kentucky I have been fortunate to have supportive colleagues both in and outside my department. The College of Arts & Sciences has provided support at various points, making research for this book possible. The Gender and Women's Studies Department has been an ideal and supportive home in which to pursue my research interests; the Social Theory Program provided me with the opportunity to team-teach a graduate seminar that touched on several of the topics in this book; and the Latin American, Caribbean, and Latino Studies Program has provided me with opportunities to share my research with both colleagues and students working in the same regions of the world as I do. The College of Arts & Sciences provided two Summer Research Fellowships that allowed me to travel to and spend time in Peru, Germany, and Canada for this book project. The Marie Rich Endowment also provided me with funds to facilitate research for this book.

In Lima, my time as an invited visiting professor in the Gender Studies Program at the Pontificia Universidad Católica del Perú during the summer of 2013 provided me with a perfect opportunity to extend my stay in Lima and begin interviews for this project. I am grateful to Fanni Muñoz, director of the Gender Studies Program, for inviting me. During my time in Lima, my parents' support and the support of Margarita Quispe were invaluable in helping me have the time I needed to conduct research, getting my children to and from school, keeping them happy, fed, and safe, and providing us all with a home in Lima.

I am indebted to several colleagues for their insightful feedback on earlier versions of book chapters. In particular, Sarah Lyon, Kristin Monroe, and Karen Rignall, who read parts of the manuscript, provided support and very helpful feedback as I worked on this project. I am also thankful to Srimati Basu, Lisa Bjorkman, and Karl Swinehart for comments on an earlier version of the introduction. Other colleagues who have helped me think through this research at conferences and other venues include Florence Babb, Pascha Bueno-Hansen, and Sylvanna Falcón. Florence Babb in particular provided very helpful, constructive feedback on the manuscript and has been a source of much appreciated collegiality and support as my research has developed. I am also thankful for the feedback and suggestions received from a second anonymous reviewer. At the University of Illinois

Press, I could not have asked for a better editor than Marika Christofides. I am also very grateful to Dawn Durante at the University of Illinois Press for her encouragement and to Mary M. Hill for copyediting. Thank you to everyone who contributed to this project. All mistakes remain my own.

PERUVIAN LIVES
ACROSS BORDERS

INTRODUCTION

Transnational Lives
Home, Privilege, and Exclusion

Sitting on a sofa in his cozy living room in a bright Surco apartment during the Lima winter of 2013, Marco describes himself as open-minded and tolerant of others with different backgrounds and beliefs. He and Chabela, his wife, decided a few years earlier to return to Lima to be closer to family and to make Lima home for their children. He attributes his open-mindedness to his exposure to and daily interactions with persons from different backgrounds during close to two decades in the United States. Marco then confides in me that he regrets that he has again embraced racist attitudes and behaviors since returning to live in Lima, concluding that "Peru has made me racist." He describes how in his everyday life in Lima seeing people "urinate on the streets, throw bottles on the streets, they insult you, take the gun out, they go in to rob" contributes to the everyday insecurity he and his family experience and to the change in his views. Referring to his racialized descriptions of those who litter, yell, and commit crimes, toward the end of the interview I asked, "And why do you think the people you are describing are always cholos [of mestizo-indigenous background] or black?" "Why are they cholos? Because they are people who live outside of Lima, [and] they have very little education, that's all," Marco replied.

Marco's descriptions of the behaviors and attitudes of Peruvians whom he considers to threaten his family's well-being underscore both his family's sense of insecurity and his belief that some racialized Peruvians refuse to or are incapable of belonging to the more educated, cosmopolitan world he and his family inhabit in Lima. This is a sentiment echoed in many of the narratives I heard from middle- and upper-class transnational Peruvians who described themselves as open-minded and tolerant. It was a preliminary analysis of these narratives that I planned to present at a conference two years later and seven thousand miles away in Zagreb, Croatia, in the summer of 2015. Zagreb was a relatively short train ride from Munich, my family's temporary summer home where I planned to meet and interview Peruvians about their life in Germany. It was also the farthest from Lima I had presented research related to this book.

On that first night in Zagreb, I pulled the white curtains back and opened the heavy window to let air into the hot, stuffy hotel room. Looking down from the sixth floor of my hotel, I saw a band playing in Jelacica Square. To my surprise, the words and music to "La flor de la canela," the most well known Peruvian waltz, filled the room.[1] I took a deep, slow breath and felt nostalgic, comforted, and grateful all at once through the sounds, sights, and smells of homes—imagined, far, and near. These were the sorts of associations with home I had carried with me as my family and I had emigrated from Peru when I was a child, even as in the back-and-forth between the United States and Peru I had added other symbols to my repertoire of home.

The next day, during a brisk walk to the hotel, I spotted a man with a brightly colored red, orange, and purple "Hecho en Perú" (Made in Peru] woven textile bag across his chest, standing a few feet ahead of me. I stopped suddenly and automatically blurted out, "¿Son peruanos?" (Are you Peruvian?) to him and his companion. "¡Sí!" they responded, a little surprised. "Soy peruana" (I'm Peruvian), I offered, and the three of us instantly took a step toward each other. Smiling, one of the men initially commented that "no pareces" (you don't look it), which I awkwardly attempted to brush aside by joking about the clothes I was wearing and the circumstances surrounding my stay in the city. For the next twenty minutes, standing in sunny, windy downtown Zagreb, I learned about the two men's lives. They had emigrated from Peru to Brazil years earlier, and they now studied and lived in Brazil. They had traveled to Croatia for a conference, on the other side of the country and a week earlier, and were enjoying a few days of leisure as tourists before returning to Brazil when I ran into them. We commiserated about how we missed certain foods and family and about the next time we each hoped to be in Peru. I asked them about their plans to return to Peru. Less than twenty-four hours in Croatia, a country with a very small immigrant population (and one predominantly from neighboring countries of the former Yugoslavia), and I had already stumbled on connections to Peru twice.

Migrants experience complicated and sometimes unexpected relationships to home, as Marco's and the Zagreb experiences suggest.[2] This book is not solely about Marco's return migration to Lima, nor is it about my own migration story of back and forth between Peru and the United States, with short stays elsewhere, yet Marco's views and my short stay in Zagreb echo several themes middle- and upper-class Peruvians discussed with me in speaking of their transnational lives and connections to Peru, whether in Zagreb, Munich, Toronto, Austin, Lima, or other settings I visited during research for this book. These themes include longing for family and home; gendered, racialized, and class identities; danger and security; connections among Peruvians abroad; language issues; music, food, and other symbols of home; national identity; and return.

Placing in critical dialogue claims of openness and tolerance with Peruvian gender-racial-class hierarchies, I examine the limits of belonging constructed by transnational Peruvians from social classes that have historically held social power and the role of the policing of borders and exclusionary practices in this form of cosmopolitan belonging. I am referring here to the sort of self-identification of openness Marco embodies coupled with the racial and class hierarchies his comments underscore in the lives of Peruvians whose international mobility is facilitated by middle- and upper-class status and attachments to multiple homes, such as in my case and those of the two Peruvian men I met in Zagreb. At its core, this book argues that to claim belonging is to exclude and that transnational middle- and upper-class Peruvians engage in subtle and more direct policing of borders of belonging even when there are no physical borders as a way to claim and maintain social status—even as they too experience exclusion because of their racialization, language skills, or accent. This form of exclusionary belonging relies on local configurations of power based on the politics of class, race, gender, and sexual identity in Peru, yet it aspires to and commonly includes claims of openness and tolerance across borders. Critical engagements with various dimensions of everyday life among transnational Peruvians in the following chapters examine how individuals negotiate and seek to maintain socioeconomic status and cultural capital grounded in local Peruvian configurations of power within transnational fields and through cosmopolitan aspirations.

Marco's self-identification and comments and my experience in Zagreb underline some of the assumptions about unspoken differences and identities that these sorts of transnational experiences and policing involve and the value of an intersectional approach to Peruvian transnational lives. Against a complex web of Peruvian racial-class-gender hierarchies even a brief meeting thousands of miles away from Peru can be informed by very real (to Peru) markers of status. It was also status markers that Marco's racialization of dangerous others points to, as they make clear who belongs in and who should be excluded from open, tolerant spaces. In Zagreb, resources associated with middle-class status allowed the two men and me to travel to Croatia as academics and tourists. Earlier in our migration trajectories, it was middle-class status, educational attainment, and language skills as native Spanish speakers fluent in other languages that facilitated emigration from Peru. During my return visits to Lima, my shared middle-class status with those I interviewed also likely facilitated their openness toward me and my access to them—a topic I turn to later in this section.

Shared middle-class status is only part of the picture, however. Peruvian racial-class hierarchies that cross borders can also inform initial perceptions of one another among Peruvians. The men in Zagreb were both mestizo and significantly shorter than me, and in recognizing Peruvian textiles in their outerwear I did not hesitate to assume they could be Peruvian. One man's remark that "no pareces" when I identified as Peruvian was similarly likely specifically directed at my racialization based on my physical appearance (tall, lighter skin). At that moment, affective attachments—an area I return to shortly—to my own constructions of Peru as home informed my decision to assert my deeply held identity as Peruvian by dismissing his comment as I pointed to a more superficial aspect of my appearance, my clothing, rather than address our racialization of Peruvian identities more critically. In retrospect, it seems fitting that this meeting took place in Croatia, which came into being as a result of ethnic conflicts among states in the former Yugoslavia. An insider/outsider binary fails to reflect the lived hierarchies attached to social status and ethnic identities as these shaped access to citizenship rights in the former Yugoslavia and now in Croatia as it negotiates the arrival of newcomers and migrants as a member of the European Union (since late 2013). Insider/outsider binaries of belonging similarly rarely reflect the complicated practices, contradictory ideologies, and everyday challenges and conflicts transnational Peruvians negotiate in constructing belonging both in Lima—as in Marco's case—and in other parts of the globe.

Among the Peruvians whose migration trajectories I examine in this book, return as a possibility, an impossibility, or a reality looms large. The lens of return provides one way to understand what transnational Peruvians desire, reject, or feel ambivalent about in constructions of home and Peruvianness. A close look at individual lives across settings and affective and material attachments to and practices in those settings exposes the lived realities of everyday negotiations surrounding return to a home that is fundamentally made up of "processes of inclusion or exclusion" (Brah 1996, 192) based on hierarchies of gender, location, language, race, sexual identity, and class.[3] Here I examine how a place recognized as home can have contradictory meanings for different groups of people, as well as for the same person. As a lens, then, desired, rejected, imagined, and physical return brings to the forefront evolving constructions of and meanings associated with Peruvianness, belonging, and home. The chapters that follow reflect the experiences both of those who have returned to live in Peru after years abroad and of those who continue to live outside Peru. They underscore how, far from referring to a coherent group with similar traits, the term "migrant"—and, even more specifically, "middle-class migrant" and "upper-class migrant"—encompasses a broad range of identities and experiences.

Employing return as a critical lens, *Peruvian Lives across Borders: Power, Exclusion, and Home* presents an intentional departure from the more prevalent focus on international labor migrants from lower and working classes in migration scholarship, particularly among anthropologists. This book draws on the transnational lives of middle- and upper-class transnational Peruvians. Migration research has tended to focus on the movements of largely unskilled, low-income migrants (Coles and Fechter 2008) even as those of middle- and upper-class background have comprised and continue to comprise a significant number of migrants. Anthropological studies focusing on women commonly examine women from lower economic classes, and little attention has been given to the study of everyday practices and agency of those in more powerful positions (for an exception, see Ong 1999). In anthropology, the study of those with high socioeconomic status and, more specifically, of elites has tended to be limited to studies within particular "local" contexts rather than transnational spaces and dynamics (for Peru, see Fuller 2002; Kogan 1998). In her study on gender relations within Lima's upper classes, anthropologist Liuba Kogan (1998) noted that the absence of academic studies of the upper classes until at least the 1990s led some researchers to draw on novels for details of upper-class lives.

I suggest that a critical examination of middle- and upper-class Peruvians' migration experiences reveals as much about individual trajectories and class dimensions of migration as about broader constructions of Peruvianness and home that inform and have repercussions for the everyday lives of Peruvians across multiple differences and spaces. Put another way, my perspective is that it is important and necessary to analyze migration trajectories of Peruvians of various backgrounds—including those who have traditionally held more social power, as examined here—if we want to understand the workings of racial-gender-class hierarchies as these continue to be reinforced, challenged, and transformed. In writing this book, I purposely engaged with the areas of contestation and reinforcement of existing racial-gender-class hierarchies in everyday life because of what they divulge about the limits of inclusion. Chapters bring to the forefront ideas and practices that rely on discourses and experiences of social status by middle- and upper-class transnational Peruvians to justify the exclusion of other Peruvians from realms of belonging and reinforce their own status and belonging. The effects of the resulting exclusion against and by middle- and upper-class Peruvians and accompanying symbolic violence are far from limited to one class, social identity, or location. As I underscore throughout the book, the goal here is not simply to propose that more affluent Peruvians also experience discrimination and exclusion. I engage in a critical analysis of how and what the rich tensions and nuances between belonging and exclusion in the transnational lives of middle- and upper-class Peruvians tell us about the social hierarchies and accompanying ideas and practices that inform the everyday lives of Peruvians.

Social and economic upward mobility, or the maintenance of status, is a significant factor for migrants across socioeconomic backgrounds. I propose that it is through a transnational, intersectional lens that we are best equipped to examine "tensions between different hierarchies and criteria of status and privilege as travelers move from one context to another" (Amit 2007, 2). Taken together, studies of diverse groups of migrants provide us with more holistic understandings of social configurations of power, belonging, and exclusion among any one national group both within and beyond national borders. In this sense, it is not only possible but also necessary and valuable to critically examine and deconstruct the forms of power, belonging, and exclusion negotiated by middle- and upper-class migrants in their transnational journeys.

Belonging, Peruvianness, and Home

Mobility is commonly portrayed as the antithesis of belonging (Fallov, Jorgensen, and Knudsen 2013), yet in practice mobility opens up new possibilities for reimagining and reinscribing emotional and material attachments associated with home(s)—including when, as I discuss below, one's sense of attachment and belonging to that home is perceived as incomplete or illegitimate by others. For Peruvians I interviewed, leaving their home in Peru, and most often in Lima, to settle temporarily or permanently elsewhere involved feelings ranging from sadness to uncertainty to relief, yet it certainly did not result in feeling homeless. Migrants feel at home in more than one place and move from one place to another as they create or maintain multiple attachments. This is the case even as and when their affective and material attachments to one or more places are contested by those around them.

The politics of belonging has been a central topic in scholarship on transnational identities (Yuval-Davis 1997, 2006). Moving away from conceptualizations of home and belonging as essentially sedentary, bounded, and centered in only one place, I approach home and belonging as grounded in shifting, fluid, and potentially plural attachments across time and space (Andits 2015; Glick Schiller and Fouron 2001; Nowicka and Cieslik 2014; Raffaeta and Duff 2013; Ralph and Staeheli 2011). That belonging and identity are shifting and plural should not be taken to mean, however, that they are deterritorialized in ways suggested in previous approaches (i.e., Appadurai 1996; Glick Schiller and Szanton Blanc 1994). I emphasize here that the ability to travel back and forth between Peru and elsewhere strengthens a multiplicity of attachments as it fortifies the particular shapes of affective and material connections to specific places within and outside Peru.

In practice, these politics of belonging mean that Peruvians within and outside of Peru are invested in policing boundaries of belonging even as their own belonging may be challenged by those around them. Kathy Davis and Lorraine Nencel (2011) observe that their positions as privileged middle-class white U.S. academics working in the Netherlands and integrated by most measures do not prevent strangers and acquaintances from regularly pointing out and asking about traces of an accent from someplace else or about their immigrant status. These questions serve the purpose of reminding them that they cannot fully belong.[4] In contrast to the home they left in the United States, where they did not face these questions because of their unmarked status as white middle-class women, in the Netherlands their whiteness and class status are not sufficient for them to pass vis-à-vis unmarked mainstream national identities there. After three decades of feeling at home in the Netherlands, a country popularly touted as particularly open and tolerant, their own sense of attachment and their everyday practices over time are not sufficient to guarantee their recognition as fully belonging in the eyes of those around them who identify as native Dutch. The chapters that follow engage with many instances of Peruvians similarly experiencing feeling both at home and excluded in spite—and precisely because—of their own self-identifications with privileged status groups and plural attachments to homes.

Who is and is not Peruvian and what should and should not be considered Peruvian are publicly and privately debated and negotiated across platforms. In December 2014 a YouTube video titled *You Know You Are Peruvian When*, featuring a young Peruvian American mestiza woman discussing symbols of Peruvianness, made its debut. In the three-minute, thirty-second video, a young woman dressed in a red-and-white Peru soccer jersey holds up and shares with viewers a succession of colorful Peruvian artifacts, such as Inca Kola, candy, dolls, religious icons, and clothing items. She also recites rhymes and jokes. She comments on the artifacts against the backdrop of a pale beige wall in her bedroom. The English-language video has been shared thousands of times and has received overwhelmingly positive comments by Peruvians. The public Facebook page of the group Peruanos en el Extranjero (Peruvians Abroad) includes many of these comments by Peruvian parents with children born in the United States who found the young woman's interest in and connection to Peru particularly endearing.[5] Other Peruvians mentioned that they personally identified with and enjoyed watching and listening to her characterization of Peruvians' objects of longing and nostalgia. Others, however, complained that the young woman should have spoken in Spanish if she was truly Peruvian, disapproved of her accent when she did speak in Spanish, and generally questioned her authenticity as Peruvian. The young woman's mention of key Peruvian symbols such as Inca Kola, *pollo a la brasa* (rotisserie chicken), chullos (alpaca or wool hand-knit Andean hats), typical national dances and music, and several other foods, places, practices, and words did little to convince some that she too belonged to the same imagined community (i.e., Anderson 1999) other Peruvians claimed.

In the YouTube video case, as in other cases that appear in this book, belonging becomes as much about one's own emotional attachments as it is about everyday practices and the policing of borders by others who identify as Peruvian to determine who should and should not be included in desired constructions of home. Reading some of the negative comments about the young woman's language use and abilities, I was reminded of comments I had heard growing up during middle-class gatherings and much more recently from some Peruvians I interviewed that reflected disapproval of Peruvians who left Peru and did not teach their children Spanish. In the majority of these cases, the criticisms were directed at poorer Peruvians and their children. In this sense, it is worth noting that Peruvians I spoke with consistently shared with me and showed pride in the fact that they spoke Spanish at home with their children. In addition to consolidating their own sense of home and attachments to Peru through the maintenance of Spanish in the home, these statements served to separate these Peruvians from "other" (lower-class, poorer) Peruvians.

YouTube provides a web-based, media-sharing global platform for the negotiation and discussion of what it means to be Peruvian and to represent Peru through such videos, yet it is not the only site for the discussion of belonging and what it means to be Peruvian. Peruvian gastronomy, examined in chapter 5, provides another global platform—sometimes also through the virtual world, other times through physical manifestations—through which to negotiate representations of Peru. More broadly, migrants' everyday life within and outside of Peru as it intersects with family dynamics and labor, public places and street harassment, experiences of safety and danger, and other seemingly mundane practices also engages in and contributes to constructions of what it means, or rather what an individual believes it should mean, to be Peruvian—as the following chapters examine. In all these cases, constructions of Peruvianness draw on, reinforce, and destabilize configurations of power rooted in lives in and imaginings of Peru, often specifically in the country's capital. Here, as in other spaces, social hierarchies are central to processes of belonging.

As is the case for belonging, home is rarely uncomplicated. Whereas for some, home is associated with feelings of safety and security, family, and happiness, for others, it might be associated with insecurity and exclusion. Most often, conceptualizations of home are messy (Ahmed et al. 2003): home can simultaneously be a place of safety and danger and of love and rejection. Living abroad allowed some to enjoy aspects of home they cherished, such as immediate family and Peruvian food. It also allowed them to distance themselves from violence in the form of homophobia, street sexual harassment, and petty crime. Individuals missed their families in Peru and reminisced about childhood memories, yet they also shared shifting and sometimes contradictory feelings about Peru as home as they enlisted their own changing constructions of home. Themes that regularly appeared in the narratives of those I interviewed as they spoke of Peru and a possible return included fear, security and insecurity, longing, and exclusion.

In paying attention to the role of emotions and emotional attachments in migration trajectories, Jayani Bonnerjee draws on Elspeth Probyn's work to approach belonging within transnational lives "as a complex overlap between 'being' and 'longing'" (2013, 432) in his study of Anglo-Indian identities in Toronto. In discussing migration in the context of their lives, Peruvians I met routinely discussed both how they *felt* and what they *did*. This book pays attention both to emotional attachments and to pragmatic behaviors and decisions to reflect the intimate ways in which these are interlinked in migrants' everyday lives. In this sense, emotions and emotional attachments are not simply psychological states but intimately connected and central to social and cultural practices of boundary maintenance between "us" and "them" (Ahmed 2004). Emotional attachments in particular have received little attention in studies of migrants' conceptions of home (Ralph and Staeheli 2011). Individual well-being, however, can be subjectively expressed through and reflected in the embodiment and management of emotions, and emotions can provide information about the contexts in which they occur (Tapias 2015). Here I therefore approach emotions, emotional attachments, and everyday practices as central to conceptualizations of home. For those

I spoke with, how secure or insecure they felt in Lima and other places of residence could be as significant in their conceptualizations of home and decisions to return to Peru as the longing for particular people, places, and objects and their physical experiences of danger and safety there.

Since 1996 the Peruvian government has made it possible for Peruvians to hold dual citizenship. This facilitates legal issues such as inheritance and property ownership for many transnational Peruvians, yet it does not decrease the complexities of affective and material attachments associated with belonging. Skype, Facetime, Facebook, texting, Instagram, and other social media may facilitate the maintenance of some affective ties, as they provide ways for parents to see and communicate with their children in their new homes, migrants to stay involved in community events from afar, and friends, family, and acquaintances to keep track of, visualize, and instantly comment on the whereabouts of those who are thousands of miles away. These forms of technology may also carry unintended emotional and practical consequences. In her book on working-class Peruvians from the Mantaro Valley who left the country between the late 1980s and 2005, Ulla Berg (2015) observes that migrants prefer visual technologies as modes of communication to maintain ties to their communities of origin. However, cherished family videos and Skype sessions may inadvertently provide evidence of possible extramarital relationships, remind migrants of individuals or places they would rather not remember, and provide evidence that remittances were used in ways that differ from the migrants' intended purposes in sending them. They work against the very secrets and white lies transnational migrants may rely on for their own well-being and that of the family from which they are apart, as Maria Tapias (2015) also found in her research on women's well-being in Bolivia.

Approaching Return

Return to a home may be temporary or permanent, voluntary or involuntary, individual or familial. One may return to one's ancestral land or country of birth and to the specific community of origin or another community in the country of origin. Some returns come after years or decades without return visits; others are the culmination of shorter, more regular visits. For some, short visits may substitute for a permanent return. Return may be desired and possible. It may also be rejected or impossible because of individual circumstances or as a result of broader social, economic, and political conditions (Long and Oxfeld 2004). Even when return is desired and planned, the experience of return may be a difficult one. Writing on West

Indian return migrants to Barbados, George Gmelch notes that over half of the returnees he interviewed "were so dissatisfied during their first year at home that they believed they would have been happier abroad" (2004, 213). For many others, however, the challenges combined with the rewards of return create incentives to stay.

In contrast to the more widespread view, even among migration scholars, that romanticized visions of home heavily inform decisions to return or not return among voluntary migrants (e.g., Constable 1999; Conway 2005; Ralph and Staeheli 2011), in this book I maintain that migrants take into consideration multiple factors in deciding if and when to return and for how long, so that their decisions are better understood as resulting from the intersection of emotional attachments and pragmatic strategies. This does not mean that migrants will not be disappointed with or surprised by aspects of their return experience when these do not match some expectations or hopes. It underscores, however, that just as the division between home and not-home and insider and outsider is simplistic and misses the complexity of everyday life, so does the approach to voluntary return as due largely to romanticized views of home. In the narratives in this book, individuals and families negotiate longing and nostalgia as they grapple with the changing, complicated realities they expect in life postreturn. Significantly, these negotiations are facilitated by the resources available to Peruvians I interviewed. As middle- and upper-class Peruvians, many could afford to regularly visit Peru. These short-term return visits assisted migrants in molding their attachments both to their community of origin and to their current place of residence and in determining or preparing for practical challenges postreturn (Carling and Erdal 2014). Chapters 1 and 2 examine the class dimensions of return more closely.

Focusing on young software professionals who return to Bangalore after many years abroad, Carol Upadhya notes that they "return equipped with self-proclaimed enlightened, liberal, and forward-looking orientations and practices, which form a lens through which they judge India's disorder, rampant corruption and *chalta hai* (easy-going) attitude" (2013, 154). Similarly, professional Peruvians in their twenties who return to Lima after studying abroad draw on and adapt ideas and practices from throughout their migration trajectories to approach everyday life in Lima. In this sense, they remake home. They simultaneously express commitments to contributing to their society of origin and identify elements they aspire to change in their society. For several Peruvians, these elements included what they identified as chaos and disorder, lack of civility in everyday interactions, racism, sexism, and homophobia. None of these elements inspired nostalgia or longing, yet they were clearly recognized as part of the reality of home. As middle- and upper-class migrants, these Peruvians' social and economic position facilitates return as part of a fluid migration trajectory in which return is not the inevitable endpoint of mobility. Multiple returns are possible: some are temporary, others are permanent, and some begin as the former and end up as the latter, and vice versa.

Migration and Intersectionality: Configurations of Power and Transnational Lives

Intersectionality is among the most celebrated theoretical and methodological approaches within feminist research, even as emerging research in the field of gender and women's studies continues to struggle to fully engage with intersectional analyses that move beyond a gender-plus-one-social-identity approach and apply these transnationally (Bahkru 2008; Chakravarty and Frank 2013; Collins 2012; Kitch and Fonow 2012). The meaning of the term "intersectionality" varies across policy documents (Yuval-Davis 2006). In the United States, intersectional approaches developed largely as a reaction to and critique of the assumption of universal sisterhood espoused by white middle-class feminists. Kimberlé Crenshaw (1991) coined the term to refer to the ways in which African American women's identities and experiences of oppression are founded on multiple intersecting markers of difference that include gender, race, and class. Further exploring differences among women, Patricia Hill Collins (1998) and bell hooks (1989) similarly conceptualize interlocking systems of domination whose effects can be felt at both the community and the individual levels among marginalized groups. In a similar vein, the earlier work of Cherríe Moraga and Gloria Anzaldúa (1981) calls attention to multiple yet mutually distinct oppressions among white heterosexual women, heterosexual women of color, and lesbian women of color. In Peru, Marfil Francke's (1990) concept of *trenzas de dominación* (braids of domination) directs our attention to the intersections of race, class, and gender in indigenous women's experiences of oppression. These forms of oppression aren't simply vestiges of the colonial past. They are continuously reconstituted and reinvented to naturalize persistent social hierarchies that privilege those in positions of power (Reygada 2010; Stern 1999).

Intersectional approaches have been employed to examine a variety of multidimensional experiences, including those associated with Latino masculinities (Alcalde 2014; Hurtado 1998; Hurtado and Sinha 2008; Rios 2011) and immigrant, lesbian, and minority battered women in the United States

(Sokoloff 2008). In the context of Latin America, intersectional approaches have been applied in studies of different groups of women, including in Peru (Alcalde 2010; Boesten 2010, 2014; Bueno-Hansen 2015) and Guatemala (Menjivar 2011), to name only a couple of locations. While approaches developed in the United States have focused mainly on minority populations, outside the United States intersectional approaches under various names have more broadly engaged with analyses both of minority groups and of those groups that traditionally have more social power and cultural capital. Together, intersectional studies underscore the mutual yet varied constitutiveness of social identities both within and across borders.

In approaching migration, including return, through an intersectional lens, I am interested in how gendered, racialized, class, and sexual identities inform the experiences of belonging and home for Peruvian migrants within and across their communities of residence outside Peru and upon returning to Peru for those who return. The intersectional approach my research engages with reflects what Sarah Mahler, Mayurakshi Chaudhuri, and Vrushali Patil have called a "transnational intersectional approach" that examines "the articulation of various axes of differentiation not just within but simultaneously across national borders" (2015, 101). Floya Anthias's (2013) "translocational lens" further calls attention to the varied and potentially contradictory meanings associated with migrants' social identities across locations. In Anthias's work, as in my work, critical attention to layers of power and social hierarchies—of gender, race, class, and sexual identity—is a central aspect of a transnational intersectional lens. The positioning of migrants' perceived and self-defined identities in hierarchies of power in Peru and abroad informs access to desired affective and material resources and opportunities.

Migrants are racialized, classed, and gendered in different locations and contexts, and they negotiate and attach meanings to their identities in relation to particular social, cultural, economic, and national contexts. A person may enjoy privileges associated with her class status in Peru yet feel marginalized because of her accent, work, or racialization in her community in the United States. Another person might feel safe walking hand in hand with his same-sex partner in downtown Toronto yet be attacked or discriminated against if he does the same in his neighborhood in Lima. This person might feel he belongs in Lima because of his family ties and familiar environment there. He will also recognize that everyday life once he returns to Lima will include forms of exclusion and discrimination because of his identification as a gay man. The decision to return in this and other cases cannot be narrowed down to a single identity or factor or to purely emotional attachments or experiences (feeling at home, feeling discriminated against or marginalized) or material experiences (being physically attacked, having access to cheaper household labor) by themselves.

I am among a growing group of "native anthropologists" living outside Peru (see also de la Cadena 2000; Garcia 2005; Gandolfo 2009; Li 2015; Mendoza 2008; Vásquez del Aguila 2015) who complicate the insider/outsider binary in doing research in and on Peru. I am a Peruvian middle-class immigrant who has become a U.S. citizen and is married to a U.S. citizen, is a parent to second-generation children, and is the daughter of return migrants, so to state that the broad topic of migration and return migration informs my life is somewhat of an understatement. Yet I am not alone in having a transnational family, in the general contours of my transnational family life, or in conducting research in Peru. And it is the specific emotional and pragmatic attachments that provide my transnational life with its general shape and me with a sense of home: a husband from the United States; one child born in Peru and another in the United States; and, more broadly, close family both in Peru and in the United States. Travel, visits, and communication via phone and social media are critical to maintaining my attachments and sense of home.

The broad strokes of my story may have similarities with those of other Latin American migrants and transnational Peruvians in particular, but this book is not about my life as a Peruvian migrant, nor is my goal here to present generalizations applicable to all Peruvian migrants.[6] Those I spoke with were more interested in sharing their own stories about their migration experiences than in asking about my background and life. It would be disingenuous of me to assume, however, that perceptions of me did not inform how much others initially trusted or distrusted me when they agreed to meet and share their stories and information with me.

As I walked to cafés, homes, restaurants, office buildings, malls, and many other places where interviews took place and as I interacted with Peruvians across settings I was keenly aware of privileged aspects of my own identity—which include my middle-class background and professional position—and that these aspects facilitated my access to and travel for several interviews. More often than not, my middle-class background and perceived whiteness in Peru meant that I could easily signal my familiarity with the clubs, streets, restaurants, and schools those I spoke with mentioned through an appropriately timed nod, smile, head tilt, or brief comment. Demonstrating familiarity with the social worlds in which Peruvians I spoke with circulated and having personal experiences of living transnationally helped build rapport in many cases. Sometimes the trust placed in me meant that a person would make openly racist comments about other Peruvians or minority groups abroad under the assumption that I shared these views. More often it meant that the person would discuss personal successes and challenges in the context of migration and then reflect on these experiences. The stories shared with me make clear that professional and familial material successes are also commonly underpinned by affective and material experiences of discrimination, racism, sexism, and insecurity. Knowledge of shared identities as migrants likely also facilitated openness toward discussing frustrated attempts at fitting in and experiences of discrimination, misunderstanding, and marginalization.

The transnational experiences of belonging, privilege, and exclusion I examine in the following chapters vary, and none is on its own representative of all Peruvians, of all middle- or upper-class Peruvians, or of men or women as a group. As a whole, however, these stories push us to continue to expand approaches to transnational lives. They encourage us to recognize and more fully and critically examine the changing and sometimes contradictory identities and experiences both within a single person's migration trajectory and in living transnationally.

Negotiating Class

Crossing borders brings opportunities, and it also means that differences that mark an individual or family as high status in one place may not be recognized in another. Among *limeños* abroad the first questions commonly heard during initial meetings tend to include "What part of Lima are you from?" and "What school did you go to?" These questions are more about the assessment of cultural capital and social position than about the automatic feeling or identification of some inherent, shared Peruvianness. In her study on Caribbean migration, Karen Fog Olwig eloquently discusses how middle-class migrants are "quite conscious of their relative position in society in the place of origin as well as the migration destination" (2007, 90), since they, like many other migrants, move in part to improve or at least maintain their status. Middle-class Caribbean migrants in Olwig's study sought to distinguish themselves from the lower-class Caribbean migrants with whom they were commonly grouped by others in the United States. Angela Torresan (2007) similarly found that middle-class Brazilian immigrants in London emphasized their class status from Brazil, particularly when the type of work they engaged in did not reflect the social standing with which they identified.

In Toronto, some middle-class Peruvian migrants I spoke with engaged in low-status work that included newspaper delivery and house cleaning. These types of work did not reflect their perceived social status in Peru and did not change their self-identification as middle class. In South Florida, middle-class Peruvians who had never felt marginalized in Peru regularly experienced marginalization due to their undocumented status after the expiration of their tourist visa. Yet, even as they experienced marginalization they had been impervious to previously and as their low income prevented them from maintaining the middle-class lifestyle they had become accustomed to in Peru, they identified as middle class (Sabogal 2012; Sabogal and Núñez 2010). Unlike in class-conscious Peru, however, Peruvians' self-identified middle-class status in the United States and Canada does not typically include relying on domestic workers, and this results in intrahousehold, gendered negotiations of chores and expectations, as discussed in chapter 2.

Peru has been and continues to be a class-conscious, hierarchical society. Most Peruvians I interviewed came from the capital, Lima, and identified as middle class. In Lima, a person's district of residence, school attended, educational attainment, professional employment, family and ethnic-racial background, income, and membership in social clubs all inform that person's positioning in social hierarchies. With few exceptions, Peruvians I interviewed had the cultural capital and economic resources to travel internationally without major obstacles and with supporting legal documentation. Given the variations of class within Lima and fluidity of class transnationally, examining the role, perceptions, and fluidity of the experience of class among mostly middle-class and some upper-class Peruvians exposes conflicts, persistence, and transformations in configurations of power and social relations in Peru and abroad.

There is no official definition of "middle class" in Peru, as in many other places. Nonetheless, according to the popularly used contemporary categorization of Peruvians into socioeconomic groups for purposes of marketing and polls, the Peruvian population is often categorized into A, B, C, D, and E groups. Those in group A are the wealthiest, and those in the B and C categories are middle class. In 2011 almost 40 percent of the population could be categorized as middle class (groups B and C) according to this categorization (Jaramillo and Zambrano 2013).

Until World War I, there was little recognition of a middle class (Parker 1997). Reflecting the hierarchical structure of society, those at the top were typically white (and some mestizo) and simply referred to themselves as *gente decente* (decent people), whereas those at the bottom of the hierarchy were mestizo and indigenous and were referred to by the self-identified *gente decente* as *gente del pueblo* (village people) (Parker 1997). Peru has moved away from this seemingly simple class binary, in part facilitated by mass internal migration to cities, especially Lima, since the 1950s. What has remained constant is that one's social standing is determined by a combination of factors that go beyond income. As a recent study of the vast San Felipe apartment complex community in the Jesús María district of Lima underscores, the complexities and conflicts within the middle class are vast. In this apartment community, middle class includes both "old" middle-class families long established in Lima and first-generation, upwardly mobile families who have more recently migrated to the capital from other parts of the country or from shantytowns in other parts of the city (Pereyra 2015).

Previous research on Peruvian migration has examined some of the contexts in which Peruvians live and create a sense of belonging, including in the United States (Berg 2015; Paerregaard 2014; Vásquez del Aguila 2015), Japan (Paerregaard 2008, 2014; Takenaka 2009; Takenaka and Pren 2010), South Korea (Vogel 2014), Spain (Paerregaard 2014), Italy (Napolitano 2015; Skornia 2015; Tamagno 2003), and Chile (Garcés 2015; Nuñez Carrasco 2010; Paerregaard 2009, 2014). Anthropological research on Latin Americans' transnational migration (i.e., Berg 2015; Boehm 2012, 2016; Paerregaard 2014; Pribilsky 2007) has tended to focus on labor migration among working-class migrants (but see Sabogal 2009). South American middle classes have only recently begun to receive anthropologists' sustained attention, such as in recent ethnographies of emerging middle classes in Bolivia (Shakow 2014; Pellegrini Calderón 2016), a re-examination of the middle class in Peru (Huber and Lamas 2017), and the more focused ethnography of the San Felipe middle-class residential complex in Lima (Pereyra 2015) mentioned above.[7]

Attention to the everyday lives and dynamics within the middle classes has long been advocated (e.g., Nader 1969) as a way to understand the processes connected to the exercise of power in everyday life, a topic in which anthropologists have historically been interested (e.g., Mintz 1960; Wolf 1982). I am not suggesting, however, that it is more or less legitimate to examine one group of Peruvians (middle, upper, or working class—inasmuch as these terms themselves are porous and messy) over another. Stretching my own research to also include middle classes and those in higher social and economic positions provides me with a broader view to contribute to analyses of power in everyday life.[8] The focus on particular groups in this book reflects the need to approach and examine inequalities—racialized, classed, and gendered—through multiple lenses. By critically examining inequalities and power asymmetries from multiple perspectives, we gain a broader, more complete view of these asymmetries. This book, in particular, contributes to recent efforts to critically understand how social inequalities are renegotiated, challenged, and reproduced transnationally in the lives of privileged social groups (e.g., Twine and Gardener 2013). Here much of the emphasis is on those traditionally viewed as holding substantial social and economic power. As I underscore, middle-class Peruvian migrants, whether self-identified or identified as such by others, are far from monolithic in their views and experiences.

Peruvian Migrants across Settings

Historically, middle- and upper-class Peruvians have had more access to international migration than poorer Peruvians. Throughout the twentieth century, it was more common for Peruvians with fewer socioeconomic resources to engage in in-country migration to Lima—a topic I return to in Chapter 1. However, since World War II, international migration increasingly included working-class populations. For example, Quechua-speaking women from rural areas in the highlands traveled to the United States to work as domestic servants, and working-class Peruvians from various regions traveled to Paterson, New Jersey, to work in the booming textile industry there. The United States continues to be the most popular destination for Peruvians, yet by the late 1980s Peruvians had become increasingly interested in European, Asian, and South American destinations. Immigration laws passed by the Italian, Japanese, and Spanish governments to encourage the migration of unskilled foreign workers, and of Peruvians of Japanese descent in the case of Japan, facilitated emigration for some. In Japan, Peruvian men sought work in factories, whereas Spain and Italy attracted Peruvian women more for work as domestic servants (Paerregaard 2014). South American destinations such as Chile and Argentina became particularly appealing in the 1990s for those without significant economic resources as migration restrictions and costs to the United States and Europe increased (Nuñez Carrasco 2010). Whereas Peruvian migration has historically been dominated by the middle classes, in Chile the Peruvian population is predominantly lower class in large part due to the affordability of this trip compared to other, more distant international destinations (Garcés 2015; Nuñez Carrasco 2010).

Today over 232 million people live outside their country of birth (Mahler, Chaudhuri, and Patil 2015).[9] Peru's rate of out-migration is among the highest in Latin America, with from 7 percent to more than 10 percent of Peruvians living abroad (Takenaka, Paerregaard, and Berg 2010, 5; UNFPA

2012, 19).¹⁰ Lima, where most of the Peruvians I interviewed lived or had lived, has the highest rates of emigration nationally (OIM/INEI 2010). These rates of emigration mean that 10 percent of Peruvian households have at least one member abroad (OIM/INEI 2010), and these households are routinely engaged in transnational negotiations and communication. In this context, middle-class migration continues to be significant: between 2000 and 2003, approximately one-third of emigrants were professionals and technicians from the middle classes (Powell and Chavarro 2008).

Length of time abroad for Peruvians varies: 47 percent of Peruvians tend to stay abroad for over three years, 25 percent stay abroad between six months and a year, and 27 percent stay abroad between one and three years (Durand 2010). Peruvians live in a range of countries, yet not all destinations are considered equal. The prestige attached to remittances reflects a hierarchy of places in the Peruvian imagination.¹¹ Karsten Paerregaard (2014) found that among the countries he studied, salaries in Japan were highest; followed by those in Italy, Spain, and the United States in the middle; with salaries in Argentina and Chile at the bottom.¹²

At the same time as the economic crisis in the European Union deepened, entry into the United States became more difficult for those without sufficient financial resources. About 250,000 Peruvians returned to Peru between 2001 and 2011 (OIM 2012). In 2013 Peru's Law of Incentive to Return Migration was modified under pressure from migrants-rights groups to lift some of the legal and economic barriers and to provide additional benefits to promote and ease migrants' return. As the political and economic situation in Peru has stabilized and improved, return migration has become a more likely possibility for some. Just between 2007 and 2009, eighty thousand Peruvians returned to Peru (OIM/INEI 2010).

The Peruvian migrants I spoke with were concentrated in four countries: the United States, Canada, Germany, and Peru. The United States, Canada, and Germany are high on the migration hierarchy, yet each has distinct immigration policies, cultural practices, and concentrations of immigrant groups that in part shape the ways in which Peruvians experienced their daily lives. In all of them, however, middle- and upper-class Peruvians commonly lived through their own racialization for the first time. They experienced marginalization and (unwillingly) embodied an "other" even as they sought to set themselves apart from those they had typically racialized and discriminated against in Peru, as examined in chapter 1. The specific settings of reception in each of the three national contexts I engage with in this study, in addition to Peru for return migrants, provide unique opportunities for understanding transnational Peruvian lives through intersectional lenses, as examined in the following chapters. I outline some important general characteristics for each context below. It is also worth noting here how each context contributes to our understanding of specific areas of Peruvian transnational experiences.

Given the country's large Latino population and history of discrimination against Latinos, as discussed more in chapter 1, the United States is especially useful for examining experiences of racialization for Peruvians. In this sense, the United States context in particular presents greater opportunities for understanding how those with higher status (middle- and upper-class Peruvians) experience situations in which they are marginalized (as racialized Latinos) more than in Germany and Canada. I underline that U.S.-based experiences of marginalization do not necessarily increase transnational Peruvians' tolerance toward others or result in Peruvians leaving behind Peru-based social hierarchies.

The backdrop of Canada's official multiculturalism provides a particularly provocative way of examining the persistence of Peruvian racial and social hierarchies even in contexts with official multicultural policies, a larger Latin American middle class within a smaller Latin American population, and less overt discrimination than in the United States. Several of the Peruvians I interviewed in Canada had negative opinions of how Peruvians are treated in the United States, and they contrasted this treatment to their lives in Canada. Aldo's views of the United States, where no one wanted to know about "your history, your language, it is so ignorant on their part, I think it is very ignorant.... They tell you to forget about Peru in the United States," was representative of the views of Peruvians I spoke with in Canada, who considered Canada a more tolerant, less biased place to live for Peruvians than the United States.

Studies of Latin Americans in Europe have more frequently focused on more common Latin American destinations, particularly Spain, given its colonial connections to Peru. Spain's financial crisis, beginning in 2008, however, created conditions in which Peruvians who had immigrated to Spain decided to move elsewhere for better economic opportunities. Some returned to Peru (e.g., Berta in chapter 3), while others moved on to countries with more economic stability and opportunities in Europe, as is the case of Germany (Domingo, Sabater, and Verdugo 2015). Germany in particular presents a strong contrast to Canada's multicultural policies, the United States' large Latino population, and the United States' and Peru's lack of state parental leave and childcare programs. In the discussion of women's autonomy in the context of migration in chapter 2, I discuss how Germany's government programs may impact women's professional lives and autonomy—especially in cases in which women have very young children—in ways not experienced in these other settings. As contexts of reception and everyday life, the United States, Canada, and Germany also present different requirements for naturalization through residence, as noted in what follows.

The United States

The United States and Canada are among the largest immigrant destinations in the world. North America contains approximately 34 percent of all Peruvians living abroad, with the United States having the greatest concentration of Peruvians outside Peru (Altamirano 2000, 2010; IOM 2012). Peruvians commonly seek citizenship in the United States (Durand 2010), where they may do so after a minimum of five years as permanent residents.[13] The majority of Peruvians in the United States arrived since 1990 (Berg 2015). Among those I interviewed, at the time of the interview six Peruvians lived in the United States, and eleven had returned to Lima after living in the United States. Among survey participants, which I discuss more in the next section, thirty-nine lived in the United States. Mexicans and Central Americans comprise the largest groups of Latin American immigrants in the country, yet Peruvians are in the top five South American immigrant groups based on size. Peruvians make up approximately 16 percent of South American immigrants in the country (Zong and Batalova 2016).[14]

By 2050 Latinos are expected to make up one-fourth of the U.S. population. The term "Latinos" is popularly used to refer to recent immigrants from the over two dozen countries that constitute Latin America, as well as to U.S.-born citizens of Latin American descent. Latinos of varying national backgrounds thus constitute both the largest domestic minority group in the United States and the largest immigrant group. In the United States, native-born Americans' stereotypes of immigrants vary according to immigrants' perceived ethnic identity, race, place of origin, and legal status (Lu and Nicholson-Crotty 2010; Valentino, Brader, and Jardina 2013). Todd Hartman, Benjamin Newman, and C. Scott Bell (2014) emphasize that prejudice and antipathy specifically toward Latinos plays a significant role in support for restrictive immigration policies. Over the last two decades, media depictions of immigrants have turned increasingly negative in the country and have included the association of immigrants with the spread of disease and as particularly dangerous and polluting (Esses, Medianu, and Lawson 2013). And it is Latinos and, more specifically, Mexican immigrants who are almost exclusively associated with the terms "undocumented" and "illegal" and who are depicted as a national threat both by politicians and in the popular media (Chavez 2008; Esses, Medianu, and Lawson 2013; Santa Ana 2013).

Some Peruvians reported frustration that in their communities in the United States they would sometimes be assumed to be Mexican when they were overheard speaking Spanish. This frustration resulted from what they perceived to be a misrecognition of their affective and material attachments to Peru. Others reported feeling amused that they were not identified as Latin American because they did not look the way people in their communities expected Latin Americans to look—again, the Peruvians I interviewed were generally light skinned and relatively privileged socioeconomically. Tatiana, a tall, slender woman with blue eyes and light brown hair in her early forties, did not feel discriminated against in her small city in the United States, yet she noted that even after she had lived in the city for almost a decade, cashiers and other city residents would do a double-take and seem confused when she spoke with an accent or introduced herself as Peruvian or Latin American.

Canada

In Canada, Latin Americans make up only a small percentage of immigrants and come from over twenty countries (Veronis 2007). Unlike in the United States, in Canada there are very few Mexican immigrants. The majority of immigrants in contemporary Canada come from Asia. Latin Americans have generally arrived as political refugees from Chile, Argentina, and Uruguay in the 1970s and from Central America, particularly Guatemala and El Salvador, in the 1980s; for economic reasons as professionals; and for family reunification. In the 1990s Latin American immigrants consisted mainly of professionals arriving under the country's skilled worker immigration category (Veronis 2007, 2010).

Canada admits approximately 0.8 percent of its population annually as immigrants, and Canadians have shown widespread positive support for immigration (Ferrer, Picot, and Riddell 2014). Unlike in the United States, in Canada multiculturalism has been the official immigration policy since 1971, and civic duties and people's sense of belonging are formally prioritized over assimilation (Armony, Barriga, and Schugurensky 2004). Immigrants may apply for citizenship after four years of continuous residence in the country. During his work on Anglo-Indian identities in Toronto, Jayani Bonnerjee frequently came upon the discourse of multiculturalism as "an image that was part of the everyday language of the city, appearing in conversations, in the daily media and amidst several festivals that celebrated Toronto's (and Canada's) multiculturalism" (2013, 434). However, multiculturalism as an official policy does not necessarily result in racial harmony, the absence of discrimination, or the dismantling of structural inequalities (Falcón 2016).

Immigration policy in Canada is broadly divided into three categories in admitting immigrants: humanitarian, economic, and family. Among Peruvians I met with, the most common categories through which they had migrated were economic opportunities and family reunification. Within the economic program, potential economic contributions are central, and highly skilled and professional immigrants are prioritized. Piero left Lima for a high-level executive position at an international bank in Toronto in the early 2000s, after the peak of political violence in Peru and well into the country's more politically and economically stable years. When the family found the house they wished to buy shortly after arriving in Toronto, he offered the seller an extra $5,000 to move up the move-in date. Piero had a well-paying and prestigious job in Lima, yet the offer of further career advancement and what he describes as the extraordinary security in his daughters' everyday life in Toronto convinced the family to make Toronto their permanent residence.

Latin Americans are concentrated in three main areas in Canada: Montreal, Vancouver, and Toronto. The Toronto Metropolitan Area has the largest concentration of Latin American immigrants, with a Latin American population of over 150,000 (Veronis 2010, 177). Among those I interviewed, at the time of the interview twelve Peruvians lived in Toronto. One man was preparing to return to Lima at the time of the interview in Toronto, and he met with me for a second interview the following year in Lima. Among survey participants, fifty-five lived in Canada, most of them in the Toronto area. As in the case of Peruvians in the United States, both those who planned to return and those who did not maintained connections to Peru and had affective, social, and economic attachments to Peru.

Peruvians in Toronto identified as having arrived during different waves of Peruvian migration. One man explained that "some of us are from the Velasco wave, others from the Alan García wave, others the Fujimori wave," referring to the three presidencies during which Peruvians he had met in Toronto had arrived in the area.[15] Peruvians had left Peru for Canada largely because of the economic and political situation in Peru during these periods. During Velasco's presidency, from 1968 to 1975, rural-to-urban migration was more common than international migration, and international migration was largely reserved for the upper classes. It was during this time that the government expropriated property from many upper-class families. Alan García's first presidency, from 1985 to 1990, witnessed a sharp increase in emigration because of worsening economic conditions resulting in the worst economic crisis in decades, paired with rising political instability and violence. Alberto Fujimori's presidency, from 1990 to 2000, was characterized by increasing political violence between the Peruvian military and the Maoist-Leninist group Sendero Luminoso (Shining Path).[16] The structural adjustment policies he put in place resulted in the "Fuji-shock" and continued political violence. The widespread economic policies and increasing political violence by the Shining Path and the state led to massive internal displacement and an increase in international emigration. Indeed, the most common reason for leaving Peru has been the widespread political violence and economic instability of the period.[17]

Germany

In the European Union, estimates suggest a total of about three million Latin American immigrants, and a significant number of those have arrived since 2000 (Yépez del Castillo and Herrera 2007). Latin Americans arrived in Europe during three main periods. In the 1960s and 1970s, Latin Americans fled the dictatorial regimes of the Southern Cone. In the 1980s, predominantly middle-class Latin Americans arrived in Europe to pursue higher education degrees and because of increasing poverty in their home countries. Since the 1990s, Latin Americans have migrated to various European destinations mainly for economic reasons, in search of work and better opportunities for their families (Yépez del Castillo 2007).

In Germany, where Latin Americans make up approximately 1 percent of the immigrant population (Gruner-Domic 2011), the post-1990 flow of emigration from Latin America was motivated by economic need, family reunification, educational aspirations, and political asylum. Acquiring citizenship in Germany requires more years of residence than in Canada and the United States: immigrants must have lived in the country for at least eight years before applying for citizenship. Since 2000, German citizenship has also been possible based on birthplace, rather than only based on previous German lineage in cases in which at least one parent has lived in the country for at least eight years prior to the birth of the child. The largest immigrant groups in the country are from Turkey, Eastern Europe, and the former Soviet Union. Unlike immigrants from Turkey, immigrants from the latter two areas tend to be ethnic Germans. Among Latin Americans, the largest immigrant groups are from Brazil, Colombia, Peru, and Cuba (Hernández 2007). Among those I interviewed, at the time of the interview six Peruvians lived in Germany (in Munich), and four had returned to Lima after living in various parts of Germany.

During the summer of 2015, in a sunny biergarten by a small subway station on the outskirts of the city, I met with the current and former president of the Peruvian Cultural Association in Munich. Over beer and a large dish of pretzels, cheese, and onions, they graciously discussed with me the association's events (some of which I had participated in that summer), its origins in the late 1980s, and its plans for the future. When I asked how Peruvians were perceived in the area, Joaquín and Estela quickly responded that the racism commonly associated with the treatment of *Ausländer* (foreigners) was reserved largely for those assumed to be from Turkey. They agreed that, for Peruvians, as Estela explained, the more common attitude was to be viewed as exotic yet in a positive light, as in "You're Peruvian? How great!" This attitude is not afforded to those assumed to be from the much larger immigrant group, from Turkey. Originally arriving in Germany as guest workers and against the backdrop of Germany's long history of viewing immigrants as temporary sojourners and maintaining restrictive immigration and naturalization policies, Turkish immigrants are still considered as the most different from the nonmigrant German population in comparison to other immigrant groups (Schunck, Reiss, and Razum 2015).

The association, which seeks to promote Peru's culture, language, and music, organizes events throughout the year and boasts about 150 members. The members, the majority with German Peruvian families, attend various events with their families, particularly the association's most popular events: the Independence Day Parade (July 28), the Inti Raymi (Sun Festival) in June, the procession of the Señor de los Milagros (Lord of the Miracles) in early October, and the Día de la Canción Criolla (Day of the Criollo Song) in late October. These events, organized to bring Peruvians together, are characterized by large crowds and camaraderie yet also by complaints about how Peruvianness is unevenly represented.

Joaquín and Estela shared stories about how in spite of efforts to be inclusive and attentive to the requests of the relatively small Peruvian population in the region, without fail at every event someone feels their region of Peru or cultural background has been excluded. When for one event the hired band played music from the sierra, some people from the selva complained that hegemonic Peruvian culture excluded them. When at another event the food represented dishes from the coast, others from different parts of the country similarly complained of exclusion. Joaquín explained that he now attempts to hire at least two bands to represent at least two different types of music for events. These efforts to include more symbols of national identity help appease Peruvians' demands for broader representation among cultural associations and groups yet, as the following chapters discuss, do not address the more profound schisms and forms of exclusion in everyday life that Peruvians experience in Peru and abroad.

Peruvianness in Munich or anywhere else in the world is rarely fully inclusive. Indeed, this book suggests that particularly within Peru, inclusiveness is not a desired goal for many Peruvians. Joaquín and Estela, like other

Peruvians I met abroad and after their return in Lima, insisted that they would not have learned as much and as directly about differences among Peruvians had they not left their initial home communities and moved to unfamiliar settings. Leaving one's place of origin is not a prerequisite to confronting and potentially understanding differences among Peruvians, yet in these cases it was in these settings abroad, and later again in Peru, that several individuals expressed their first encounters with othering—of themselves by others. As Manolo in Munich put it, "It is a little sad," because "you are [considered] an outsider" in Lima and abroad, even when Peruvians felt distinctly at home in those spaces.

Getting Here and There: Tools and Pathways

As an anthropologist with an interdisciplinary background in Latin American studies and in an interdisciplinary gender and women's studies department, my approach to identities and everyday practices in the realm of Peruvian migration and return migration relies on an eclectic mix of methods and a transnational intersectional framework.[18] I draw on interviews and participant observation in the United States, Canada, Germany, and Peru; survey results from Peruvians in various parts of the globe; interdisciplinary literature on Peru and Peruvian migration; and my own longitudinal research in and on Peru to examine migration, including the idea and practice of return. I bring to the forefront ways in which transnational Peruvians across settings recognize and negotiate configurations of power based on social divisions and identities. Together, the chapters that follow examine ways in which belonging does not imply unproblematic inclusion, security, or rights for those who do not conform to dominant norms.

In spite of various differences, including age, gender, sexual orientation, marital status, place of residence, religion, and political ideologies, one area in which all agreed was that living transnationally involved a complicated mix of longing, pain, challenges, and joys that don't simply disappear once one settles in a new home or returns to another home. In addition to multisited fieldwork, interviews, and cultural texts, I draw on an online survey—a large one for a qualitative researcher—as part of a multiprong approach to transnational lives.[19] Distributed and completed in 2013, the survey provided me with a broad picture of Peruvians abroad and their views on return and was completed by 113 respondents.[20] Survey participants included 57 men and 53 women whose ages ranged from early twenties to late seventies in the United States, Canada, Germany, Australia, Spain, Switzerland, Mexico, and Argentina. Asked if they planned to return to Peru to live in the future, the majority (82 percent) who completed the survey responded they did not plan to return. The survey provided a broad picture of Peruvians abroad, including demographic details about age, time abroad, educational background, and marital status. It was also an important step in preparing for interviews and site visits. Questions (including open-ended questions) on the survey provided me with glimpses into more complex issues such as reasons for leaving Peru, plans to return or not return, experiences of discrimination in Peru and abroad, how ideas about race and gender may have been impacted by migration, and symbols or other factors respondents associate with Peru.[21]

In this book I am equally interested in understanding why some Peruvians want to and do return and why other Peruvians do not plan to return, and I draw on interviews and participant observation in Peru with return migrants as well in Canada, Germany, and the United States with Peruvian migrants. In both cases, as the following pages examine, everyday experiences of security and insecurity, family, and belonging play a central role in decisions and experiences of temporary or permanent returns or in the rejection of return as a possibility. Interviews with Peruvians who had returned, those who planned to return, and those who did not plan to return were central to my analysis of Peruvian transnational lives.

Short annual trips and a four-month Lima research trip in 2013 to focus on return migrants, a ten-day research trip to Toronto in 2014, a two-month research trip to Munich in 2015, and shorter trips within the United States in 2014 and 2015 provided opportunities to conduct interviews with forty-eight Peruvians on their migration experiences, including plans for or experiences of return. I conducted twenty-four interviews with return migrants in Lima and twenty-four interviews with Peruvians living abroad. Among those I interviewed, at the time of the interview six Peruvians lived in the United States, eleven had returned to Lima after living in the United States, twelve lived in Canada, six lived in Germany, and four had returned to Lima after living in Germany. Among those I interviewed who had returned to Lima after living abroad in places other than the United States, Canada, and Germany, the locations included Argentina, Australia, Colombia, the Dominican Republic, France, the Netherlands, and Spain. Interviews took place in Lima, Munich (Germany), multiple cities in Texas and Kentucky (United States), and Toronto (Canada).

This book draws heavily on analyses of interviews complemented by participant observation. While some interviews took place in homes, many—as the reader will notice—took place in coffee shops in the middle-class and upper-class neighborhoods Peruvians I interviewed resided in or frequently visited. In requesting interviews, I asked each person to suggest the most convenient place for him or her to meet me, and I offered to come to his or her house. During this research process, I found myself visiting more coffee shops than I had previously done, including during any other sort of research on or with Peruvians.

The choice of sites for and behaviors within these meetings and interviews also constituted an important window into markers of status and power relations within everyday, class-based, gendered social practices. First, they provided those I met with the opportunity to show me the sorts of (hip, trendy, classic, and/or well-established) places they frequented and in which they felt comfortable or wished to be seen. Second, meetings and interviews reflected gendered norms and gendered power relations. For example, men who were significantly older than me routinely insisted on paying for my coffee drink, even though as the researcher I offered to pay for theirs and had been the one to request the meeting. In one case, an upper-class Peruvian man sent me the name and address of a new and very expensive trendy restaurant in Lima when I asked him about a convenient place for him to meet me for the interview, and he suggested that we meet there during his lunch break. Even as I ate my beautifully presented, small quinoa risotto in the Miraflores restaurant, I suspected that when the bill came he would insist that he pay for it. I requested to pay for our meal as a token of appreciation for sharing his time with me for the interview, yet he informed me that when he made the reservation he told the waiter to bring him the bill. Significantly, women I interviewed, even when significantly older than me, did not try to pay or insist on paying for my coffee or food. In those cases, it was I who was expected to show respect, professionalism, and gratitude by taking care of the drink or meal during the meeting or interview. In meetings with older upper-class men, in particular, taking care of the bill signaled gendered norms of courtesy and the men's high economic and social status.

The popularity of meetings in coffeehouses stood in contrast to my previous research in Peru on women's experiences of violence (see Alcalde 2010), when interviews most often took place in women's homes, at public parks, and in offices and were complemented by participant observation in shelters, police stations, and other spaces women visited. During that research process, I visited neighborhoods and parts of Lima that I had not visited or known well previously and that were predominantly inhabited by poorer Peruvians.[22] As a middle-class Peruvian and one who had lived abroad for long periods of time, I had not become familiar with these areas during family return trips or my everyday life in Lima. In contrast, the research process for this book led me to neighborhoods in Lima with which I was often familiar, even if only by name or superficially. I had heard of many of the neighborhoods the Peruvians I interviewed lived in, and I had visited friends and relatives and attended events and restaurants in others: Miraflores, San Isidro, Surco, Barranco, La Molina, and San Borja. I explored many new streets before and after interviews as I surveyed the neighborhoods and reflected on individuals' experiences. While many of these neighborhoods did not have physical gates around them, the security guards on the corners and at the entrances of many apartment buildings served similar functions to the gates. In this way, middle-class neighborhoods in Lima reflect the global phenomenon among middle classes of not only seeking comfort and exclusivity but attempting to keep unwanted others out of their neighborhoods and lives, often through gated communities (Zhang 2010).

On the one hand, in connection to "studying up" groups with more power, it is valuable to note that middle-class Peruvians may have preferred to meet at coffeehouses in order to control the amount of information about themselves they wanted to expose to my prying eyes and ears, for convenience, and because those I interviewed generally did not know me well. This last point is further reinforced by my observation that the majority of the times (about one dozen) that I was invited into people's homes for interviews or to meet them initially happened when an acquaintance had personally introduced and vouched for me, making the invitation less risky. On the other hand, as someone whose research has focused on Peru for almost two decades and as a middle-class Peruvian, I am able to fully participate (and observe) in middle-class and upper-class spaces such as clubs, neighborhoods, and social events that move my observations beyond those spaces afforded through individual interviews. This last point is particularly relevant when we consider Shamus Khan and Colin Jerolmack's (2013) excellent point that what people say is not necessarily or even often the same as what they do. In their analysis of Khan's (2011) ethnography of an elite boarding school in the United States, at which Khan interviewed the students, they underscore that "elites are often spoken to (interviewed) but rarely observed" (Khan and Jerolmack 2016, 12). Khan (2011), for example, found that while students consistently spoke of their hard work and of meritocracy in interviews, his observations revealed a very different picture in which the select few students admitted to the school rarely studied for as long as they said they did.

My ability to observe and move in and out of spaces in which those I interviewed regularly found themselves meant they might run into me as they went about their everyday lives after the individual interview. During one of my return visits, an aunt and uncle invited me and my family to the Club Regatas as their guest to eat at one of the restaurants in the club. After the meal, we stopped by the beach there so that my younger son could play in the sand. Walking away from the sandy beach with shoes in hand and looking for a place to dry my son's wet clothes, I ran into a woman I had recently interviewed. She was there with her family as well, and after a brief, friendly conversation about the meals we had just enjoyed with our families we each went our way. In another instance, this time in Toronto, I visited a friend and her family in their home in a hip downtown neighborhood. Just a couple of minutes after we all left their house to walk to a restaurant in the neighborhood, we ran into a woman named Alicia, whom I had interviewed the day before, with her husband and a group of their friends. It was perhaps not surprising that my U.S.-born, Canadian resident friend and her family and Peruvian-born, Canadian resident Alicia and her husband were, indeed, neighbors, since they were all late thirty-somethings and early forty-somethings with similar educational backgrounds and interests. We happily chatted and made introductions, and then each walked in the direction of our chosen restaurant.

Journey Map and Themes

Peruvians live in many parts of the globe, and in these chapters it is the experiences of Peruvians who have returned to Lima and of those who continue to live outside Peru in Germany, Canada, and the United States that invite us to critically discuss what it means to be Peruvian both here and there and how incorporating the experiences of the middle classes and, to a lesser extent, the upper classes enriches our understanding of transnational lives and migration. The picture that emerges, the Peruvianness across borders and then back to Peru (and potentially out again), is not a tidy one but a fluid, jagged constellation undergirded by hierarchies of race, class, gender, and sexual identities that Peruvians challenge, resist, and reinforce. Chapters chart a path from Lima as the site of return to settings in Canada, Germany, and the United States and back again to Lima to examine spaces of contestation and reinforcement for what should and should not be included in constructions and everyday practices associated with Peruvianness.

Chapter 1, "Privilege, Racialization, and Exclusionary Cosmopolitanism in Transnational Trajectories," brings to the forefront power relations at stake in redefining realms of belonging and inclusiveness among Peruvian migrants. It introduces exclusionary cosmopolitanism as a theoretical framework for approaching transnational Peruvian identities. Within transnational Peruvian and, more specifically, *limeño* spaces, cosmopolitan belonging is often shaped by existing hierarchies: some migrants belong, while others are denied inclusion by middle- and upper-class *limeños*. The chapter examines racialization and racial hierarchies in Peru, particularly in Lima, and the construction and treatment of indigenous internal migrants as the historically inferior other for middle- and upper-class *limeños*. It brings into the discussion of cosmopolitan belonging how processes of racialization and othering also impact international migrants who had previously considered themselves to be part of the unmarked privileged middle and upper classes in Lima. In this chapter I suggest that while being cosmopolitan typically means thinking of oneself as a citizen of the world, we should not assume that being cosmopolitan includes views of others as belonging to that same cosmopolitan world. In practice, openness in the context of migration from and return to Peru may be more about distance from or tolerance toward the intolerance of others of similar class and racial backgrounds than about inclusiveness that defies existing Peruvian racial-class hierarchies. This conceptualization of cosmopolitanism illuminates the role of local configurations of power in Peruvian transnational lives. Through this style of exclusionary cosmopolitanism, middle- and upper-class transnational Peruvians simultaneously proclaim openness and reinforce their own superior high social standing. The approach to cosmopolitanism introduced in chapter 1 informs the discussion of transnational lives in the remaining chapters of the book.

Chapter 2, "Gendering Return: From Middle-Class Señoras to Migrants without Domestic Help, and Back," introduces return in the Peruvian middle-class context before moving on to more specifically examine everyday gendered and class intricacies for women throughout their migration trajectories. It focuses in particular on the role and absence of domestic servants in middle-class women's lives and the roles women embrace, resist, and renegotiate both outside Peru and after returning, as well as on women's experiences of autonomy and professional lives as these are impacted by migration trajectories. In chapter 3, "Gendering Everyday Violence and *Seguridad* across Spaces," it is not the political violence and economic insecurity in the 1980s and 1990s that motivated many to leave that receive sustained attention; instead, it is the more mundane forms of verbal violence, street harassment, and everyday anxieties that shape interactions with partners and children among return migrants that are central. The chapter explores relationships within the family, as well as migrants' behaviors and experiences in public spaces as these are informed by concerns about violence and security both in decisions to return and in postreturn everyday life. We read about the ways in which safety is gendered and is a major concern for return migrants. Family members and acquaintances warn women return migrants in particular about their increased vulnerability. Warnings about and the experience of street sexual harassment provide additional insights into the role of gender, race, and class in discussions and experiences of safety among return migrants within and outside the family. Discourses that discipline women specifically and present this control over women's movements as necessary for women's safety, as well as the street as a dangerous space in which middle-class anxieties about class, race, and gender intertwine, feature prominently in this chapter.

The intersectional approach to return and migration continues with the discussion of gendered hierarchies and security in chapter 4, "Heteronormativity, Homophobia, and Home." Chapter 4 focuses on quotidian technologies of exclusion against migrants who identify as gay, lesbian, and bisexual. Drawing on interviews, newspapers, ordinances and bills, novels, and field notes, I underscore how forms of exclusion, violence, and insecurity can undergird and even define belonging in the context of return. I also examine how oppressive practices within Peruvian migrant groups outside Peru may reinforce exclusionary practices. More broadly, I suggest that LGB individuals may find themselves in the difficult position of accepting violence against them—homophobic practices, jokes, and discrimination—in order to be at home with their families, in their homeland, and within immigrant communities, which leads to exclusion and a lack of rights in everyday life. In this chapter, return migrants both experience and perpetuate exclusion. The cases in this chapter underscore the return context as one in which homophobia permeates everyday life in public and intimate family settings and in which LGB Peruvians are subjected to exclusionary incorporation into the nation upon their return.

Chapter 5, "The Taste of Home: Nostalgia, Pride, and the Limits of Inclusion," invites us to reflect on some of the forms of exclusion and privilege examined in earlier chapters in the more mundane yet increasingly central space of food in constructions of Peruvianness. I discuss how a new, cosmopolitan image of Peruvians that comes out of recent nation-branding projects and culinary representations legitimizes the privileges and high social status middle- and upper-class transnational Peruvians seek to maintain abroad. Rather than unite Peruvians across class differences, the gastronomic boom and its manifestations in practice reinforce social hierarchies in which middle- and upper-class transnational Peruvians are at the top—therefore also reflecting the sort of exclusionary cosmopolitanism I argue is central to middle- and upper-class Peruvian lives. In this sense, food becomes a powerful site for the construction of particular brands of Peruvianness in Peru and abroad. In the concluding chapter, "Persistent Hierarchies and Transnational Lives," I reiterate the more prominent threads throughout the book and further examine the processes of exclusion at the heart of Peruvian racial-gender-class hierarchies in the realm of migration and return migration.

CHAPTER 1

Privilege, Racialization, and Exclusionary Cosmopolitanism in Transnational Trajectories

Alicia sat beside her teenage stepsister under a beach umbrella enjoying the view and the shade. Seeing an attractive man walking near them, she turned to her sister to nudge her to notice the "super hot and muscular" man. Her stepsister, whom Alicia was visiting, asked Alicia which man she was referring to, and Alicia told her she was referring to the man carrying and selling baskets. Incredulous, her sister exclaimed, "*Imbécil*, how can you like him? He's black!" As we sat sipping tea in a coffeehouse in wintry downtown Toronto, Alicia explained that it was precisely the type of racism and class bias expressed by her sister that troubled her most during return visits to Peru. Alicia visited and reconnected with extended family in Lima every two to three years. She had no plans to return to live in Lima.

A few months later and almost four thousand miles away, Marina and I sat in another coffeehouse in humid, gray Lima. Marina had recently returned to live in Lima from the United States, and here too the conversation soon turned to the forms of racism she perceived around her. She explained that she felt particularly frustrated that her boyfriend's father routinely made racist remarks. Yet, reflecting on the situation, she explained that she had become convinced that it was necessary for her to "think of being tolerant with the person that in the end is so intolerant" now that she lived in Lima again. Put another way, she believed she should be more accepting of her boyfriend's father's racism. Both Alicia and Marina expressed disagreement with the racism they identified in everyday life in Lima, and as middle-class white women from Lima, neither personally experienced racism there. For Alicia, living in Toronto provided the desired distance from behaviors and comments she found particularly frustrating. For Marina, openness and tolerance must be, paradoxically, directed at those who practice discriminatory behaviors to ease some of the frustration she feels as an individual about widespread systemic racism.

This chapter examines changing understandings and negotiations of race, racism, and class as Peruvians adapt to new settings outside Peru and through return journeys. It examines the racialization of poorer Peruvians in Lima and the racialization of the previously unmarked white middle classes beyond Peru's borders. Most significantly, it introduces a form of exclusionary cosmopolitanism that informs transnational experiences included here. The first part of the chapter examines racialization and racial hierarchies in Peru, particularly in Lima. I examine the ways in which racialization is tied to the construction and treatment of indigenous internal migrants as the historically inferior other for *limeños*, in particular in relation to middle- and upper-class Peruvians' perceptions of themselves. I then turn my attention to how processes of racialization and othering impact international migrants who had previously considered themselves to be part of the unmarked privileged middle and upper classes in Lima.[1] The third part of the chapter more directly engages with migrants' cosmopolitan aspirations and experiences, critically examining both the forms of openness migrants aspire to and the contradictions inherent in everyday practices. I argue that while to be cosmopolitan typically means to think of oneself as a citizen of the world, it should not also be assumed to include views of others as belonging to that same cosmopolitan world. In practice, openness in the context of migration from and return to Peru may be more about distance from or tolerance toward the intolerance of others of similar class and racial backgrounds, as in the case of Marina, than about inclusiveness that defies preexisting Peruvian racial-class hierarchies. This conceptualization of cosmopolitanism as exclusionary relies on and reinforces unequal power relationships so that middle- and upper-class transnational Peruvians simultaneously proclaim openness and reinforce their own superior social position. Belonging, in this sense, is intimately tied to racist and class-based exclusionary practices that have their roots in Peru and that Peruvians seek to translate across borders as a way to maintain and reinforce their social status and cultural capital, even as they become racialized as migrants.

Everyday Racism: Race and Racialization in Peru

Racism is part of everyday life in contemporary Peru (Callirgos 1993; Golash-Boza 2010; Oboler 2005; Portocarrero 1993; Vásquez del Aguila 2015). Racialization, a relational process whereby groups—and their assumed phenotypic characteristics—become associated with positive or negative meanings and social worth relative to other groups, has a long history in Peru and the region. Unlike South Africa's more widely recognized apartheid system, however, in contemporary Latin America social divisions based on race may not appear as evident. And it is precisely this "ambiguity and relative openness" of racial and ethnic markers that allows for "a veiled form of racism that finds its greatest power in the flexibility of its terms" (Reygada 2010, 30). Andean research makes visible widespread everyday discrimination and violence against those who are ascribed identities as indigenous or black even as the existence of racism is denied (Alcalde 2010; Boesten 2010, 2014; Bueno-Hansen 2015; de la Cadena 2000; Ewig 2010; Radcliffe and Westwood 1996; Rahier 2003; Seligmann 2004; Theidon 2013; Wade 1997; Weismantel 2001). In her research on the Andes, for example, Mary Weismantel noted that although "people are notoriously unwilling to use racial terms of any kind as self-descriptors," she observed widespread racism against those identified as indigenous or black (2001, xxxiv).

In the Peruvian national imaginary, the country's geographic regions represent distinct forms of racialization that differentiate and impose hierarchies onto broad categories of Peruvians (Alcalde 2010; Greene 2007; Orlove 1993). The regionalization of race means that negative connotations of backwardness and ignorance are popularly attributed to the highlands and jungle regions, whereas the coast, where Lima is located, is associated with modernity. This division is part of a broader historical nationalist project of modernization that has increasingly relied on a racialized distinction between the urban and whiter coast as exemplified by Lima and the more rural and indigenous rest of the country (Stepputat 2005).

In contemporary Peru, television shows commonly represent indigenous Peruvians and Afro-Peruvians through caricatured characters, such as Paisana Jacinta (Peasant Jacinta) and Negro Mama (Black Mama), who appear as less intelligent than and at best as sidekicks to white and mestizo Peruvians (Falcón 2016). My memories of spending weekends at my maternal grandmother's house in Lima in the 1980s include trying to fall asleep with the blasting sounds of laughter coming from the television in the background, which was often turned on to the popular *Risas y salsas* (Laughter and dances) on Saturday evenings. The skit-based comedy show featured stereotypical images of indigenous Peruvians, Afro-Peruvians, women in general, and those with disabilities. It held the honor of being the most popular show in Peru for several years during the 1980s.

The structural racism and violence inherent to the regionalization of race also positions some Peruvians as less worthy of access to citizenship and mobility than others. In practice, this means that poorer Peruvians from the Andean provinces or from the capital's *pueblos jovenes* (young towns, shantytowns) will confront multiple obstacles to apply for and obtain a foreign visa through official, state-sanctioned means (Berg 2015). These barriers make it necessary to go through complex and expensive informal brokerage systems in which prospective migrants may be encouraged to adopt more European-sounding names to increase the probability that they will gain access to necessary official migration documents (Berg 2015).

The depth and history of racial hierarchies were as apparent in the country's internal conflict largely between the state, the Shining Path, and the Movimiento Revolucionario Túpac Amaru (MRTA) from the early 1980s until roughly 2000 as they are in more recent hiring practices and everyday jokes. Focusing on the period between 1980 and 2000, Jelke Boesten (2014) analyzes sexual violence, particularly gang rape, perpetrated by the Peruvian armed forces against civilian women during the armed conflict. Drawing on testimonies compiled through the Truth and Reconciliation Commission from women and soldiers, Boesten's analysis and Pascha Bueno-Hansen's (2015) research emphasize that violence was founded on existing hierarchies of race, class, language, gender, and location. Put simply, soldiers routinely drew on women's racial background to determine whom to sexually abuse and how. Poor indigenous women were deemed as rapeable by lower rungs of soldiers, often in groups, while mestiza and whiter women were reserved—also to be raped—for those individuals with higher status in the armed forces.

While different from the more direct and visible forms of violence against indigenous women by the military, the Shining Path, and the MRTA, the less visible forms of structural racism apparent in hiring practices also reflect the devalorization of indigenous bodies. Peru has had an antidiscrimination law (Law 28867) since 2006, yet it has had little effect on hiring practices. To examine the role of racism in hiring practices in Lima, Francisco Galarza, Liuba Kogan, and Gustavo Yamada (2012) sent close to five thousand CVs to twelve hundred entry-level jobs advertised in Peru's mainstream newspaper, *El Comercio*. The CVs were identical in terms of qualifications, education, and work history, yet they differed in two significant aspects. First, the CVs differed in the gender of the applicant. Second, some CVs were of applicants with last names popularly associated with indigenous Peruvians, while others were of applicants with typically (white) European-sounding last names. The study revealed that men received 20 percent more interviews than women and that applicants with "white" last names received 80 percent more interviews than those with indigenous last names. Additionally, those assumed to be indigenous women received a much lower response rate compared both to indigenous men and to white women. Put another way, indigenous Peruvians continue to face structural obstacles to social, economic, and migratory mobility. The transnational intersectional approach introduced in the previous chapter further underscores the significance of considering more than only one identity in understanding the effects of racial-gender-class hierarchies on Peruvian experiences. In seeking employment, as in other areas related to mobility, indigenous women in Peru confront significant obstacles that cannot be attributed solely to race or gender.

In spite of this sort of evidence of widespread discrimination, denial of the existence of racism is pervasive—particularly among the middle and upper classes. Focusing on racism in everyday life, Tanya Golash-Boza (2010) finds four main arguments that *limeños* rely on to deny the existence of racism. In speaking with Peruvians in varied settings, I too came across these arguments. First, some *limeños* might point to the multiracial nature of their own extended families. Second, they might point to their multiracial or multicultural group of friends. Third, they might insist that stereotypes about Afro-Peruvians and indigenous Peruvians actually reflect reality. Fourth, they might argue that racism is about individual behaviors and that they as individuals do not practice those behaviors. In the case of racism against Afro-Peruvians, Golash-Boza (2010) notes that jokes that equate blackness with criminality are common and that depictions of Afro-Peruvians as hypersexual, ignorant, and primitive abound in the media. These sorts of stereotypes in part inform attitudes such as those expressed by Alicia's stepsister at the beginning of the chapter and often travel with Peruvians on their transnational journeys.

The denial of racism observed by Golash-Boza has also been noted by others and is featured prominently in the Peruvian documentary *Choleando*, which came out in 2012. The documentary, framed around the broad questions of whether or not racism exists in Peru, places at the center Peruvians discussing their views on racism. While they do not examine the myriad manifestations of racism in everyday life, the interviews in the documentary underscore the strong and often contradictory opinions Peruvians hold on the topic. Taken together, Peru's history and the opinions and experiences of Peruvians in the film and of people Golash-Boza and others—including myself—have interviewed underscore what Peruvianist scholars have long discussed: that masculine, fair skinned, and urban continue to be the norm in Peru and that racism is pervasive and has been reproduced in multiple forms since colonial times as a way to exclude other identities—particularly *indio* and *cholo* identities—from the national imaginary (Bruce 2007; Portocarrero 1993; Quijano 2000).

On Hierarchies: Imagining and Interacting with Internal Migrants

Migration is an integral aspect of Peruvian lives and has a long history. The presence of migrants—international and internal—is ubiquitous in Lima, where most of the individuals I spoke with came from or returned to. However, not all migrants are considered equal: migrants who travel overseas are generally viewed more positively than internal migrants from the Andes, who tend to be viewed with disdain by *limeños* (Nugent 1994). The placement of poorer indigenous internal migrants near the bottom of the social and racial hierarchies that the middle and upper classes call upon is central to transnational Peruvians' marking of their social status within and outside of Peru.

In Lima, interactions with internal migrants tend to be limited to unequal relationships in which internal migrants have significantly fewer economic resources and are employed by middle- and upper-class Peruvians as domestic servants or encountered in the service sector. The relationship to internal migration of Peruvians whose transnational lives this book examines was commonly, although not always, characterized by the perpetuation of discrimination against internal migrants. Few, if any, spoke of seeking out friendships with internal migrants while in Lima, although several interacted with and developed friendships with Peruvians from outside of Lima once they were abroad, usually in the context of Peruvian migrant associations.

Today, transnational families may have members both spread across national borders and within Peru. At any given point, international migrants may also become internal migrants and vice versa: a man from Ayacucho may immigrate to the United States after an initial migration to Lima; a woman from Huaraz living in Germany may move to Lima and then to her hometown a few years later. Internal migrants may find migrant associations or clubs with individuals from their specific town or village more easily than international migrants, who more often participate in migrant associations composed of Peruvians from across the country and with more diverse class and racial backgrounds.[2]

International migration is easier to keep track of than in-country migration in part because of national border controls, regulations, and immigration agreements between countries. In terms of scale, however, internal migration is significantly more widespread than international migration.[3] In spite of its prevalence globally, in-country mobility garners significantly less scholarly attention than international migration, to the point that the term "migration" is most commonly used to refer to international migration exclusively (Skeldon 2006).[4] Research on (international) migration rarely includes discussions of more common internal migration in Peru or elsewhere.[5] Yet, like international migrants, internal migrants seek to improve their and their children's lives by moving closer to spaces with increased economic opportunities and resources.[6]

Internal migration in Peru as elsewhere is commonly a first step in trajectories that include immigration to another country (Altamirano 2010; Berg 2015; King and Skeldon 2010; Paerregaard 2008, 2014). In Lima, internal migrants made up almost half the city's population by 1991 (Kokotovic 2007), and the percentage has continued to increase. Currently, about one-third of Peru's population is concentrated in the capital. To live in Lima has long been a sign of modernity and urbanity, and the middle and upper classes have sought to distance themselves from newer migrants, whom they commonly view as culturally and racially inferior.

Lima's wealth is concentrated across a number of neighborhoods that include Miraflores, La Molina, Monterrico, San Isidro, Surco, and San Borja. Surrounding or near these and other neighborhoods, as well as the main cathedral and plaza downtown, are a series of formal and informal settlements. Peruvian American novelist Marie Arana's description of San Isidro encapsulates some of the inequalities that are central to the spatialization of wealth in these neighborhoods: "The streets here were clean, hosed down by gardeners every morning; the walls freshly painted every Spring. Standing guard in the magnificent doorways of the commercial establishments were armed sentries in handsome uniforms, whose only apparent charge was to shoo off the beggars who stumbled in now and then" (*Lima Nights* 2010, 11). Walking through Miraflores, the district where my childhood home is located, it is possible to see the gardeners and maids Arana also refers to in neighboring San Isidro and in her novels on middle- and upper-class Peruvians' lifestyles hosing down and sweeping streets early in the morning, making sure the stench of opened garbage bags and stray cats' urine from the previous night is gone. These are increasingly rare sights in my parents' neighborhood, however, where the growing commercial centers Arana refers to are accompanied by casinos and high-rise apartment buildings where single-family homes once stood. The guards in these new commercial centers, in addition to keeping away beggars, act as a sort of social status police, questioning those they suspect of not belonging in these centers.

Many of the internal migrants whose families settled in and developed squatter settlements on unwanted desert land travel to these commercial centers on weekends, sometimes to be met with suspicious looks and increased surveillance. Among those older settlements, some dating to the 1940s and 1950s, many have consolidated and now boast city services, property titles, and brick houses. More recent *pueblos jovenes* continue to appear in more marginal locations. During the 1980s and 1990s, when terrorism and state violence led many to leave the country, displacement due to political violence led to internal migration to Lima. Newer periurban settlements have higher percentages of migrants than Lima's urban areas, and residents have comparatively less access to health care services and higher rates of poverty (Antiporta et al. 2015). Unlike middle- and upper-class Peruvians, who rarely visit periurban settlements, those who live in these periurban neighborhoods visit wealthier neighborhoods regularly both for leisure on weekends and during the week to work, often in the homes of wealthier Peruvians and in newer shops in commercial centers.

The vast majority of Peruvians I discuss here lived abroad with the backing of legal documentation and at a much higher economic cost than internal migration. As migrants, however, they may not have access to some rights and protections afforded to citizens in the United States, Germany, and Canada. As Ulla Berg (2015) has similarly shown for Peruvian indigenous and mestizo immigrants from outside of Lima, it is only in theory that all Peruvians have access to the same citizenship rights in their home country. As is clear here and in the following chapters, not all Peruvians can in practice count on the same rights in Peru, and some return migrants may experience exclusionary incorporation within their own hometown, as examined in chapter 4.[7]

When I asked transnational Peruvians how, in light of their experiences of migration and in some cases of marginalization and exclusion, they now viewed internal migration in Peru, the responses varied widely. On the one hand, there was widespread agreement that in general both internal and international migrants likely faced discrimination and exclusion. Typical responses echoed one person's view that "it is similar in terms of discrimination. People from the sierra experience discrimination in Lima, as Latin Americans experience discrimination in the United States," and that these experiences of discrimination in the context of migration to the United States and elsewhere may change one's self-perception and position in society. Transnational Peruvians further agreed that both forms of mobility required adaptation and learning new practices and customs. On the other hand, transnational migrants understood their own position of privilege within the context of migration and experiences of discrimination, and they struggled to maintain those privileges and to differentiate themselves from Peru's internal migrants.

Transnational Peruvians explained that in view of their own economic resources and in stark contrast to internal migrants whose villages or homes were destroyed through political violence, "I have the privilege to go back home." Transnational migrants also generally found themselves in environments of increased racial and gender tolerance outside Peru in spite of individual experiences of marginalization, whereas internal migrants often confronted less overall tolerance in the Lima setting. As this and other chapters make clear, the discrimination experienced by internal migrants commonly originated in the middle- and upper-class racist practices transnational Peruvians I interviewed embraced or, at the very least, did little to transform. One person explained that "if you have one rose you think it is beautiful and unique, but in a field of roses it is nothing." Going from feeling both unmarked and privileged in Lima to being viewed as an outsider in other countries led many to question their own practices, unearned privileges, and expectations in "a field of roses." These critical self-reflections were far from universal, however, and reflecting on one's privilege does not automatically or necessarily translate into tolerance and the embrace of differences. In other words, feeling discriminated against as an individual outside Peru does not necessarily lead to a reconceptualization of one's place in or desire to transform Peruvian racial-gender-class hierarchies.

Becoming Latinos: On Racialized Identities and Pushback against the Fluidity of Class

Through Peruvian migration to the United States, many middle-class Peruvians have experienced disjunctures that may not be readily understood by those who stayed in Peru.[8] In Florida, middle-class Peruvians experienced significant anxiety as they sought to reconcile their class backgrounds, professional experience, aspirations, and everyday life in Peru with the opportunities and challenges they faced in their new communities (Sabogal 2005). As members of privileged groups in Lima, few middle- and upper-class Peruvians had experienced the sort of racialization in everyday life they confronted outside Peru, particularly in the United States, as discussed in this section. The performance of their class identities was also challenged. For example, being middle class in Lima had meant relying on the cheap labor of poorer Peruvians as gardeners and domestic servants, yet abroad many could not afford to hire household workers and took on these and other tasks themselves in addition to seeking outside employment. The growing international migration of indigenous and at one point working-class Peruvians has further contributed to a broadening of middle-class transnational

Peruvians (Berg 2015). This broadening of the middle class may in particular challenge the forms of self-identification whiter and wealthier Peruvian migrants abroad had clung to as a way to differentiate themselves from less affluent and less white Peruvians both in and outside of Peru.

The significance placed on class status by migrants themselves is something Aldo alluded to when he explained that at the beginning of Lima visits his children typically go to the kitchen to serve themselves and clean up, as they do in their home in Toronto. By the end of the visits, however, the children have adapted to their privileged status in Lima so much that they expect a domestic servant to bring them their food and to pick up and take their dishes to the kitchen, and to wash them. Aldo reminds them that these behaviors are not what he and their mother expect of them in Toronto, yet he also confided in me that this is to be expected in Lima, given their social position there. His wife, he adds, tells him to "not meddle" so much with how her family—with whom the family stays during visits—behaves, including expectations regarding domestic servants.

Middle- and upper-class Peruvians rarely brought up being the targets of racism or class bias in Peru.[9] In speaking of their experiences abroad, however, migrants openly discussed discrimination against other Peruvian migrants they knew, as well as their own experiences of exclusion and marginalization.[10] Cases of direct discrimination were typically based on migrants' perceived accents and identification as Latino. Peruvians I spoke with expressed frustration at being categorized as Latino and the assumptions that were made about them based on the negative connotations associated with Latinos as a group.

In Lima, three women return migrants in their twenties recounted experiences of feeling discriminated against in the United States. These experiences were based largely on their inclusion in a broader Latino category. Over the last decade and a half, in the United States media depictions of immigrants have become increasingly negative and have included the association of immigrants with the spread of disease (Esses, Medianu, and Lawson 2013) and as particularly dangerous and polluting (Cisneros 2008, cited in Esses, Medianu, and Lawson 2013). Latino immigrants, and Mexicans in particular, are commonly viewed as criminal, untrustworthy, a security threat, and being in the country to take away jobs from citizens (Chavez 2008; Golash-Boza 2012; Hitlan et al. 2007; Timberlake and Williams 2012). As Ruben Rumbaut (2009) reminds us, the media, academics, and laypeople alike routinely use the term "Latino," an ethnic term, in ways that racialize Latinos. It is therefore common to read news stories and scholarly pieces about the Latino vote as compared to the black vote and the white vote, as if all three referred to racial groups. And by the middle of the twentieth century, "illegal" in particular had become associated with racialized Latinos in the popular imagination, particularly with Mexicans (Getrich 2013; Hallett 2012). Today, Latinos throughout the United States are perceived as belonging to the "race" associated with illegality (Hallett 2012).

Marina, who went to the United States for her university studies, narrated how when she visited her aunt at a café where her aunt worked one of the customers asked her aunt in front of Marina if Marina knew English and had come to the country in search of a job. Marina believed that "those things are super discriminatory: because I am Peruvian I only go to the United States for a job?! So those things would happen to me." In her U.S. college she confronted a similar situation: "There were a lot of children of immigrants from Puerto Rico, the Dominican Republic, and it was as if you are packaged in the same category as them, but you never feel identified with them. They don't have the same experiences." At times people she met would seem surprised and openly tell her that she was not the "typical Latina." Marina's comments underscore her own position as an English-fluent, middle-class Peruvian dissatisfied with the homogenization of Latinos and the imposition of a pan-Latino identity on her. As a middle-class, white Peruvian woman, a U.S.-imposed Latina identity marginalized her in a way she had not experienced in Lima. It was precisely her privileged background that she hoped to reassert by separating herself from "other" Latinos who did not have her privileged educational and socioeconomic background. She felt frustrated that her privileged position could not be as easily perceived in the United States as in Lima. It is precisely this frustration that she cannot assert her higher social status that also stands in stark contrast and opposition to the openness to and tolerance of different identities she proclaims and with which she identifies, which I discuss later in this chapter.

Recognizing the fluidity of her identities as white and privileged in Lima and as a racialized Latina in the United States, Marina explained that while living in the United States, she would "take advantage of returning [to Lima] every time I had vacations." Visits to Lima meant access to privilege and so to feeling more comfortable because she was not marginalized. Marina contrasts her own sense of national identity to the homogenization of Latinos across nationalities and places of origin in the United States and her own privileged class background and language skills background with the identity that is projected onto her by strangers on the street, as well as at her university. She pushes back against the imposition of a panethnic identity in part as a way to exalt her own privileged position compared to other migrants. My interpretation of her experiences underscores both how she experiences exclusion and, significantly, how she asserts her own belonging to a higher social status as a way to push back on exclusion. In pushing back against her marginalization, however, she is marking herself as different from, and therefore excluding, other Latinos (e.g., those who do come to the United States for work and are undocumented) from the group with which she identifies or feels she belongs.

María José similarly discussed how, when she was growing up in California, people she met assumed she was Mexican because she spoke Spanish. Although she would initially make a point of telling them she was Peruvian and pointing out differences in national identities, as she came to know more Mexicans and Central Americans she began to learn more about their histories, and "as I got older I no longer cared" if people identified her as Mexican. Seen as perpetually embodying the "other," María José commented that she was either identified as Mexican or asked, "You look so exotic! Where are you from?" Unlike Marina and many other Peruvian migrants I spoke with, María José now prefers to identify as Latina. She identified as middle class, as was the case for other Peruvians I spoke with, yet her family's middle-class status was significantly more recent than that of other Peruvians I spoke with who had more established *limeño* ties. Because María José's extended family did not live in one of the traditionally middle- and upper-class neighborhoods in Lima, she had experienced more egalitarian interactions with Peruvians of more diverse backgrounds while in Lima as a child than other Peruvians whose journeys I examine here.

Speaking of her experience on a college campus in the United States, Lucy also expressed frustration that she was perceived as different from and exoticized by those around her. This was something she had not experienced in Lima. She told me that one night as she was walking across campus a drunk white fraternity student came up behind her running and yelled at her, "Are you Japanese?" She has no Japanese ancestry, and she identified this incident as part of a broader pattern of homogenization of nonwhite persons that assumes that if you are "not white," then any guess about your "strange race" is valid. Because she was perceived as a woman of color in the United States, she explained, she came to be particularly wary of drunk white men on campus. She was concerned that they might perceive her "otherness" as a signal of inferiority and as a license to disrespect or sexually assault her.

Lucy's exoticization was also evident off-campus. During her visits to friends' homes over the Thanksgiving break, Lucy was attributed a broader racialized identity as a non-U.S. other. During her first year in college in the United States, she accompanied a college friend to her house for the break. During that Thanksgiving meal "I remember that her aunt asked me if there were cannibals in Peru, and she asked me if I was from the jungle, and for me that was, uff. Comments like that . . . are super ignorant, as if Peru were a country of exotic savages." Lucy was particularly annoyed that her friend and the family hosting her identified themselves as leftist and liberal, just as she and her family identified themselves in Peru, but that they would hold such stereotyped views about Peru and Peruvians. To her, being liberal and leftist should be synonymous with openness and the rejection of stereotypes. What also stands out here is that Lucy directly connected her and her family's upper-middle-class status to their leftist political views and self-proclaimed tolerance and curiosity and could not as easily fathom that other forms of openness would not recognize her high status in this cosmopolitan world. In a similar way to how internal migrants in Peru may be popularly associated with exotic (and therefore inferior) practices, Lucy as a racialized Latina in the United States was assumed to belong to a society with exotic, backward practices by self-proclaimed open-minded individuals in her new community.

Iván also went to university in the United States, and he brought up how others' perception of him as a racialized Latino impacted how he came to think of himself and his experiences. Now a college professor in the United States, reflecting on his years as an undergraduate in the United States, Iván narrated: "I remember it very clearly that I went to the college, I didn't know this girl and she confronted me and told me, 'You're a Latino man, don't get close to me!' And at the same time, the other defect is that there's this idealization of the Latino man, sexualized. It's a very confusing issue. . . . Your opportunities lie within the parameters of negative stereotypes." On the one hand, a young woman he did not know warned him to stay away from her: she viewed him as potentially dangerous and violent because he was first and foremost a Latino man to her. On the other hand, later in his college studies he was stereotyped as a "Latin lover" and assumed to be sexually savvy, desirable, and available.

Regardless of how he viewed himself, these objectifying stereotypical understandings of Latino masculinity had the potential to shape how others interacted with and treated Iván. In this divergence between his white, middle-class identity in Lima and his perception as a predatory Latino man in the United States, Iván's experiences mirror those of other privileged migrants for whom migration becomes their first experience in the embodiment of otherness. The gendered consequences of racialized stereotypes of Peruvian migrants were just as clear in Lucy's case, where an imposed identity as Latina made her feel more vulnerable to assaults and harassment, as in Iván's case. Lucy and Iván had little power to change how they were initially perceived by those around them.

As a university professor, Iván held more power to address and challenge stereotypes as he taught courses related to Latino studies. His courses regularly attracted Latino students. To him, not only self-identifying and being identified by others as Latino but also focusing on Latino issues in his research and teaching meant that "to me to be Latino here [in the United States] is not something I find problematic; instead, for me it is an opportunity to explore" Latino identities from multiple perspectives. Through his teaching, he was also able to "teach courses in which the students are constantly reflecting on that [Latino] identity, [so] it is both personal and academic." In his classes, stereotypes of Latinos could be openly and critically discussed and contested through discussions and readings. A Latino identity, although broader than the more specific "Peruvian" identification transnational Peruvians generally hold on to during their early emigration, allowed him to form relationships and alliances he had not previously considered easily attainable. Once he decided to embrace his identity as Latino he felt he could more easily "move, politicize, and find common experiences with people who think differently, and if we did not have that identity [in common], I would not be able to relate to and hang out with them." As we sat in a street-corner café on a hot summer day, Iván brought up how much he enjoyed spending time with Latino friends who did work very different from his and who came from different social and national backgrounds, including construction workers and other day laborers in his neighborhood. Iván embraced the Latino identity others had imposed on him during at least the last decade and a half he had spent largely in the United States, yet it was not one he had originally sought. As did many other Peruvians, Iván initially only identified as Peruvian. As time went by, he realized that in the United States he was "Latino" to others, and it was only when he returned to Peru for visits or was among other Peruvians that he could more easily identify specifically as Peruvian.

As I sat across the small table from Iván during the interview, I realized that Iván's answers and comments also touched on many of my own experiences as a Peruvian woman who identifies as Latina in the United States and regularly conducts research on and teaches Latino issues as an academic and whose courses attract Latino students. Like Iván, my interest in Latino identities is both personal and academic, and I come from a middle-class background in Lima. Although this did not arise during the interview, there is an additional point worth considering here, one that Iván's—and my own—experiences underscore: among Latinos, some privileged identities within the broader "Latino" identity allow us to move in and out of various groups more easily than others. For both Iván and me, our educational background, employment position, immigration status, lack of accent when speaking English, and fair skin allow us to move among different groups more easily than some other Latinos. For example, the Latino day laborers Iván had become friends with were dark skinned and spoke very little English, and some were undocumented. Their experiences moving smoothly through different spaces among both Latinos and non-Latinos would very likely be significantly more challenging and even dangerous (due to the threat of deportation) than my or Iván's movements in these same spaces. Whereas for Iván, and for me in many ways, embracing a Latino identity may be primarily "an opportunity to explore," for others that same broad Latino identity may intersect with other identities they hold and result in much more oppressive and difficult experiences as Latinos.

Similarly to Iván, me, and other transnational Peruvians, Dario, who returned to Peru after his graduate studies in the United States, explained that he had never felt Latino until he was treated as Latino in the United States. For Dario, Latino was an identity with negative associations, and an identity foisted on him rather than willingly embraced by him. Writing on Iranian middle-class men who migrated to Europe, Fataneh Farahani (2013, 2015) similarly notes that as middle-class heterosexual men, Iranians she interviewed were part of an unmarked group in Iran and had the experience of being viewed through the lens of stereotypes and treated as "other" for the first time when they immigrated to Europe. The experiences of Iván, Dario, and others discussed in this section similarly underscore the racialization processes previously unmarked migrants may experience. They also illustrate how racialized stereotypes of Latinos in the United States are gendered.

Peruvians I met in Munich brought up negative stereotypes of Latinos less often than did Peruvians in the United States and Canada. Nonetheless, the effects of racialization also informed Peruvians' experiences in Germany, particularly for those who stood out from the majority of Germans around them because of their physical appearance or language. I heard the same story from three people in Munich: a Peruvian woman they knew had recently gone to the airport with her two young children to board a plane to Peru for a brief vacation to visit family. Airport personnel did not believe the children she was with were her children and demanded proof that she was their mother. The woman, whom I met during my visit to Munich, is mestiza and has dark skin. Her husband is German and white, and their children had whiter skin than she. The children have German passports, and her passport is Peruvian.[11] This sort of situation, several Peruvians told me, was not uncommon when Peruvians of indigenous and mestizo background attempted to travel with their whiter German Peruvian children.[12] Those who shared this story with me also noted that they had not personally experienced this sort of situation when traveling with their children.

Embodying the Other through Language

Back in Lima, my interview with Olivia included a discussion of patterns of discrimination she too had observed against immigrants during the five years she lived in Germany. Olivia, who speaks German fluently and self-identifies as white, had not personally experienced discrimination. However, for her it was clear that for the "Turkish, the Arabs," there is a different sort of treatment, because they do not blend in as well as she considers she did and because there are so many more people from Turkey than from Latin America in Germany. Whereas negative stereotypes were commonly associated with the significantly larger Turkish immigrant population, Latin Americans comprised a very small population about which Germans had not yet developed widespread stereotypes and that did not have the same associations with guest workers and difference as Turkish immigrants—as discussed in the introduction. Latin Americans constituted a relatively small population, and some had arrived as political exiles during the right-wing military dictatorships in the Southern Cone in the 1970s. They had been welcomed by solidarity movements in Germany.[13] The only time Olivia had felt discriminated against was because of her accent when she spoke German.[14]

Discrimination, or the possibility of discrimination, based on foreign language skills and accents appeared as a common theme in interviews. Juan, a longtime resident of Munich, was convinced that "if you do not know German, regardless of how many degrees you have in Peru, you are an ignorant person to them." Juan had struggled to learn German during his first few months in Germany. Although he had become fluent in German, in reflecting on his own experiences and those of other Peruvians and Latin Americans, he considered language as the greatest barrier he had faced to fitting in and being recognized as an equal in everyday life in Germany.[15]

For Federico, who returned to Peru after earning a doctorate and working as a professor in U.S. universities for several years, even before he was seen, his accent marked him as "other" and became a cause for discrimination in the United States. During his early days in the United States he had attempted to call a taxi service to schedule a pickup from his apartment. In spite of his efforts to enunciate his words and calmly ask the woman on the other end of the line to repeat herself so he could understand, she became frustrated with his language skills and hung up on him after telling him, "We don't need people like you in this country!" This experience is similar to that of Fernando in Toronto, who explained that although he never felt discriminated against because of how he looked, since he didn't look "too *cholito*," when he spoke it was clear to others that he was, in fact, Latino because of his accent, and it was at that moment that he felt marked as an outsider.

Thirty-two-year-old Patricia in Texas similarly noted that although she had not felt discriminated against, she had seen how people treated her older sister. Her sister arrived in the United States and learned English at age fourteen and had an accent when she spoke English. Both sisters had lived in the United States for most of their lives, yet Patricia was never asked where she was from, whereas for her sister, this was a common question. Regardless of how at home her sister felt, the regular questions from strangers about where she was from underscored her suspected outsider status.

In these cases, regardless of how they view themselves, it was through speaking that these Peruvians became marked as different and felt most vulnerable. Critical commentary by Kathy Davis and Lorraine Nencel (2011) on their positions as U.S.-born middle-class migrant women in the Netherlands for over three decades brings to the forefront the role of white privilege in some transnational lives. In a cowritten piece also mentioned in the introduction on their experience of being continuously questioned about their perceived accents, the scholar-migrants observe that "it had been our privileged position as white middle-class immigrants that had allowed us to believe that we could just slip into the Dutch community effortlessly," adding that their "expectations concerning integration were not only naïve but also a product of white privilege and Eurocentrism" (2011, 475). Peruvians similarly expected a more seamless, and privileged, integration into their new communities, yet their accent, if not their skin color, marked them perpetually as "other" in ways they had not expected and against which they pushed back—such as through Marina's reassertion of her privileged position through return visits to Lima or Iván's critical discussions and deconstructions of stereotypes of "Latino" in his courses.

Recognizing Prejudices

Patricia tells me that racism is widespread in Lima but that it is class bias that she has come to recognize as a problem through her interactions in and out of Peru. She explains that she views *limeña* society as very *clasista* and that this even shapes how Peruvians interact abroad: "Something I can't stand and that's bothered me my whole life, you meet a Peruvian and [the Peruvian] asks you where you're from, from which neighborhood, which school did you go to, that's always so important for us." As noted in the introduction, the answers to these questions determine whether or not the people in the conversation belong to the same social group, shaping future interactions. In meeting Peruvians abroad, these questions have indeed been among the most common ones initially asked of me. They position Peruvians within particular spaces and, therefore, help determine their place in racial-ethnic and class hierarchies. The repetitive nature of these questions across spaces, rather than a curiosity, is better understood as a pervasive form of policing of ethnic-racial and class boundaries in Peru and transnationally.

Liliana is among the small group of Peruvians I interviewed who were originally from outside Lima. Similarly to Patricia, she notes that widespread racism combines with other forms of discrimination to cement exclusionary practices. She migrated to Lima for her university studies. There, she was asked about where she came from by students originally from Lima—the majority—who would look down on her and other students from the provinces. Tired of being treated as inferior, she would point out to her classmates that although they considered themselves *limeños*, it was very likely that their parents or grandparents were also from the provinces or somewhere else, because there is "no one who is pure, pure *limeño*." In response, some classmates would reply that they were certain that their family's last name came from Spain. In calling upon their Spanish heritage, they distanced themselves from indigeneity and internal migrants and reinforced their identities as legitimate *limeños*. Patricia's and Liliana's comments underscore the intersecting roles of class, race, and location in Peruvian hierarchies.

Recently returned from the United States, Dario, a heavyset dark-haired university professor in his midforties, expresses satisfaction with his personal and professional life in Lima and frustration with the rampant racism in the city. For him, the racism of everyday life had become much more visible, and unacceptable, since he returned from his graduate studies in the United States. He pointed out that "here, everywhere you hear sexist and racist insults, and it's shocking because people do it so naturally, and no one sees anything wrong with that." When I asked him if he could think of any examples he had recently encountered he replied that almost daily, as he moves about the city, he hears "cholo de mierda" (shit *cholo*), "serrano tenías que ser" (you must be *serrano* [a person from the highlands]), and "mujer tenías que ser" (you must be a woman) as insults toward those who are perceived as doing something undesirable. In the first two insults, the regionalization of race is quite clear, since the insults are founded on the person not being a true *limeño*. In the third case, the insult is based on the person being in the wrong because of the absence of masculinity. These insults had not been directed at Dario, yet they were directed at those near him, the first two typically at those assumed to not belong in Lima: either recent or assumed to be recent internal migrants. As he and I walked from his tall apartment building in Jesús María, where we met and chatted for a few minutes, to a nearby coffeehouse for the interview, and later as I walked to the main street in the neighborhood to catch a *combi* (a small public bus), I could also hear yelling and insults in the heavy traffic of some of the streets we crossed.

Twenty-six-year-old light-skinned Bárbara echoed the view that she perceived racial-ethnic hierarchies much more clearly after returning to Lima: "Here you do feel the discrimination, that if you are not blond or white," you are excluded, she explained. She too had recently returned from studying in the United States. She worked for a nonprofit agency when we met. As in Teresa's and Dario's cases, Bárbara did not feel she was the target of racist behavior in Lima, yet she witnessed racist behaviors and attitudes around her. She did, however, experience other forms of exclusion and marginalization as a bisexual woman, as discussed in chapter 4.

Speaking of her visits to Lima with her children, fair-skinned, blue-eyed Tatiana tells me that she feels happy that her children's public school in the United States exposes them to more diversity than they would be exposed to if they attended an elite private school in Lima, as she and her husband had done. Her statement might seem odd, given the wide range of identities in Lima, so it is worth noting here that elite schools in Lima rarely represent the range of diversity among Peruvians. Instead, they cater to (mostly) white wealthy *limeños*. Speaking of her son's experience and contrasting it to her own experiences in Lima, Tatiana explains that "here his classmates are Asian and from India, and he loves that, because someday he may end up working with them, and if this were Lima, someone would be saying that he was the *chifa* [Chinese restaurant] owner" if he had a Peruvian classmate of Chinese ancestry. Tatiana hopes her son will reject the overt and more subtle forms of racism she became accustomed to growing up in Lima. She regrets that even in her mother's home, it is clear to her and her children the different ways in which people are valued when they see how the extended family treats domestic servants during their visits. Tatiana wants her son to be successful and open to the range of international identities he may encounter in the course of a successful cosmopolitan career. Tatiana refers to international diversity rather than intranational diversity, since the latter is popularly considered inferior to the former. It is also worth emphasizing here that it is precisely this sort of privileged, controlled exposure to diversity that can be easily transformed into social capital (i.e., as understanding and appreciation of diversity) by cosmopolitan groups to further enhance their own privilege. Social capital gained through familiarity with diversity, however, does not require any sort of profound engagement with other people or advocacy to end the discrimination of those "others" considered diverse.

Discrimination against women working as domestic servants is rampant and stood out as a common theme in the discrimination migrants identified in Lima, particularly in their extended families' homes. In Toronto, Julián, who had arrived in Toronto in late 1980s with his wife and children, commented that he found it uncomfortable to watch his sisters and mother-in-law exploit domestic servants in Lima during his visits. The women who work as domestic servants in extended family homes typically come from provinces outside of Lima. As internal migrants, some lack family networks and support in the capital and are more vulnerable to exploitation. Thinking of his visits to Peru from Munich, Manolo too was particularly frustrated with how domestic servants continue to be treated in relatives' homes and told me his German wife had been surprised at what domestic servants are asked to do in Lima. One of his cousins, he added, found the idea of changing diapers so disgusting that she refused to change her infant daughter's diapers and instead demanded that one of the domestic servants be in charge of doing that.[16]

Discrimination against domestic servants was also apparent during beach vacations. Speaking of his time in Lima, Iván remarked that he finds it very difficult to be in Asia, an exclusive beach resort south of Lima where his family and friends vacation, because of the widespread racism he sees there. Asia is a popular summer beach destination for *limeños*, about ninety kilometers from Lima and consisting of numerous beaches along eight kilometers of coastline. Until 2007, posted rules in Asia denied domestic servants and nannies access to the ocean during the daytime, when wealthy families enjoyed the beach. The campaign Empleada Audaz (Audacious Maid) in January 2007 resulted in a mass protest in which hundreds of domestic servants and their allies, dressed in the typical uniforms imposed on domestic servants, demanded access to the ocean and an end to discriminatory practices.[17] The main goal of the campaign was to raise consciousness about the pervasive racism many Peruvians faced on an everyday basis. Speaking to me in 2014, Iván commented that he still saw discriminatory practices in Asia. Although beaches are public, in practice, access to them continued to be restricted by the demands of individual families on the nannies and domestic servants they employed, and treatment of domestic workers remains poor.

To reach the Asia beaches, middle- and upper-class beachgoers in private cars compete on the road in a zigzag with *micros*, public buses, and taxis, all zooming by to reach the next passenger, stop, or beach as fast as possible. Those leaving Lima to spend a few days in Asia pass by several shantytowns on the desert dunes by the highways on their way there. Traffic can make the popular journey last up to three hours during particularly busy periods. At the end of the road trip, those staying in Asia settle into expensive beach houses and their own microworld of leisure, away from the busy streets. Armed with beachwear and often accompanied by domestic servants and nannies, *limeños* tired of leisure time on the beach can also visit exclusive nightclubs, shops, and restaurants in the Asia shopping center.

Critical Reflections, People of Color, and the Rejection of (Some) Prejudices

Lucy, who shared the story of being asked about cannibals and her jungle life in Peru by her hosts in the United States during the Thanksgiving break, went on to discuss how her experiences of feeling exoticized and discriminated against by white Americans in the United States had impacted the way she viewed herself and the people around her. In Lima she belonged to a privileged group in which racism and class discrimination were not directed at her, but in the United States she seemed exotic to some. In searching for spaces in which she felt comfortable, she learned about and began to identify with concepts such as "persons of color" in college, and these helped her to more critically examine and reflect on her experiences in the United States. The fluidity of identities from white and middle or upper class in Peru to a person of color in the United States is similarly reflected in Marie Arana's memoir, *American Chica: Two Worlds, One Childhood*. Like many Peruvians I spoke with, Arana notes that her American Peruvian heritage brought her privilege in Peru and exoticization that sometimes resulted in marginalization in the United States.

In spaces in which she and other persons of color could discuss their experiences at her U.S. university, Lucy found points in common both in how she and others experienced college life and in the circumstances under which they felt threatened in everyday life outside of the university setting. This recognition of common experiences did not, however, mean she embraced a Latina identity or renounced any privileges associated with her position in Lima. It is her experience of embodying otherness that she refers to in telling me that she now better recognizes the racism that pervades everyday life in Lima and that affects other Peruvians most profoundly.

On a warm evening in a cozy Italian restaurant in Munich, white, light-haired Manolo referred to his own childhood and youth in Lima before traveling to Argentina and then settling in Germany as sheltered and full of racism. Reflecting on how his daughters' childhood and their views are different from his own at their age, he lamented his own racism as a young man in Lima. To Manolo, his years in Germany have been critical to his changing worldview. He attributed his growing and less judgmental respect toward those who are different from him to his experiences in Germany, where he noted that he learned to refer even to the trash collector as *Herr* (Mr.) as a sign of respect. He explained, "I feel terrible regret about how I treated the domestic servant" in his house. He believes that although his own attitudes have changed, his friends from school in Lima have maintained the racism of their younger days. This view—that one's attitudes have changed but those of other Peruvians who have stayed in Lima have not—was a common one.

Iván made a similar comment as he discussed invariably feeling uncomfortable with his childhood friends' racist behaviors during visits to Lima. Until he left Peru to go to college in the United States, Iván explained, he had "certain privileges, very spoiled, and I was very comfortable in that life." Although he did not attribute his critical introspection to the U.S. environment, he recognized that the migration process presented him with new opportunities to question identities and privileges he had previously taken for granted. He now distances himself from the entitled and racist behaviors he had previously enjoyed. To him, his thirty-something-year-old friends from an elite British school in Lima "have not changed, they continue to think the same way as when we were sixteen" about race and class. Like Lucy, Iván now employs the term "people of color" to reflect his own evolving views about identities and oppression. Unlike Peruvians who are typically discriminated against because of their geographic origins (highlands or jungle areas), race (not white or mestizo), or language (Quechua or another indigenous language), Lucy, Iván, and other transnational Peruvians whose experiences I discuss count on resources that allow them to move freely between spaces in which they may be marginalized and more familiar privileged spaces in Lima.

For Marco, it was during his time in the United States that he had the opportunity to reevaluate the hierarchies he had long taken for granted and that he now views as marking whiteness as safe and positive and all else as potentially dangerous or inferior: "Here, let's say, they are more closed-minded about the 'be careful to not be around him, you know he's not *blanquito* [white],' that type of thing. There [the United States], no, we are friends, we are more 'open mind,' that's how you say it. So the *negrito*, the *cholito*, and the *blanquito*, we are the same. And that did change in me, because I was racist when I lived here [before]." Migrants carried ethnic-racial hierarchies with them across borders. These hierarchies, and migrants' former position within Peruvian social hierarchies, however, made little sense outside their lives in Peru.

In their attempts to initially apply Peruvian ethnic-racial hierarchies to new settings, several people mentioned that it was their children who most strongly challenged their views and pushed them to recognize their own prejudices. Carlos explained his daughters' influence in his way of thinking: "To tell you something that sometimes shocks you, especially at the beginning when we first arrived, for example, to see a black man [*un morenito*] with a white girl. So we made the comment, and they immediately stopped us, our daughters. They've educated us, and we've learned from them." Migrants referred to their children as the driving force behind their changing attitudes toward racial difference—at least racial difference outside Peru. The dynamics surrounding racial, cultural, and religious differences were commonly brought up as something that had been shocking at first and that migrants slowly became more open to. Some migrants embraced difference as they became more critical of the racial biases they had brought with them and the negative effects these had on others and on their family in adapting to life in a new setting with its own set of differences.

Cosmopolitan Aspirations and the Parameters of Exclusionary Cosmopolitanism

Like Tatiana, Carlos, and other Peruvian migrants with whom I spoke, Ana María brought up her children's openness to others with pride and noted how it helped her and her husband reflect on and shape their own attitudes and behaviors in Toronto. The Peruvian social divisions founded on ethnic-racial hierarchies she and her husband had grown accustomed to in Lima required significant revisions in their new community. Speaking of her children's views and the long history of racism in Peru, Ana María poignantly recounted how a few weeks earlier her eight-year-old daughter had scolded her because she had commented that it was odd that one of her daughter's classmates wore a head covering. Her daughter, indignant that her mother would comment on that, replied, "It's part of her culture. What's wrong with that?!" For Ana María, her daughter's response was a positive sign of her openness.

Ana María felt proud of her daughter's openness. She also recognized the limits of her own tolerance, adding that "in the end the racist parameters stay with us. I mean, in the end, you have the friend, and you're thinking that they may get married in the future, and that will not sit well with you." In bringing up her concerns about possible outcomes of her daughter's openness to difference, Ana María speaks to the persistence of ethnic-racial hierarchies. For her, unfamiliar nonwhite people may be acceptable coworkers and friends in the same way Tatiana appreciated international forms of differences among her son's classmates, but she continued to have strong reservations about anyone *too different* as an intimate partner for her children. Ana María's comments and those of other Peruvian migrants discussed in this chapter and throughout the book open the door to examine the role of cosmopolitanism in these migration trajectories. They present situations in which migrants applaud tolerance and openness yet may also qualify these forms of tolerance as they seek to be both cosmopolitan and to hold on to social divisions that recognize their own superior status based on Peruvian racial-class-gender hierarchies. It is this rich tension between the desire to belong and be open to new forms of difference and the desire to assert one's higher social status by excluding others based on assumed racial and class differences rooted in Peru that shapes exclusionary cosmopolitanism.

Cosmopolitanism tends to be analyzed in depth as an attitude, value, or state of mind yet less critically examined in connection to accompanying concrete social practices and behaviors tied to specific individuals. In approaching cosmopolitanism and proposing exclusionary cosmopolitanism as a useful concept for understanding the experiences of middle- and upper-class transnational Peruvians, I am responding to calls to "make cosmopolitanism a valuable analytical concept" by resisting its appeal as a largely abstract fantasy rarely tied down to real people and practices (Skrbis, Kendall, and Woodward 2004, 119). It is individual practices, behaviors, and even views, I posit, that are often in tension with claims of openness as a state of mind popularly associated with elite travel and approaches to difference in the world.

Given the robust body of interdisciplinary scholarship on cosmopolitanism, a brief discussion of cosmopolitanism is useful here to further situate my approach to exclusionary cosmopolitanism as it intersects with previous approaches. Since Immanuel Kant's essay "Perpetual Peace" (1795), written over two hundred years ago, cosmopolitanism has been conceptualized from multiple perspectives. Cosmopolitanism has been variously defined as a state of mind of the well traveled who are comfortable in diverse cultural settings (Hannerz 1996) and enjoy feelings of citizenship and belonging that transcend nation-states (Calhoun 2002). It has also been identified as a set of predispositions that allow both an understanding of local practices and an openness toward an increasingly interconnected world (Ahmed et al. 2003). Nina Glick-Schiller (2015b) approaches cosmopolitanism as an aspirational outlook that does not negate disparate pasts, cultural practices, and identities yet that looks beyond national and religious allegiances to include shared moments of recognition, commonality, and kindness. Kwame Anthony Appiah's view that "there is much to learn from our differences" (2006, xv) underscores a now commonly accepted view of cosmopolitanism as a moral orientation that seeks out the positive value of human, particularly cultural, differences in the modern world. As Appiah also observes, however, power relations and hierarchies are not divorced from this moral orientation, and it is possible to see in the cosmopolitan a "posture of superiority towards the putative provincial" (2006, xiii).

Anthropologist Pnina Werbner (1999) pushes back against the trend to associate cosmopolitanism with global travel, viewing it as openness not limited to immigrants or elites. In her study of nonelite Latin American women in Germany, anthropologist Sandra Gruner-Domic (2011) also resists the common trend of associating cosmopolitanism only or mostly with elites and interprets cosmopolitanism as individual competencies to create and engage in inclusive social relations. Geographer Daniel Hiebert (2002) similarly takes an ethnographic approach to cosmopolitanism, emphasizing that in the community context he focused on in Toronto, it includes everyday acts of hospitality toward people of different cultural backgrounds within the constraints of national borders. In their recent edited volume on cosmopolitanism, anthropologists Nina Glick-Schiller and Andrew Irving (2015) agree that displacement or travel is not a prerequisite for cosmopolitanism.

While some approaches challenge cosmopolitanism's traditional association with elites, and others push back on the centrality of travel or migration to cosmopolitan outlooks and practices, few engage with openness equally critically as a central component of these varied approaches to cosmopolitanism. As in Ana María's case, however, openness may be selective, partial, or limited. Here it is worth remembering Glick-Schiller's warning that power must not be overlooked in approaching cosmopolitanism, since even when cosmopolitans are not elites, they speak "from a position of unequal and superior power—the power to define who and what is different and to grant or not grant humanity to others" (2015b, 32). Sara Ahmed and colleagues similarly underscore that "home and migration cannot be adequately theorized outside of these spatialized relations of power" (2003, 6). In his ethnography of an elite U.S. boarding school, Shamus Rahman Khan (2011) aptly describes "privilege" as the combination of rhetorically embracing openness while protecting the status quo. It is this qualified openness and often reinforcement of one's own privileged positions vis-à-vis others that are central to exclusionary cosmopolitanism.

Selective openness in this way facilitates the maintenance and application of Peruvian gender-racial-class hierarchies abroad. Recognizing the limits of expressed openness draws attention to the role of power within cosmopolitan outlooks and allows us to see how transnational Peruvians determine acceptable and nonacceptable forms of difference. On the one hand, the cosmopolitan outlooks embraced by migrants' children and by some migrants themselves may present them as postracial, postgender, and postclass individuals. On the other hand, the intersection of particular gender-race-class identities is precisely the defining factor for desired exclusion in many of these cases.

Peruvian migrants may feel that they are part of a greater community of global citizens across borders. Being part of a larger, greater, and more cosmopolitan community does not, however, negate their own forms of self-identification, which are based in part on Peruvian racial-class-gender hierarchies that place them in positions of power above others. This simultaneous sense of tolerance and self-identification founded on dominant Peruvian hierarchies makes it possible for some to perceive a black man as an acceptable classmate or coworker and reject the same man as an appropriate spouse for a child, regardless of a shared common humanity. Similarly, friendships across class lines may be welcomed outside Peru even as relations of power and divisions that characterize interactions across class lines are reinscribed during visits and extended stays in Peru.

After eight years in Germany, Manolo felt content with his professional life, incorporation into a German community, and travel, but he dearly missed socializing with other Peruvians.[18] He therefore decided to find and get to know other Peruvians in the city. His attempts to make meaningful connections with Peruvians near him were difficult because he did not feel he had much in common with other Peruvians he met. He enjoyed meeting other Peruvians, making jokes, and celebrating Peruvian holidays together. These meetings in large groups, however, provided only superficial connections that rarely resulted in more than occasional multihour get-togethers to celebrate Peruvian holidays.

Manolo's experience illustrates some of the ways in which Peruvian racial-class-gender hierarchies manifest themselves transnationally. The Peruvian-ness Manolo and other Peruvians shared through food, jokes, and small talk and their sense of connection became increasingly limited as biases held about each person's social background surfaced. These biases tended to come out in jokes or unexpected comments while drinking among *patas* (buddies, friends) who otherwise spoke of feeling comfortable and respected around each other. Manolo had attended elite private schools and frequented elite social clubs in Lima, and he migrated with significant economic resources. Peruvians he met in the 1990s in the Munich area tended to have grown up in shantytowns and attended public schools, and sometimes they had parents who worked as household workers in the neighborhoods Manolo grew up in. The size of the Peruvian population in Munich was very small in the 1990s, and Manolo did not find much in common with other Peruvians because of their significantly different class backgrounds. The opportunities to socialize among Peruvians across class and geographic lines in ways that are typically avoided in Lima was also alluded to by many other interviewees. Peruvians in the United States, Germany, and Canada similarly commented that "different social classes get together here," "food unites us," and "being outside Peru unites us."

Like Manolo, Iván spoke both of these new opportunities to socialize with Peruvians across class lines outside Peru and of the obstacles to developing and maintaining these relationships. During his time outside Peru, he had lived both in Germany and in the United States, where he currently lives and works. Referring to his earlier stay in Germany, Iván described how one of his closest friends there was also Peruvian. Unlike Iván, who, like Manolo, grew up in an upper-class household in Lima, his friend was from the Amazon "and had had a very different life from mine. There were no schools, we were not alike, but we became friends, and the result was a friendship that would have been impossible in Peru." Iván, like many other Peruvians I spoke with, was aware that even when Peruvians of different social classes shared the same space in Lima, these interactions tended to be limited to hierarchical, racialized encounters of employer/employee and customer/seller that rarely developed into relationships of mutual understanding and respect.

During his regular trips to Peru, Iván felt uncomfortable with the insistence on distance from others from lower social classes and the racism he routinely witnessed among his relatives and acquaintances. These practices are instrumental to maintaining racial and class hierarchies that prevent the sorts of friendships he and his friend had the opportunity to forge in

Germany. Like Manolo, Iván sought out opportunities to travel to see new places and people. Unlike Manolo, Iván made a point of also traveling within Peru as a way to escape the confines of Lima society once in Peru. It was during these in-country trips, particularly to places tourists avoided, that he found opportunities to converse with and learn about differences among Peruvians. He acknowledged that these short exchanges did not result in the establishment of "real ties" but that the trips and exchanges provided him with, as he put it, "possibilities to talk with people who are outside the small world in which I am" during his Lima visits.

Iván's emphasis on openness through interactions made possible by in-country travel rather than travel outside the country is not the most commonly recognized form of cosmopolitanism, yet it reflects Hiebert's focus on the significance of local-level interactions. In his ethnographic study of an internationally diverse neighborhood in Toronto, Hiebert (2002) argues that cosmopolitanism is manifested through cultural outreach, curiosity, and hospitality in everyday interactions between individuals and families from diverse national and cultural backgrounds. These interactions may include such simple actions as the exchange of recipes and fruits and vegetables from different parts of the world, as well as information about these and conversations that enhance understanding across difference.

For Hiebert, as for Iván, cosmopolitanism is "a way of living based on 'openness to all forms of otherness,' associated with an appreciation of, and interaction with, people from other cultural backgrounds" (2002, 212). This form of local cosmopolitanism includes everyday acts of hospitality toward people of different cultural backgrounds within the constraints of national borders and is what is most lacking in the forms of cosmopolitanism embodied by other middle- and upper-class Peruvians. Yet even for Iván, embracing differences among Peruvians has little effect on the everyday manifestations and maintenance of racialized hierarchies among acquaintances and friends in Lima. Put another way, it is worth noting here both that definitions of cosmopolitanism do not typically include effecting change in how others behave and that in the context of Peruvian racial-class hierarchies embracing difference does little to transform these hierarchies. The particular parameters of Peruvian transnational cosmopolitan outlooks are born in part from the persistence and embeddedness of internal hierarchies in transnational trajectories, a topic I turn to more in the following section. Transnational Peruvians typically both feel uncomfortable with pervasive forms of racism in Lima and benefit from the structures and unequal systems that maintain these forms of racism during visits and postreturn.

Cosmopolitan Parameters:
Everyone but the *Cholo de mierda*

In *The Peruvian Notebooks*, Peruvian novelist Braulio Muñoz introduces us to Anthony Allday, a Peruvian migrant in the United States who feels "lucky to have been born white, like his mother" (2006, 79). Anthony believes that looking white can open doors for him that being identified as indigenous would not. In the United States, Anthony avoided "travel on trains and buses because he disliked meeting poor Blacks and Latinos" (2006, 79), and he worked to distance himself from other Peruvians. Yet as he attempts to rebuild his life in the United States and distance himself from his indigenous past, he feels he cannot fully escape his own racialization and on at least one occasion laments that he looks "like a cholo de mierda" (2006, 278) even outside Peru.[19] The rejection of the *cholo de mierda* by this fictional character reflects a broader process of racialization and discrimination through which some Peruvians are both the privileged and the discriminated-against migrants, a process also apparent in the experiences of Peruvian migrants I met. In Peru, however, *cholos* are popularly assumed to be recent migrants from other parts of the country or to live in the settlements historically developed and inhabited by internal migrants.

"Cholification," the "processes of indigenous mobility, urbanization, and migration" (Greene 2007, 340), reflects cultural-racial processes in Peru that complicate nonindigenous/indigenous and urban/rural dichotomies. Broadly, it is a term popularly employed to refer to someone of indigenous background whose upward mobility, migration, or language identify her or him as mestizo (Quijano 1980). In contemporary Peru, the term *cholo* is also a packed concept. On the one hand, it is routinely used as an insult to refer to a person's inferiority due to her or his indigenous roots. On the other hand, the term *cholo* has also acquired positive connotations as more people proudly self-identify as *cholo*. In appealing to a broad Peruvian base, former president Alejandro Toledo (2001–2006) proclaimed for himself a *cholo* identity and was recognized as El Cholo publicly. In spite of Toledo's strategic use of a *cholo* identity, *limeños*, particularly those of white, middle- and upper-class background, applied the term *cholo* negatively to Toledo, as when he was referred to as a *cholo de mierda* (shit *cholo*) (Alcalde 2010).

In Canada, Fernando explained that multiculturalism as an official policy in his everyday life meant that "in a school, seated together we have the Chinese, the black [person], the *cholo*, all equal." This sort of recognition of equality within diversity proved particularly difficult to embrace and apply not only inside but also outside of Peru. Multiculturalism could mean, as it did for Gabriela, a long-term resident of Toronto, that "what is beautiful about this country is that because it is a country full of immigrants, then the accent, the color, that [discrimination], I haven't experienced." For her, the range of nationalities, languages, and skin colors made it easy to feel she belonged and was respected in her country of residence. She emphasized, however, that education and social position are key to being accepted, noting her belief that as long as one presents oneself as educated, there are no problems, because Canadians are open, tolerant people. Gabriela's qualification of openness associated with some types of immigrants (those who are educated) and not others (those who do not appear as educated) is echoed in Hernán's remarks about his own self-identified racism and illustrates the sorts of exclusionary cosmopolitanism to which I refer in this book.

Hernán stated that, according to his wife, he was very racist. To him, he explained, his racism had to do with two factors. The first, which he considered "not very important," was skin color. He would meet someone and see her as "*cholita*," and his wife would ask, "Where do you see that she is *cholita*? You are very sensitive to the issue of skin color." Hernán agreed with his wife's assessment. Second, and what was more important, according to Hernán, was the quality of a person. After asking me to please pardon his language, he proceeded to explain that there was an important difference between "the *cholo*" and "the *cholo de mierda*." Whereas he claimed to not feel hostility toward *cholos*, and he did not believe he treated people badly because he considered them to be *cholos*, he did feel justified in his rejection of some *cholos* who held certain attitudes: those who treat people badly because they see that person as white or as a bureaucrat. With *cholos* who held these attitudes, Hernán stated, it was impossible to reason. Hernán's views directly draw on and seek to justify prevalent racism in Peru and reinforce and naturalize his own privileged position by presenting certain identities (*cholos*) as anathema to modernity, civilization, and desired forms of Peruvianness—all factors his narrative suggests he and those like him more adequately embody.

In both Gabriela's and Hernán's assessments of their own openness and the openness they attribute to Canadians, Peruvian racial-class hierarchies support rather than challenge Gabriela's and Hernán's inclusion in an open, cosmopolitan world. The cosmopolitan world they aspire to through concrete practices and beliefs in everyday life is in practice an elite one to which only a select few can belong. According to this conceptualization of openness, migrants may belong to this cosmopolitan world as long as they are clearly positioned near the top of the Peruvian social hierarchy, one in which Gabriela and Hernán are visibly recognized as desirable migrants and their privilege in Peru is recognized across borders. Additionally, the racialization of some Peruvians as irrational and disrespectful of these hierarchies is used to justify their exclusion from this cosmopolitan—civilized?—community in and out of Peru; they are labeled undesirable and unacceptable. Like Hernán's references to irrationality, these characterizations deny some Peruvian identities fluidity even in contexts of continuing physical and migratory mobility. Middle- and upper-class Peruvians can thereby both be "very open" and exclude others from proclaimed worlds of tolerance.

The identification and singling out of some Peruvians as undesirable by categorizing them as *cholos* is something Marina discussed as particularly noticeable after her return to Lima. As noted in the opening paragraphs in this chapter, she explained that whereas for her being outside Peru had resulted in her rejection of the types of racism that mark some people as *cholos* and *indios* as a way to deny them basic forms of respect and rights, for her boyfriend's father these forms of racism were accepted, and he practiced them. She explained, "It's a fight with him, because I see he is very open, but if someone cuts him off in the car, it's '*cholo*,' '*indio bruto*' [brute/stupid Indian]." For Marina, her openness and tolerance contrasted to the racist behaviors and attitudes that she regularly witnessed and that bothered her. More significantly, in spite of his routine racist comments, she insisted that her boyfriend's father was "very open."

In reflecting on the racism she witnesses, Marina laments the racism yet significantly concludes, "I abhor anything of that type but I will also be more tolerant of those things, I have to think of being tolerant with the person that in the end is so intolerant." In this case, openness and tolerance is directed at those who practice discriminatory behaviors and whose attitudes place some Peruvians outside the realm of belonging. The view of *cholos* as somehow outside the realm of acceptance for upper- and middle-class *limeños* is also reflected in the work of Berg. In her book she examines how Peruvian migrants confronted "centuries-old urban constructions of indigenous Peruvians and their urban *cholo* counterparts as rural, backward, and essentially unfit for citizenship, metropolitan modernity, and international travel" (2015, 5). Because of these prejudices, those who returned to Peru were sometimes made fun of as "Americanized *cholos*" (Berg 2015), as if they were putting on airs and pretending to be something they could never be because of their *cholo* identity. In these narratives, there are limits to the fluidity of *cholo* identities, and being identified as *cholo* is rarely viewed in a positive light.

Persistent Exclusions in a Cosmopolitan World

This chapter examines how exclusions founded on racial-gender-class hierarchies underpin Peruvian lives and are both destabilized and reinforced through mobile lives. The cases examined emphasize that to move away from Peru tends to make a person more aware of her or his own social position in Peru, yet this process does not necessarily promote more openness and tolerance toward others. For many middle- and upper-class Peruvians, living transnationally means searching for ways to maintain and make visible their high-status identity both in and outside of Peru. In the realm of the everyday, middle- and upper-class Peruvians' desires for maintaining social standing attributed to them in Peru reinforce the exclusion of other Peruvians from the realms of belonging through racist practices that contradict claims of tolerance central to cosmopolitanism.

Gruner-Domic's observation that "migration may require an individual to change but does not necessarily lead to the migrant adopting a cosmopolitan position" (2011, 476) speaks both to the forms of marking differences Peruvians experienced abroad and to the very broad, sometimes contradictory meanings associated with cosmopolitanism in migration literature. This chapter invites us to engage with the intersecting ways in which being at home may simultaneously entail both professing and practicing openness and reinforcing and reproducing power relations based on Peruvian configurations of power along racial-ethnic and class hierarchies. Rather than suggest that these are therefore not cosmopolitan positions, I underscore that these practices encourage us to consider the role of power, exclusion, and belonging founded on social hierarchies within lived cosmopolitanism.

It is the rich tension between belonging and privilege, on the one hand, and exclusion and marginalization, on the other hand, that characterizes many migration trajectories. Migration may bring about situations in which those who identify as middle or upper class find themselves viewed as nonwhite and Latino and therefore as outside the privileged mainstream for the first time. Outside Peru, some migrants may have significantly increased opportunities to socialize with Peruvians across class lines, they may engage in types of work they would not have accepted in Lima because of their class status, and they may be surprised to find that their accents mark them as outsiders. In reflecting on and gaining a deeper understanding of their own vulnerability, privilege, and shifts in status, they may question their own position within Peruvian racial-gender-class hierarchies and more widespread prejudices and discriminatory behaviors against others. They may point to experiences of participating in alliances and friendships across class lines with other Peruvians abroad, their own marginalization and exclusion as migrants, and their adaptation to non-Peruvian worldviews on class, gender, and race. Over and over again, Peruvians brought up that migrating had provided them with new opportunities to appreciate and accept differences.

It is worth emphasizing nonetheless that in many cases openness to difference was primarily selective and reinforced existing hierarchies and Peruvians' own positions of privilege within them. Identifying and examining selective openness makes visible the power relations at stake in redefining the realms of belonging and inclusiveness in connection to Peru and more broadly within transnational social fields. These relations of power are grounded in specific contexts and histories and always already enmeshed in preexisting inequalities and forms of exclusion.

My approach to cosmopolitanism within Peruvian migration experiences among middle- and upper-class Peruvians does not equate openness to inclusiveness. Some Peruvian migrants may perceive themselves as citizens of the world, yet this does not mean that they view all Peruvians as being equal and that existing racial-ethnic and class hierarchies at the center of dominant narratives of national identity will be suspended or rejected. One person's questions about another's neighborhood and school in Lima may be an effort to create links between migrants, yet it is also, more significantly, a particular *limeño* way to approach difference and police boundaries transnationally. These boundaries are founded on particular Peruvian class and racial-ethnic hierarchies. In a central way, these boundaries are deeply connected to the racialization of poorer indigenous internal migrants in Peru by middle- and upper-class *limeños*.

Return migrants may paradoxically begin to accept racism—their own or that of others—as a form of tolerance. This form of tolerance in practice reinforces the power that migrants of middle- and upper-class backgrounds have over who is and is not fit to belong in an open, cosmopolitan world. Just as for Hernán there is a *cholo* and a *cholo de mierda*, for Gabriela there is an educated, and therefore acceptable, immigrant and an uneducated one who is unable or unwilling to overcome the negative qualities of his or her group. Yet as Berg's (2015) observations about "Americanized *cholos*" underscore, some may view the inferiority associated with being *cholo* as unchangeable. Cosmopolitanism in these narratives signals openness toward one's own experiences of perceiving difference and othering across borders but does not necessarily or usually result in openness to question hierarchies in which upper- and middle-class white Peruvians are positioned as privileged or that recognize higher status among Peruvians who previously had been looked down upon.

Cosmopolitanism may therefore frame both Marina's and Lucy's experiences of identifying as Latinas or as persons of color in the U.S. context, rather than more narrowly as Peruvians, in a setting in which middle-class and upper-middle-class migrants are not the privileged whites. It may also frame Hernán's discriminatory behaviors toward other Peruvians he considers inferior. Within transnational Peruvian and, more specifically, *limeño* spaces, cosmopolitan belonging is often shaped by existing hierarchies, and those who move back and forth may choose to reinforce rather than disrupt those hierarchies: some Peruvians belong, and others are denied inclusion within realms of tolerance.

CHAPTER 2

Gendering Return
From Middle-Class Señoras to Migrants without Domestic Help, and Back

I met Ana María in a small, busy café near her home in a suburb of Toronto on a chilly, sunny day. The pungent smell of espresso, mixed with the sweet aroma of fresh pastries, surrounded us as we chatted about her life in Lima and Toronto, her new business in Toronto, and the multitasking central to her many roles. After she described a typical day for her in Toronto, I asked her how she compared it to her everyday life in Lima. Her response astutely sums up what many women I met with repeated over and over: "Here you have to be a superwoman, a wonder woman that has to do everything. In Peru you can hire someone to help you in the house, and you can go to work and come back calm, and you play with your children. Here you have to organize yourself to be mother, housewife, to work outside the home, to do everything. You are everything!" In bringing up hiring domestic servants in Lima and the need to be a "superwoman, a wonder woman" in Toronto, Ana María points to two key areas that inform the negotiation of gender roles in the context of migration among Peruvians I met with in the course of this project. The first is the presence of paid domestic labor in middle- and upper-class family dynamics and the effect of this on women's responsibilities and relationships in Peru and abroad. The second related area is women's increased autonomy, accompanied by the expectation that women will "do everything" in the absence of domestic help in new settings. Outside Peru, women who had viewed domestic servants in Lima not only as a necessity (an often taken-for-granted one) but as a marker of social status expressed anxiety and concern about suddenly being personally responsible for various household duties their family had previously assigned to nonfamily members. In new settings, the negotiation of household duties previously assigned to domestic servants rose to the center of women's concerns in managing the household and could reshape relationships with partners.

While nationally Peruvian women are almost exclusively responsible for housework (Anderson 2007), class status and economic resources mean that middle- and upper-class households rely on the cheap paid labor of poorer women in managing households. It is therefore poorer women who typically do the bulk of the housework in Peru, often taking care of their own households in addition to working for middle- and upper-class families. Women I met with in Lima, with a couple of exceptions, did not typically regularly perform the cleaning, cooking, and shopping on which their households relied on a daily basis. In Lima among middle- and upper-class Peruvians, then, wealth allows individuals to delegate household work to those outside the family. If there is gender equity in this arrangement, it is reserved for middle- and upper-class women and men whose social status and wealth allow them to avoid this work and assign it to poorer women and men.

Although both men and women in Lima are freed from household labor, middle- and upper-class women and men engage with its management to different extents. Women typically engage in household management more so than their husbands. Women I met felt pride in overseeing and managing decisions about whom to hire and what the hired domestic servants should do, buy, cook, and even eat each day. They also openly acknowledged that relying on domestic servants in Lima improved relationships within the family because the women did not have to negotiate and often argue about the distribution of household chores or childcare with partners. Domestic labor by others provided women with more flexible time to spend with their children and on their personal well-being.

A good amount of scholarship has focused on gender roles in the context of emigration, but there has been less interest in examining gender roles within return migration literature as migrants readapt to social, class, and cultural norms. As I examine in this chapter, for middle- and upper-class transnational Peruvians, access to and dependence on domestic servants play a significant role in their own gendered, class-based behaviors. Far from celebrating a straightforward homecoming, narratives of return underscore ambiguity and challenges in an everyday life that is significantly shaped by gender and class standing.

Returning to Lima for some signified reclaiming the privileges of their Lima class status—including relying on the subordinated status of other women working as nannies and domestic servants—at the same time as their relationships with extended families and partners continued to change. Whether in Canada, Germany, or the United States or back in Peru, home soon became a site of renegotiation of gendered expectations between intimate partners, as well as of reevaluation of one's self as a gendered, classed, racialized person. The connections between home and homeland, in this sense, become fluid as one and both become sites for the reproduction, disciplining, and surveillance of gendered bodies and their connections to both family and national affairs (Grewal 1996, 2006; Sagar 1997). This chapter introduces return in the Peruvian middle-class context before moving on to more carefully examine everyday gendered class intricacies for women in particular and how these undergird emigration and return. Women's migration narratives point both to broader societal inequalities that shape the performance of middle-class gender roles and to significant transformations in terms of autonomy, family relationships, and professional opportunities.

Return and Middle-Class Migration Trajectories

Return migration has received little scholarly attention, yet it is not a recent phenomenon. Of the fifty-two million migrants who left Europe between 1824 and 1924, at least one-third returned to their country of origin permanently (Wyman 2005). Increasingly recognized as an important aspect of global migration flows (Hansen 2008; Ní Laoire 2008; Phillips and Potter 2009; Sussman 2010; Teo 2011), return migration began to receive scholars' attention in the 1960s. Migration scholarship in the twentieth century tended to focus on assimilation and integration (Vertovec 2001). In the late twentieth and early twenty-first centuries, transnational approaches grew in sophistication in response to previous trends to accentuate the significance of everyday life, cross-border attachments, and continuous mobility in the lives of immigrants (Glick-Schiller and Fouron 2001; Nowicka and Cieslik 2014; Portes, Guarnizo, and Landolt 1999; Ralph and Staeheli 2011; Sassen 1998). More recently, an increasing number of journal articles on return migration to various parts of the world spanning Cyprus (Teerling 2011), Central Asia (Agadjanian, Gorina, and Menjivar 2014), and Hong Kong (Yan, Lam, and Lauer 2015) and recent anthologies specifically on return migration to the Caribbean (Conway and Potter 2009), Asia (Biao, Yeoh, and Toyota 2013), and multiple other places (Markowitz and Stefansson 2004) reflect growing critical attention to return as a common and sometimes repeated element in migration trajectories.

Studies of Peruvian migration have examined Peruvians' experiences abroad in a variety of settings that have included Asia, Europe, South America, and North America (e.g., Altamirano 2000; Berg 2015; Durand 2010; Escriva, Santa Cruz, and Bermudez 2010; Hernandez 2007; Leinaweaver 2013; Napolitano 2015; Paerregaard 2009, 2014; Skornia 2015; Takenaka and Pren 2010; Takenaka, Paerregaard, and Berg 2010; Tamagno 2003) but only rarely examine experiences of return migration in depth. There are no published studies specifically of return migration among Peruvians. More broadly, return migration—whether temporary or permanent—remains on the periphery of migration studies within anthropology and interdisciplinary migration research in spite of the growing attention to the fluidity of migration trajectories and transnational lives (Stefansson 2004).

Rather than approach return migration as a final, one-way movement or end point, here I engage with return as one component of fluid migration trajectories. Among Peruvians abroad and back in Peru, return was rarely treated as a final movement and reflected a more circular sense of migratory trajectories. The plurality of experiences among Peruvian migrants and returnees underscores the importance of approaching return as a complex phenomenon that defies simplistic categorizations of return as the result of successful or unsuccessful migration. Among Peruvians I spoke with and those who completed the survey, it was common for Peruvians who returned to be professionally and economically successful while abroad, challenging traditional neoclassical views of return migration as the result of a failed migration journey.[1] Before they left Peru, these individuals belonged to social groups with cultural and economic capital. They were armed with the necessary economic resources and immersed in professional networks, so a new opportunity for work or investment might lead to another migration journey and subsequent return to Peru.

Similarly, the heterogeneity of reasons to return or not return and the feelings of ambiguity in accompanying experiences defy simplistic binaries of home / not home and underscore the fluidity and circularity of return. In the online survey, the majority of respondents stated they did not plan to return to Peru to live. Survey respondents had lived abroad between two and fifty years. The average number of years abroad was twenty. Not returning to live, however, did not mean not returning at all. About half regularly returned every one to two years for visits, and about a fourth made these visits every three to five years. Transnational Peruvians used a combination of social media and communication technologies in between visits to stay up to date with family and general news.

Rather than romanticize the past and life at home, the majority of Peruvians I spoke with considered the possibility of return pragmatically and made complex decisions about the desirability and feasibility of return based on multiple factors. These factors included family abroad and in Peru, caretaking responsibilities for parents and children, security concerns, work opportunities, political ideologies, economic stability, educational possibilities, and social networks. The main reasons Peruvians did not plan to return to live in Peru were family and security concerns. About half of Peruvians who completed the survey had planned to return to live in Peru but had changed their mind and no longer planned to return to live there at the time of the survey. For many, after living outside of Peru for over a decade, returning to Peru would mean separating from their families or facing strong resistance from their families. Common responses included "I want to be close to my children and grandchildren" for those who were close to retirement age and "my family wouldn't adapt" for those with younger children. These family attachments, and the attachments children and grandchildren developed to their place of residence, had not been part of the emigration considerations and in originally planning an eventual return.

Both in decisions to return and in decisions to stay abroad longer or permanently, the desires of family and of children in particular were central. Among the small group who planned to return to live in Peru, the majority stated that their adult children agreed with their decision to return. One study that briefly discusses return migration to Peru found that return migrants to Lima experienced difficulties readjusting to a lack of organization in the city and daily life and were concerned about possible crime and safety, yet they generally viewed return migration as a positive experience because of family reunification (UNFPA 2012, 90). After decades of living abroad, however, for some there was no or little family in Peru with which to reunite.

Security concerns regarding return decisions were commonly expressed as "lack of security for my children" and references to "social insecurity." Security concerns, as discussed in the following chapters, impacted the lives of return migrants in significantly different ways, depending on the person's self-identified and perceived gender, class, and sexual identity. Often, concerns about family and security went hand in hand in considering where to live and whether or not to move. One man responded that he did not have plans to return to live in Peru because "insecurity persists, and my daughters would not be willing to move there, and I am not willing to separate from them." This was a common sentiment among Peruvians whose children had grown up abroad and now had partners and children for whom Peru had never been a place where they had lived. Because of the presence of these forms of extended family and concerns about security, several echoed the sentiment expressed by one woman that "my life is here." In these cases, return visits in addition to regular communication with relatives and friends were more desirable ways to remain connected to Peru than a permanent return. It was thus common to find that initial decisions to emigrate that had been informed by concerns over security transformed into decisions to stay, or at least to stay longer, because of ties children and other family members had developed outside Peru.

As in other parts of this book, the social and economic class position of Peruvians I am focusing on here is critical in qualifying my approach to return. The Peruvians I am focusing on by and large identify as middle and upper class, did not arrive as refugees or asylum seekers, and have the economic and social resources to migrate with visas and to not overstay those visas. Many became dual citizens of the countries to which they emigrated. Refugees and asylum seekers would have significantly different possibilities for and experiences of return. Undocumented immigrants who are forcibly returned to their countries of origin may engage in circulatory migration movements as well, yet they would face perils in crossing national borders and in everyday movements and employment that the majority of Peruvians I spoke with for this project do not experience.

Migration Trajectories through the Lenses of Gender

Migration trajectories take on various forms, just as gender roles are not uniform throughout Peru. Differences in economic resources, cultural norms, and social networks, as well as in physical settings, inform the expectations associated with women and men, so expectations for Peruvian women in the rural Andes and for urban middle-class women in Lima will differ substantially. Movement from one setting to another within Peru will also likely result in changes in status and gender roles as informed by class, place of residence, and employment. So, for example, a young woman in a high-status household in a rural community in the highlands may be perceived in the capital as having significantly lower status and confront different gendered class expectations if after moving to Lima she begins work as a nanny or cook for a middle- or upper-class family.

In Peru the period from the 1970s to the 1990s resulted in women's increased access to education and labor markets nationally (Nunura and Flores 2001), yet the access women enjoyed to educational resources and opportunities and the roles available to them in the labor market were also heavily informed by their position within existing racial-class-gender hierarchies. In spite of social changes and challenges to the broadly Catholic-infused mainstream gender ideologies, gender roles continue to be largely traditional. As María José commented about her extended family in Lima, "[They] say that this one is a *puta* [whore], and sometimes that affects me, because a woman can have the sexual life she wants, and I don't think she should be called that. And the men, no, they sleep around, and that is OK." Women's sexuality continues to be largely judged against the backdrop of patriarchal standards and expectations. Some research suggests that traditional gender roles are most strict in the upper and lower classes and most malleable in the middle classes (Fuller 2002). Across classes, however, women's sexuality is more tightly monitored than men's, and beauty tends to be associated with lighter skin. For men, it is physical strength that is largely viewed as a symbol of masculinity among those in the popular classes and employment and responsibility rather than physical strength in the upper classes (Fuller 2002).[2] In discussing migrants' experiences and referring to gendered expectations, in this and other sections I am referring to middle- and upper-class families in and from Lima. As the examples throughout the book illustrate, within this group there is significant variation.

Gendered Migration and Autonomy

While abroad, Peruvians may find and embrace new approaches to their everyday lives, family relationships, and ideas about race, class, and gender. Migration literature has emphasized two main areas in which gender roles undergo changes in the context of migration. The first is women's increased autonomy and power through increased labor market participation, for example, women who migrate to work as nannies and domestic servants and in elder care (Constable 1999; Hondagneu-Sotelo 2001; Lutz 2011). This may result in women's increased economic and physical independence from their families, as well as in new roles in the family as breadwinners. It may also necessitate the renegotiation of family relationships and mothering long distance. The second is acculturation or assimilation as individuals adapt to gender roles more in line with the gender norms of the new place of residence; often, both increased autonomy and selective acculturation may occur (Boehm 2012; Dreby and Schmalzbauer 2013; Hirsch 2003).

On the one hand, research among immigrant Latin American women, particularly Mexican women in the United States, who engage in paid work underscores increased opportunities to negotiate more egalitarian gender relations with partners (Dreby and Schmalzbauer 2013; Hirsch 1999, 2003; Hondagneu-Sotelo 2001). On the other hand, Joanna Dreby (2006) suggests that even as we recognize new opportunities for negotiating gender roles, we pay attention to the persistence and even reinforcement of traditional gender roles in the context of migration. Ricardo Contreras and David Griffith similarly suggest that women "reaffirm and reinforce traditional gender roles related to child rearing and parenting" (2012, 61) by being the primary caretakers of children once they became mothers in transnational contexts. Deborah Boehm (2012) notes that in cases in which Mexican women migrate to the United States to reunite with a partner, men may approach their partner's arrival as an opportunity to reassert masculine power in their homes as women take on caretaking, cooking, cleaning, and other household chores. Mexican immigrant women may also transition from full-time workers responsible for remittances to full-time mothers after the birth of a child, taking on traditional gender roles and losing economic autonomy at least temporarily (Alcalde 2015). Examining the role of remittances in Peruvian migration, Karsten Paerregaard (2014, 2015) finds that among the Peruvians he interviewed, remittances reinforced existing relations of gender, generation, and class prevalent in Peru. In one case, the husband's regular remittances from Japan allowed him to maintain the role of breadwinner and head of household and reinforced his wife's role as a dutiful, faithful wife in Peru for decades.

Among many of the women I spoke with, a somewhat different situation emerges. In these cases, social and economic capital informs household dynamics before migration and allows them to exercise power over household workers, as well as to engage in social activities outside the home. After migration women face new challenges and responsibilities in their roles as mothers and wives, and they work to adjust their gendered and class expectations of themselves and their partners to adapt to the demands of a new setting in which they are largely responsible for household work—at least initially. Whether in Canada, Germany, or the United States or again in Peru, it was in the home that women most strongly renegotiated their and their partners' gendered expectations.

In these narratives, the lines between autonomy, independence, and oppression become blurred. Women's narratives reveal subtle ways in which leaving Peru, settling down someplace else, and returning impact women's autonomy and identity. In leaving behind Lima, individuals also leave behind privileges they had come to count on, and this too informs family dynamics and relationships, particularly for women as spouses and mothers. In one sense, migration meant women no longer had power over the everyday practices of other women who worked for them as domestic servants. In taking on more household chores themselves, they may reflect on their own sense of self as informed by their class identity and their relationship to their partner and children in the new setting—as well as their lack of control and power over other women.

Without domestic servants, middle- and upper-class women felt weighed down by the responsibilities attached to maintaining a household, and they found it more challenging to define and view themselves in previously familiar ways. As they renegotiated household chores with their partner and children they also began to feel increasingly independent from extended family members who remained in Peru. These extended families had previously had significantly more voice in a multitude of seemingly mundane areas, such as how to structure each day, organize a room, discipline children, and prepare and serve meals. In the new setting, women often became the sole decision makers and executors in these areas. They gained independence as they simultaneously took on additional and more laborious household chores and responsibilities. Gaining independence from extended families in this context, then, meant rarely having the leisure time the women had counted on before migrating. Each day required coordination and sharing of family obligations with partners, something that had not been as central in women's premigration everyday lives.

Negotiating Gender Roles in the Home

Ana María's new roles and business led her and her husband to renegotiate the chores they agreed were necessary for their household to function. Ana María explained to me that in her view, in Peru men are much more "relaxed" about household work because they rarely engage in it, but after migrating, men become more conscious that women can't do it all and begin to share household duties. In her Lima home, Ana María had only been responsible mainly for whatever small tasks the domestic servant forgot to do. Her husband had not taken on any household chores. Months after moving to Toronto, tired of juggling so many roles and outside work, Ana María confronted her husband about the division of household chores. Several others I spoke with agreed that sharing household duties became necessary after leaving Peru in ways they had not experienced previously. Her husband could see her increased responsibilities as he also juggled his own increased responsibilities without the broader network of family and hired workers they had both counted on in Lima. They both agreed they needed to work together more closely than before to manage and meet their family's needs.

In a different part of town, Fernando also spoke of some of the differences between everyday life in Lima and Toronto for his family. In Lima, he and his wife worked outside the home and depended on a nanny and a domestic worker to help them with their young son and the house. In Toronto, Fernando described himself as "cook, plumber, and electrician," as well as cleaner, for their house. His wife, he explained, also had multiple roles in the house in addition to her part-time work outside the home. The traditional gendered and class divisions of work in the home many had lived in Lima simply did not fit their new settings, as was the case for Ana María and her husband.

For thirty-nine-year-old Liliana, migration to Germany and later return migration to Peru included a series of conflicts and negotiations with her husband about roles and contributions to the household. Liliana met her future German husband in Peru, and years later they moved to Germany as a married couple. They returned to Lima because of a family emergency. When I met her, she, her husband, and their almost two-year-old daughter were living in an apartment close to her family and had recently decided to attempt to live in Lima permanently. They had been living in Peru for a little over a year. Liliana had promised her husband that if he felt he could not adapt to Lima after living there for a few months, she would agree to return to Germany in spite of the heartbreak this would cause her.

In Germany, Liliana's husband had wanted her to look for employment as soon as they arrived. She, however, expected to spend most of her time at home, settling in and taking care of the house. She had abandoned a desirable full-time position in Lima and wanted time to adapt to her new setting and home. Additionally, she explained, her level of German when she first arrived was not sufficient for a job: "They wouldn't even accept me as a volunteer!" In Germany without a job and constantly reprimanded by her husband for not contributing to the household through paid employment, Liliana began to resent her economic dependence on her husband. As she spent her days making sure the house was impeccably clean, his complaints about her inability to find paid employment increased. Now back in Lima, Liliana has her former job again. Her husband now stays home and is unable to find employment because he has not yet mastered Spanish. He wants to stay home with their daughter, yet, as Liliana explains, for him staying home does not mean cleaning the house and cooking as she did in Germany, since they have family and domestic help to assist with those chores. Their roles are reversed, but the availability of cheap household labor allows Liliana's husband to have leisure time she never enjoyed in Germany.

Liliana has made it clear to her husband that if he wants to stay home, he needs to be responsible for some household chores. She also wants him to learn more Spanish and to look for employment outside the home. Liliana and her husband's ongoing discussions and changing expectations highlight migration as a space of constant negotiation and renegotiation of gendered roles as these are shaped by immigration policies, local settings, language barriers, cultural gender ideologies, and personal preferences and resources. In Liliana's case, she recognized that "when he met me, I was very submissive." The change in her attitudes and expectations resulted from a broad combination of factors in which emigration and return migration were important components.

Whether or not immigrant spouses are legally permitted to work also affects gender relations in the home and women's sense and experience of autonomy.[3] Among return migrants I met in Lima, Eugenia was unique in that she had returned from Colombia. Her story, however, reflected common themes of how employment opportunities as a migrant impacted her sense of autonomy. When Eugenia arrived in Colombia, to her surprise, she did not have legal permission to seek employment because she was the spouse of someone with diplomatic status. She felt "cheated" because she could not use her substantial work experience in Peru in women's development projects there, something neither she nor her husband had known beforehand. Although she felt uncomfortable about her financial dependence on her husband during her time there, Eugenia's class and educational background allowed her to find other opportunities during the years in Colombia: she enrolled in a university to earn another degree and volunteered. Eugenia would have strongly preferred paid employment during her time in Colombia, but her family did not depend on her income for its well-being. That her family did not need her to contribute financially, however, did not lessen what she perceived as the negative impact of her sudden economic dependence on her husband, a dependence that resulted directly from her migration. When we met in Lima, Eugenia had separated from her husband and once again had paid employment.

Autonomy and Adjusting to Extended Families in Postreturn Lives

In Lima, even as return migrants celebrated being close to family, they lamented how challenging it was to once again adapt to having extended family members involved in all facets of their lives. For thirty-seven-year-old Sandra, it was her return from the United States to Lima and constant family participation and opinions on all aspects of her family life that led her to "cry uncontrollably" soon after she arrived. In spite of the multitasking and housework required in living abroad, she "had already gotten used to doing things how I wanted them" in her life and in her house. She missed having the independence and privacy she had become accustomed to away from her extended family. In Lima she benefited from having "all the people who help me, who make my life easier," but this also meant that she could not expect the same amount of privacy she had previously enjoyed.

Like Sandra, many return migrants spoke of a loss of privacy and independence. Observations and complaints about relatives' unwanted opinions and advice on child-rearing and discipline, as well as unsolicited comments on individual decisions and behaviors, were particularly common areas of frustration. Olivia put it bluntly: "One thing that affects me is that my father or at least my mother meddles more in my life than when I lived far away." She had hoped that living far away for several years would make it easier for her parents to respect her decisions, yet she found upon her return that she had to "go through something like adolescence and rebellion to recover the territory that I had already won." When we met, she and a friend shared a two-bedroom apartment in an upscale building in a trendy neighborhood in gentrifying Barranco. She enjoyed being close to her family again even as she regretted that "there are other eyes always looking at you here." While she was away she had bemoaned the physical distance separating her from her family; postreturn she regretted the prying questions that came with the physical proximity for which she longed. As in other cases, return included renegotiating parameters of parent-child relationships and expectations, and this process of renegotiation rarely happened as quickly as returnees wished it would. Returnees exerted agency in many ways, including in insisting on new parameters for family relationships. They sought to enforce these parameters through regular conversations about their expectations, goals, and independence while abroad and through such actions as moving out of family homes and deciding on when and how family visits could take place after they moved out.

Similarly, Sandra explained that her mother offered unsolicited advice not only about Sandra's life but also about how she disciplined her children, and this particularly irked Sandra. Liliana brought up another point: although she enjoyed having family stop by every day and share a meal with her and her husband, for her German husband these visits resulted in "too much noise" and a lack of privacy. He regretted not having any space for himself or for their family away from Liliana's siblings, cousins, and parents. In this as in other cases, the presence of extended family provided desired assistance in childcare and household management and contributed to the return migrant's sense of belonging, but it also resulted in less privacy and autonomy for the individual and his or her nuclear family.

Class, Gender, and Domestic Servants

As is the case in urban India (see Dickey 2000) and many other urban centers around the globe, and as I have underscored for urban Peru, servants are a status marker among middle- and upper-class women and enable wealthier women to engage in status-marking activities while maintaining an organized and clean home. The employment of poorer women who are typically incorporated into middle- and upper-class households as subordinate not only economically but also in terms of race, class, and gender (Radcliffe 1990) helps mark the employing families' higher status. These are largely exploitative situations for poor indigenous, mestiza, and Afro-Peruvian women in particular that result in paltry earnings. Currently, approximately fifty thousand Peruvian women work as domestic servants, and only 8 percent of them receive a salary at or above the minimum wage (Rottenbacher de Rojas 2015). Paid domestic work makes women eligible for social security benefits, yet only 6 percent of employers have registered domestic servants as employees and contributed to their social security (Rottenbacher de Rojas 2015).

Research on domestic servitude underscores that the cheap, exploited labor of one group of women allows more privileged women to escape patriarchal constraints and exploitation (Ehrenreich and Hochschild 2003; Parreñas 2001; Romero 1992), and this was certainly the case for women and their families before leaving Peru. Once abroad, however, the status markers and resources associated with their class status ceased to include dependence on cheap household labor. There is a substantive, rich body of work on immigrants as caregivers for residents in wealthier countries (Chang 2000; Constable 1997; Ehrenreich and Hochschild 2003; Hondagneu-Sotelo and Avila 1997; Ibarra 2000; Lutz 2011; Parreñas 2001; Skornia 2015; Tamagno 2003) yet little on immigrants as employers of domestic workers. Carework, a common entry point for migrants, is widely recognized as low status (Kofman and Raghuram 2015). Immigrant women may take on the caretaking and cleaning duties of middle-class women in wealthier countries as these wealthier women enter the workforce in growing numbers. For example, the foreign-born make up 90 percent of domestic workers in Italy, 40 percent of house cleaners in France, 22 percent of eldercare workers in Canada, and 16 percent of eldercare workers in the United States (Kofman and Raghuram 2015). In her research with migrants from Peru's central highlands, Ulla Berg (2015) found that all of the women she met who had arrived in the 1970s and early 1980s had entered the United States as domestic servants. In Milan, Italy, Peruvian migrants found work in eldercare and household service (Skornia 2015; Tamagno 2003).

Before circling back to the experiences in Toronto of Ana María, whose words appear at the opening of this chapter, I introduce below the experiences of two other women of similar age and who each also have two young children. One woman recently returned to Lima, and the other lives in the United States and does not plan to return to Peru. Together, the experiences of Ana María, Sandra, and Tatiana illustrate women's changing relationship to household chores against the backdrop of Peruvian middle-class status in the context of migration and the absence of domestic workers in their households.

I interviewed thirty-seven-year-old Sandra in her modern, elegant apartment in a recently finished building in an upscale neighborhood in San Isidro in Lima. After the security guard confirmed I had been invited by a building resident, I proceeded to the elevator. The doors opened directly into her apartment, and I had the sensation of walking into a high-end furniture showroom as I stepped into her living room. As we sat on a sleek, white sofa, Sandra lowered her voice and explained that the nanny was putting the children to bed. After we had chatted informally for a few minutes, I asked Sandra's permission to record the interview. I slowly placed my digital recorder on the shiny glass coffee table. Sandra's low-key, relaxed demeanor and casual dress soon eased my worries that I might accidentally ruin something in this perfectly decorated space.

Sandra had lived in the United States for seven years with her Peruvian husband and two children. As she described her first weeks in her new U.S. city, it became clear that her arrival in the United States marked the beginning of a very different lifestyle. After visiting the supermarket nearest to her neighborhood in the United States for the first time, she quickly returned to her house and cried. Having spent her life well into her twenties as an upper-middle-class woman in Lima, she had never had the responsibility of doing her own grocery shopping or cleaning her own house. She suddenly realized how ill prepared she was to be in charge of a household. In leaving Lima, she left a space in which domestic servants cleaned, bought groceries, and organized and prepared her and her family's meals. While, as she tells me, she misses the independence she feels she gained abroad, she recognizes that it required introspection and significant changes within her to take on daily household chores while in the United States. Part of this process of accepting and negotiating with her husband new responsibilities involved in living away from Lima included recognizing the privileges, including several she and her husband had taken for granted, they had benefited from in Lima.

The family's main reasons for returning to Lima two years earlier, Sandra explained, were a job offer for her husband and the allure of raising their children in an extended family environment. Born in Lima and raised in an environment that expected and valued the involvement of grandparents, aunts, uncles, cousins, and a cadre of household workers, she had never questioned that this was desirable and the best way to raise children. She contrasted her full-time household chores and caretaking in the United States to her life in Lima, where she and her husband rely on a full-time nanny to care for their two young children. The work of another woman, who cleans and cooks, means Sandra no longer has primary responsibility for cleaning, cooking, and taking the children on playdates and is able to work part-time. In Lima, she enjoys time to relax and take care of herself and explains that she finally has time to visit a therapist when she wishes to, something she did not feel she had time or money for in the United States.

The added free time she has gained postreturn, as she distances herself from household chores and service, has come at what she considers to be a high cost: she feels less connected to her youngest child than to her older child. In the United States, she had no family and few acquaintances and friends nearby. Her days were organized around her older daughter's nap schedule and household chores. In Lima, her daughter no longer takes naps, and the nanny manages her young son's schedule. At family gatherings or children's parties at the Club Regatas, several nannies supervise and play with the children as the adults socialize.

Like Sandra, Tatiana described her adaptation to life as an immigrant in the United States as one characterized by her changing responsibilities in her day-to-day roles as wife and mother. Unlike Sandra, Tatiana does not plan to return to Lima permanently. Instead, she and her family visit family in Lima typically twice each year. When she lived in Lima, she expected her house to be clean and tidy and the meals to be well organized and prepared. After over a decade in the United States, she questions how realistic these expectations are now that she is responsible for the majority of household chores. Tatiana shows me the main floor of her house, which is located in a comfortable suburb with highly rated public schools in a midsize city in the U.S. It is a large, recent construction with tall ceilings and an open floor plan, similar to others in adjacent streets. The neighborhood boasts nature trails nearby and plenty of cul-de-sacs in which it is easy to imagine children learning to ride their bikes on weekends. She apologizes for the messy living area, and I comment on how clean and tidy it looks to me, adding that my house is rarely as neat as hers.

On another occasion when we met, Tatiana tells me that she feels uncomfortable when she witnesses relatives or friends in Lima mistreating domestic servants responsible for these household chores, and I think back to her clean house and other comments she made. On the occasions when we met she commented more than once how much work keeping up the house and cooking, on top of driving the children to and from extracurricular activities after school, and her part-time work, had become. She also said that her husband prefers that they not hire anyone to help clean the house, adding that she has more time in the United States than she did in Peru for these chores, since her outside work is part-time. The situation she described was common. I have sometimes been told by close friends that I do not have a good poker face, and from Tatiana's facial expression I assumed this was one of those times. I wanted to ask her if she agreed with her husband, but I was fairly certain I already knew the answer.

As we trade stories about how we manage our days and our children, she tells me that for her "the great difference" is that in Lima, "I would get up, the table would be set. I would say good-bye to the children, go to work. I would return home for lunch, and everything was served on the table. I returned home, and at the end of the day my mom had picked up the kids from school and done activities with them." Invisible but implied in her narrative is the domestic servant who cooks, cleans, sets the table, buys the groceries, and supervises the children when they are not with their grandmother after school. All this is done, usually, for very low wages.

In contrast to her experiences in Lima and similarly to Sandra, in the United States Tatiana feels she has a much more all-encompassing role in her children's lives precisely because she does not rely on a domestic worker and nanny to take care of household chores and the children. Reflecting on these differences, she suggests that "in Lima the mother is a spectator because you delegate so much to the domestic worker and to the nanny." While few mothers described themselves to me in these terms, the substantially increased household and accompanying childcare responsibilities for those with young children postmigration were a common concern for all mothers with whom I spoke. Once they were in the United States, Tatiana's children especially missed the nanny because "she was the person who would sit to play with them the whole day, she was there for them, to color, to play." Soon after arriving in the United States, Tatiana felt the weight of having to adapt to the demands of multiple roles she had not previously juggled.

Back in Toronto, Ana María also quickly recognized the differences in her own life in Lima and Toronto because she did not rely on the labor of a domestic worker in Toronto. After reflecting on changing household dynamics and responsibilities postmigration, Ana María decided to create her own housecleaning business. For her, she explained, it was the perfect solution because it allowed her to earn money "without having to work for someone else." As a thirty-something-year-old mother of two young children, she desired flexibility to be with her children if one of them became ill or needed to be picked up early from school or to be driven to or from an event. Her business has been successful, and three years into her venture she has a small group of five regular employees. All of the employees are recent Latin American women migrants from working-class and poor backgrounds. She caters to Canadians and to Latin American middle- and upper-class migrants.

Although she has many connections within the Peruvian communities in Toronto, Ana María tries to avoid Peruvian clients. She explained that Peruvians who had been in Toronto for years were very well off and could afford housecleaning services but that their attitudes toward her employees were embedded in Peruvian social hierarchies, not the realities of Toronto. She charges by the hour and provides clients with contracts that list which specific services are included, yet in the past Peruvian clients had expected and demanded that employees perform duties not listed in the contract and that they work longer hours than what had been agreed upon. "Not everyone, but in general they [Peruvians] have this attitude," she explained. "They imagine they can make you do work that is not included," as they would with domestic servants in Peru.

After telling me about the demands of a particularly difficult Peruvian client, Ana María added, "Thankfully, most of my clients are not Peruvian. They are Canadian, Colombian, and other Latin Americans." Since beginning her business, Ana María has also understood that when one of her employees doesn't show up or is sick, it is up to Ana María to fill in. When friends and family in Lima ask her what she does in Canada during her visits, Ana María tells them that she owns a cleaning business. When she adds that she sometimes cleans houses when her employees are not available, she is met with awkward silences and uncomfortable looks.

Ana María's experience as a transnational migrant both reinforces and challenges her middle-class status as it elucidates the connections between class and place in her performance of particular types of gendered work. In creating and being in charge of a cleaning business, Ana María embodies the successful middle-class migrant entrepreneur. In admitting that she too cleans houses and therefore engages in low-status work, however, she disrupts established hierarchies of race and class in Lima. These hierarchies mean that middle- and upper-class Peruvians in Lima rely on domestic servants for cheap labor and to reinforce their own class status and, importantly, that they do not perform this labor. Because of the negative attitudes toward domestic servants and the implicit class and power inequalities in the employer-employee relationship in Peru, Ana María's dual role as owner and cleaner is problematic for middle- and upper-class Peruvians. Because she performed this work in Canada, however, it does not have the same impact on her perceived status as it would have if she worked as a domestic servant in Lima. Similarly to Jamaican women migrants for whom social status in Jamaica continued to be tied to their previous, higher-status occupations rather than their work as domestic servants in New York City (Foner 1986), Ana María identified with her middle-class status in Lima. She viewed her business as a success in an environment in which Peru's racial-class hierarchies could not be as easily applied.

Aldo's comments about his semiannual visits to Lima from Toronto provide an additional glimpse into the embeddedness of domestic servants in middle- and upper-class lifestyles in Lima. He tells me that in spite of constant invitations to people's homes for meals during his visits, he has rarely received invitations for Sundays. Why? Domestic servants typically have Sundays off. On those days, his friends and family tend to go out to eat, and if they eat at home, they leave the dirty dishes in the sink, expecting the maid to wash them the following day. As he tells me this, I remember the many times I have heard relatives speak of planning dinners and parties for when domestic servants are available as a way to avoid setting up for and cleaning up after these events.

Negotiating Professional Opportunities as Migrants

Women's sense of autonomy and relationships with partners and families are directly connected to and impacted by professional opportunities as migrants. Throughout this chapter, issues surrounding the transformations and difficulties attached to women's and men's professional lives as migrants have appeared: Ana María's resourcefulness and frustration at managing multiple roles as she started a cleaning business in Canada; Liliana's difficulty with paid work in Germany and, subsequently, her German husband's difficulties finding work once they returned to Lima; Eugenia's profound disappointment that she could not work legally in Colombia; and Tatiana's and other women's transitions from full-time work outside the home and relying on household employees for housework and childcare in Lima to full-time household and childcare responsibilities abroad and few or no employment opportunities outside the home.

There is no dominant pattern for how migration impacts professional experiences and identities among the transnational Peruvians whose experiences I examine. Experiences of both emigration and return migration, however, consistently stress that professional lives rarely cross national borders without significant transformations. Professional commitments and transformations varied depending on multiple factors, including language skills, educational background and professional training, employment laws and opportunities for foreigners, state social programs and benefits for parents and families, and the availability and affordability of childcare in each setting. The separate stories of Tania and Julián that follow nonetheless provide at least glimpses into the sorts of negotiations and obstacles in their professional lives transnational Peruvians experienced.

For middle-class women in Lima, emigration with a partner and family could sometimes result in a pause if not a permanent end to their professional lives, although most often it resulted in significant changes in the type of work done. Among the women I interviewed, this was particularly the case for Peruvian women who lived in or had recently returned from Germany, where language skills, state programs, and employment laws for foreigners created barriers to professional integration. When Tania left Lima to move to Germany, she did so with her German husband and with legal employment permits to work in Germany. In Lima, she had lived for years supporting herself financially through a series of short- and long-term jobs mostly in nonprofit organizations. She had become accustomed to having a career and her own income. Tania had planned to stay home with her baby for the first few months while she learned German and then to find a job doing comparable work to the work she did in Lima. Soon after arriving in Germany, she confronted several challenges in finding paid employment.

Once in Germany, it took significantly longer to find a daycare facility for her child than Tania had originally expected. Spending her days caring for her baby full-time did not allow her to learn German during most of the first year there. When the family finally secured a spot at a local daycare, it was only for five hours each day. Tania spent those five hours going to, sitting in, and returning from German-language classes. Without German fluency, she would not have a chance to even be considered for the types of jobs she desired. At one point, she decided to "work at anything, even not related to my career," as long as she could work, but her lack of German fluency prevented her from applying for jobs. Even if and once she became fluent, it was unlikely that she would find a job comparable to the work she had done in Lima. Tania had begun working full-time in her area of specialization after completing coursework but before completing her thesis in Lima, meaning she did not have the university degree (*licenciatura*) that was required by many of the jobs she desired and for which she felt qualified based on her past work experience.

After two years in Germany, Tania, her husband, and their child returned to live in Lima. Within the first few months, she found full-time employment in Lima. Her husband initially had more difficulty finding work, yet his fluency in Spanish and educational background worked to his advantage in Lima, where he too secured a full-time job. For Tania, the motivation to return to Lima was largely based on professional opportunities. She did not feel her intersecting identities as woman, mother, and working professional could be fully realized in Germany because "I felt I was losing that [professional] identity. . . . I would ask myself, 'What am I going to do? Who am I? Where should I go?'" before she ultimately decided to return to Lima. While she considered the state social programs and benefits available in Germany—including healthcare coverage, parental and child benefits from the state, and state-subsidized daycare—to be significantly better than what she would have access to in Lima, to live permanently in Germany for her would have signified the end of her professional life as she knew it.[4] In Lima, both she and her husband had a better chance of thriving professionally.

Similarly to Tania, Sara returned to Lima after living in Germany for several years. Although Sara also had the required employment permit because she too was married to a German citizen, and she had the advantage of being fluent in German before arriving in Germany, her time there was spent almost exclusively with her children. The widespread expectation—accompanied by state subsidies in the form of parental and child allowances and very few daycare spots for very young children—that mothers stay home with their children for at least the first few years of the child's life meant that she had no opportunities for professional advancement during her time there. Although she would have liked to have continued her career as a teacher, during those first years she only found occasional work as a Spanish tutor, cleaning homes, and baking cakes because "I had no one with whom to leave my children, no grandmother or anyone else. There was no one, so I had no option but to stay home." Sara divorced her husband a few years after her move to Germany and returned to Peru. Now back in Lima, she enjoys a comfortable professional life teaching German.

Both Tania's and Sara's experiences mirror that of Liliana, who, as discussed earlier in this chapter, left her job in Lima to move to Germany with her German husband but returned to Peru due to a family emergency. Whereas Liliana experienced significant obstacles—largely due to language and childcare issues—to finding employment in Germany, once back in Peru she regained the position at the company at which she had worked before migrating. Unlike Tania's husband, however, Liliana's husband's Spanish skills were only rudimentary, and therefore it was now he who faced significant obstacles to finding work in Peru.

Like Tania, Julián began a career in his chosen field in Lima before completing his university thesis and earning his *licenciatura*. He and his wife faced a combination of education degree, language, and childcare challenges in Toronto. Canada provided less generous child benefits than Germany, yet their chosen new home came with a built-in network of family and compatriots. Julián's sister-in-law's family had lived in Toronto for several years before Julián and his family arrived in the late 1980s. By the time the family arrived there was already a small but well-established Peruvian community in the area—something not available to the Peruvian women I spoke with who migrated to Germany—and it included middle-class acquaintances. The network of Peruvians in the Toronto area provided Julián and his wife with important contacts for obtaining both formal and informal employment.

Whereas in Lima Julián's wife did not work outside the home, in Toronto providing for their four children required both parents to work. As Julián explained, "My first job, they paid me thirty times what I received in Lima! I thought we had it made, until I realized how much we spent and how much we paid in taxes." The significant increase in income in Toronto was accompanied by the significantly higher costs of living and in taxes. Making ends meet initially meant taking on more work and for longer hours than Julián had foreseen.

Julián viewed the various extra jobs he and his wife took on during that initial year as necessary for the transition to the new setting and did not consider that the lower-status work they engaged in affected their middle-class status. In describing a typical day during their first year, Julián explained that a Peruvian acquaintance helped them secure a newspaper delivery route to supplement their income from their two regular daytime jobs. During that first year, he and his wife took turns delivering the newspapers: "We would get up at 3:15 a.m. every day and go to bed at 9:00 at night to get up early again the following day. We had to deliver 195 newspapers during the week. I would leave at 3:45 a.m. and return at 6:30 a.m. I would arrive home, take a shower, drink my tea, go to work ... until 7:00 p.m., get home at 8:00 or 8:30 p.m., go to bed at 9:00, maybe 10:00, to get up and go to work again." They were able to save money that first year as a result of the extra work.

Rather than view the newspaper delivery route as a regular part of their life as migrants, Julián considered it and the additional extra jobs they took on as necessary but temporary deviations from their professional identities. Like the middle-class Peruvian migrants Elena Sabogal (2012) interviewed in Florida, among middle-class migrants to Toronto, lower-status jobs did not impact self-perceptions of class long established in Lima. Once his own career took off, a few years after the family's arrival, Julián and his wife decided it would be best for her to stop working outside the home and only engage in volunteer work—much the same way she would have done in Lima.

Fernando, who arrived in Toronto with his wife during the same period as Julián and his family, also faced challenges to advancing the career he had established in Lima because he too never completed his thesis. While the lack of a formal degree to accompany his years of study at the university level did not present challenges for him in Lima because of his social standing and the professional contacts he and his family counted on, in Toronto during his first years he had to take on lower-status jobs he had not previously considered in Lima. Soon after arriving he discovered that the government-sponsored language programs available to him were not his best vehicle for becoming fluent in English, so he decided to invest financially in his own future by enrolling in a local college. As he reminded himself, although the family had been well-off financially in Lima, the professional challenges he experienced were necessary and worth it in Toronto because it was there that "we came for the security of our children and for their future." Now in his sixties, Fernando is a successful businessman and feels proud that his four children have graduated from college in Canada and have successful careers of their own. With his family and his professional life now firmly settled in Canada, Fernando enjoys short return visits to Lima, but he doubts he would ever return to live there permanently.

Unpacking Transnational Trajectories: Class Background and Mobility within Gendered Fields

The journeys of transnational Peruvians underscore return as a component of rather than the necessary end point to the fluidity of migration. In many cases return was desired, yet the physical proximity of family resulted in unwanted surveillance and involvement postreturn even as migrants spoke of the importance of and their affection for their family. In many of these cases, the possibility of another return (this time to a home outside Peru) remained a possibility. For others, plans to return to Peru changed as children became adults and formed their own families, and the appearance of grandchildren further grounded the lives of older Peruvians outside Peru. Middle-class status combined with professional success in many cases facilitated shorter return visits to help keep transnational Peruvians connected to families here and there. In between visits, regular communication through social media and Skype helped migrants stay in touch and up-to-date on news and gossip with family and friends in Peru.

Attention to how the performance of class and gender is imbricated in migratory treks also sheds light on inequalities that structure everyday life premigration and that inform life outside Peru and the possibility of return. Women in this chapter experienced the fluidity of the migration process as one imbued with significant gendered consequences. After leaving Lima, the middle-class status that ensured access to cheap household labor became out of reach, and this necessitated the renegotiation of the performance of class status and of gendered household chores. Faced with having "to do everything" in the home and hold down jobs outside the home, as Ana María commented, required more than only reflecting on migrants' taken-for-granted class privileges. Women and men negotiated with each other and learned to perform tasks they had previously assigned to domestic servants and other household workers as they became the sole caretakers of children and of a household that had previously been cleaned, organized, and maintained through the cheap labor of poorer Peruvian women working as domestic servants. Particularly during their first few years abroad, transnational Peruvians faced significant challenges in their professional lives, sometimes working jobs they had previously considered too low status for them and finding their professional lives at least temporarily transformed or frustrated. In the following chapters, I delve deeper into the fluid nature of return against the backdrop of Peruvian racial-class-gender hierarchies that migrants renegotiate for themselves even as they attempt to enforce them as a way to maintain their higher social status relative to other Peruvians.

CHAPTER 3

Gendering Everyday Violence and *Seguridad* across Spaces

Chabela and Marco have been married for twenty-one years and lived in the United States for eighteen of those years. After I met them through a mutual acquaintance in Lima, they invited me to their apartment to interview them separately. On the day when I visited to interview Marco, it was early in the morning. It was also a week during which their daughters were off from school. We sat in the cozy living room by a large window that looked out onto a small park to one side of their building in Surco. The youngest daughter offered to bring me a hot drink. Their small, almost miniature, dog was curled up by her feet, and I commented on how warm the sweater he was wearing seemed. It was a chilly, gray morning, like many others in Lima. After a few minutes, the daughter got up, and Marco told me she and her sister would stay in their rooms so that we could do the interview without interruption. Their dog, perhaps hoping to stay warm, immediately jumped up to curl up beside me and stayed there almost the entire time.

After I interviewed Chabela on one of the mornings before she left for work a couple of weeks later, it became clear that Chabela and Marco agree on three and disagree on one central aspect of their migration trajectory. They agree that in Lima they and their two teenage daughters can enjoy being with their extended family more than in the United States. Both Chabela and Marco lost a parent while they lived abroad and deeply regret having lived so far from family during those critical times. Now in Lima, they feel particularly grateful for the close relationships their daughters have forged with their cousins, aunts and uncles, and remaining grandparents. Chabela and Marco also agree that their daughters have access to a better, albeit private school, education in Lima than in the United States. Their third area of agreement is that in Lima they experience a much lower sense of security in their everyday life than they did in the United States and that this shapes how they interact with each other and with their daughters. They disagree on whether or not cumulatively these experiences mean they should stay or once again leave Peru. In separate interviews, I ask Chabela and Marco if they have plans to leave Peru again. Reflecting on the three years since they returned to Lima, Marco expresses his eagerness to return to the United States, telling me, "I love my country, but I do not want to live here." Chabela acknowledges her husband's desire to return to the United States, yet she tells me that she enjoys "being back every day. I am very happy to have returned to Peru" and that she has no plans for the family to leave. One family, many journeys, two opinions, and one area of agreement: security is a concern.

Like Chabela and Marco, many Peruvians left the country to escape economic insecurity and political violence in the 1980s and 1990s. In considering a return, those I spoke with agreed that the country is more economically stable than when they left and that political violence is no longer a serious threat. As is the case in Chabela and Marco's family, it is the more mundane forms of verbal violence, street harassment, aggressive driving, and petty crime that cause concern, and these concerns shape interactions with partners and children, as well as the supervision of the latter. This chapter examines how perceptions of violence inform decisions to return or not return and how these concerns permeate postreturn everyday life. Through a discourse of danger posed by others on the street, the family home becomes a space for the renegotiation of intimate and parent-child relationships in the name of security. On the street and during family discussions of street violence, it is women in particular whose disciplining is justified as necessary for their safety. In the home, as in the street, middle-class anxieties about racialized, classed, and gendered danger become apparent in negotiating security in postreturn experiences.

Danger and Safety

Reflecting on conversation after conversation, I wondered if the dangers people who recently returned to Lima and those who lived abroad spoke to me about were based more on perception or on reality and what amount of perception and reality was involved in each case. In discussing her return to Lima, anthropologist Daniella Gandolfo writes that people she met would tell her that street crime was "worse than ever" as they warned her to leave her valuables at home when using the city's public transportation. She similarly wondered, however, if it is "really worse than ever, or is it just the ever-growing paranoia of an ever-shrinking middle class?" that magnified the dangers of Lima (Gandolfo 2009, 117). Manolo, who lives in Munich and regularly visits Lima, similarly commented that he was warned about the dangers of particular areas of Lima he went to on business by other middle- and upper-class acquaintances and relatives in Lima, yet he doubted "if these areas were really dangerous." Once he had been warned, however, he acknowledged that the possibility of danger influenced where he went and how he behaved in certain areas, since he became increasingly alert and concerned about his safety.

In this book, my main concern is on individuals' perceptions of danger because it is these perceptions that informed return decisions and permeated everyday life postreturn. In many cases, perceptions were founded on personal experiences of crimes. It is important to note, however, that the areas Peruvian migrants were routinely warned about were poorer areas and shantytowns. These unfamiliar areas are considered particularly dangerous by many in the middle and upper classes, and return migrants I spoke with are warned to avoid them. I am not arguing here that there is no danger in Lima, but I do wish to underscore the assumed correlation between danger and lower-class status and spaces in middle- and upper-class imaginaries. For many with whom I spoke, it was common and desirable to avoid these areas entirely. This limitation in movements as safety strategy is not afforded to most Peruvians, many of whom must travel long distances in public transportation and by foot at various times of the day to arrive at work sites, including in middle- and upper-class neighborhoods.

The perception and experience of danger and crime were significant factors in all of the migration narratives I heard, and the threat and reality of crime informed decisions to stay abroad and return. In Lima, insecurity is one of the main everyday problems identified by residents. In 2012, 43 percent of residents reported having been the victim of a crime (López Villanes 2014, 5). In contrast, in 2012 Toronto was the metropolitan area with the lowest overall rate in Canada (Perreault 2013), and in 2013 Munich ranked as the safest large city in Germany (The Local.de 2014). Crime rates vary by city in the United States, yet overall the crime rate is also lower than in Lima.

In Peru, the concern over *seguridad ciudadana* (citizen security) reflects in particular concerns about urban crime. In 2003 Peruvians witnessed the creation of the National Citizen Security System, through which committee and local offices on security were created and formalized (Marquadt 2012). Focusing on Peruvian migrants in the United States, Ulla Berg was told by one of the persons she interviewed that "here, in the U.S., you feel protected by the law, but in Peru it is the opposite. The law does not protect you unless you pay" (2015, 222). A recent report on police corruption in Peru found evidence of institutionalized, systemic corruption in the national police force, with documented cases of police officers accepting illicit payments

Figure 3a: Security as a central concern in elections for mayor.

and bribes (Costa and Neild 2007)—one manifestation of a much longer, more complex history of corruption within institutions and governments in the country (Quiroz 2013). Walking along the oceanfront in Miraflores in August 2014 at a prime traffic spot, I could see that mayoral candidates also sought to appeal to residents by zeroing in on voters' concerns about crime and security through billboards that directly mentioned security.

In Toronto, Aldo explained that he and his wife enjoyed spending part of the Canadian winter in Lima because of the brutal cold in Toronto but that they do not plan to return to Peru permanently primarily because of safety concerns. Piero, a bank CEO in Toronto, similarly cited safety as the main reason for not returning to Peru permanently. In 1990 in Lima Piero witnessed the murder of his boss, who was killed by a car bomb. Since then and until he and his family moved to Toronto, he relied on hired armed bodyguards in Lima. Julián similarly cited safety as the strongest determinant of his family's quality of life in Toronto compared to Lima. Hernán explained that during their visits to Lima he and his wife "know what the reality is, and we take care." In comparison, when they are in Toronto "we don't have to worry" about safety and can walk long distances without worrying about being mugged or much more.

Ana María, who is in her midthirties, views safety in Toronto as the opposite of life in Lima. Last year, during Canadian Independence Day festivities, she accidentally left her car unlocked and the window rolled down. Her laptop computer and camera were inside the car. Three hours later, when she returned to her car, both items were still there. Her mother, who was visiting from Lima, was both shocked and relieved that these items had not been stolen. Ana María tells me this story as representative of her family's quality of life in their new city. She tells me that although she had not been a victim of major crime in Lima, her cell phone and purse were stolen on the street on several occasions, and her parents' house had been broken into repeatedly. In her suburb in Toronto, she does not feel the need to continually be on the alert about possible street crimes, yet in Lima safety concerns determine much of her movement in the city, and she considers it necessary to always be alert.

"*Seguridad* in Every Sense of the Word"

For parents with small children and for those who had children while living outside Peru, a major concern in considering a possible return is how their children would or would not adapt to everyday life in Lima. Men sometimes contrasted their own childhoods in Peru with what they believed their children would experience if they returned to Peru. In some cases, migrants contrasted their own direct experiences with political violence and crime with the children's more shielded lifestyle. In other cases, migrants' comments highlight that socioeconomic status and cultural capital as middle and upper class protected them as children from multiple forms of violence and that those who felt protected as privileged children in the past in Peru do not see a way to provide their children with the same level of protection in contemporary Peru. Several parents described their own freedom from crime in the past and contrasted this in particular with their daughters' vulnerability in the present.

Sitting in a small Italian restaurant around the corner from the Spanish Catholic church at which Peruvians hold their weekly *cajón* (Peruvian drum box) and *marinera* (Peruvian coastal dance) get-togethers in Munich, Manolo and I spent three hours conversing about his life in Germany and return visits to Peru. He moved to Germany in the early 1990s. By the time of the interview, he had lived in Germany for over two decades, and he and his German wife had two daughters. Unlike most other Peruvians I spoke with, Manolo held dual European and Peruvian citizenship because of his parents. He felt privileged to have had dual citizenship from birth and noted that his migration was greatly facilitated by this. Although having dual citizenship from the time they are born is indeed not typical of most Peruvians, Manolo's concerns about his daughters in discussing a possible return to Peru echoed those of Peruvians I met and spoke with in Germany, the United States, and Canada.[1]

Halfway through our meal, I asked Manolo what he considered to be the best thing about his life in Munich. He quickly and emphatically answered, "Number one, number two, and number three: security [*seguridad*]!," adding that he meant "*seguridad* in every sense of the word: of work, of family, that there's more prosperity here, less unemployment even than in the rest of Germany, and a lower crime rate." As a father of one teenage and one preteen daughter, he contrasted his childhood and young adult concerns with political violence, kidnappings, and robberies in 1980s Lima to his daughters' experiences growing up in Munich. His daughters' easy and safe travel by public transportation, including at night with their friends, was something Manolo did not take for granted. This, he tells me, would not have been possible in Lima.

Manolo contrasts his daughters' experiences with those of a friend's daughter in Lima. He shares that his friend recently bragged that he loves living in Villa, a wealthy gated neighborhood, because he does not have to worry about his young daughter being kidnapped when she rides her bike two blocks to her friend's house. To Manolo, the luxury of living without the threat of such violence and the everyday security his daughters enjoy in Munich are what his wealthy friends in Lima attempt to purchase through long hours at work and away from their family, highly paid, competitive jobs, and isolated gated communities. In Lima, gated communities with private security guards are just one symptom of a broader system of exclusion that has intensified over time as more migrants from rural and more indigenous parts of Peru have settled in Lima and as the elite continue to solidify their efforts to gate, protect, and otherwise isolate homes, clubs, exclusive shopping centers, and schools from the growing population (Golte and León Gabriel 2011). Manolo returns to Lima every year, yet "the insecurity there does not invite me to return [permanently]." In Munich, he tells me as he finishes his bowl of minestrone, he and his family "live *seguridad* every day."

Middle- and upper-class neighborhoods in Lima have sought to distance themselves—both physically and symbolically—from areas in which poorer Peruvians live. In 2005 the wealthy La Molina district installed a metal fence along a main street to separate its residents from those in Ate Vitarte, a more recent, poorer Lima district. Residents of Ate complained that the metal fence blocked access to a main street, yet those in La Molina claimed that the fence was necessary for the security of the La Molina side (*La República* 2005). In 2011 the wealthy Las Casuarinas neighborhood in Surco erected a concrete wall to separate it from the adjacent Vista Hermosa neighborhood, one of the poorest neighborhoods. Residents of Las Casuarinas justified the ten-kilometer concrete wall with barbed wire on top as a security measure (*La República* 2015c). In June 2017 during a visit to Pamplona Alta, an established poor neighborhood on one of the hills on the other side of Las Casuarinas, residents I spoke with there disapprovingly pointed to what they and others have now long referred to as the "wall of shame," which was easily visible even from afar. While Las Casuarinas and La Molina residents insisted that security concerns justified these forced separations of areas and blocked access for poorer residents, it is impossible not to see these walls and fences as part of a longer history of exclusion, othering, and marginalization of those deemed potentially dangerous by privileged groups. Ironically, it is these same assumed dangerous others whom wealthier Peruvians seek out and rely on to work as domestic servants, cooks, nannies, and gardeners in their homes and neighborhoods.

Whereas in Lima, Peruvians tended to live in traditionally middle-class neighborhoods such as Miraflores, San Isidro, San Borja, and Surco, after they moved abroad, identifying similar middle-class neighborhoods proved more challenging. Some sought out similar neighborhoods or tried to create something similar through their network of Peruvians in new settings. Some commented that their new neighborhoods were significantly more socially and economically diverse in Munich, Toronto, and several U.S. cities than in Lima. During my stay in Toronto, I was surprised to hear a few of the people I met with refer to a suburb of Toronto as "La Planicie." In Lima, La Planicie is one of the areas in the La Molina district—a largely upper-middle- and upper-class area. It is an upscale neighborhood where celebrities are known to own homes and that boasts a large golf course and multi-million-dollar houses.

After I got off the train after a forty-minute ride from downtown Toronto to Oakville, there was no doubt that I had left the bustling city behind for something more calm and secluded. In downtown Toronto, Alicia contrasted her own choice to live in a downtown neighborhood, within walking distance to restaurants and nightlife and a university, to her uncle's choice to live in Oakville, which she jokingly referred to as Toronto's La Planicie for Peruvians. With its small downtown area and easy access to outdoor recreation, the suburban town offered a more secluded and relaxed ambiance for some. It even included, perhaps not surprisingly, a Peruvian restaurant.

During one of my visits to Oakville I also learned from a fellow Peruvian that one of the crepe shops in the town was owned by a Peruvian woman.

In speaking with Alicia's uncle, whom I also interviewed, he too brought up differences in residential preferences but expressed those differences in slightly different terms: Why, he wondered, were the generation of his children and niece so intent on spending so much money in such a small space when they could get something much bigger and more comfortable in Oakville? For the same starting price of half a million to a million dollars necessary for a small condo or home in downtown Toronto, Oakville (like La Planicie) offered large, spacious homes with large yards and significantly less traffic in a more secluded, safe area, he mused. In his case, he and his family had moved from La Molina (the district that includes La Planicie) to Oakville, and several other Peruvian families he knew had made a similar move in the 1980s. As he added, "I had my house in La Molina, my BMW, my company. I wasn't going to leave it for something different." In his case and others', the move to Toronto was desirable in large part because he believed his family could maintain the same lifestyle and social status as in Lima there, with added security and opportunities for their children.

During one of my visits to Oakville, a Peruvian man I had met offered to drive me through different neighborhoods after an interview and pointed in the general direction of where other Peruvians lived. As I left Oakville, I could see Toronto's comfortable La Planicie fade into the distance and could not help but think of a similar pattern in other cities, where gentrification attracts younger generations and families to downtown areas and the suburbs provide both larger homes and at least the idea of greater calm, safety, and seclusion. In this way, the desired comfort, seclusion, exclusivity, and promise of safety middle and upper classes seek globally through gated communities (Zhang 2010) can sometimes also be achieved through suburban towns such as Oakville.

Gated communities and private security serve the dual function of protecting middle- and upper-class families from those perceived as dangerous "others" and, equally significantly, of being indicators of wealth, thereby reinforcing high social status within Peruvian hierarchies. Gated communities in particular mark a rise in feelings of fear of crime among the middle and upper classes. In a recent study, Jan Marc Rottenbacher de Rojas and colleagues (2009) found a positive correlation between authoritarianism, intensity of risk perception, and the view of lower-status social groups as particularly dangerous. I have no evidence of authoritarian tendencies among Peruvians with whom I spoke. I bring up this finding to emphasize the broader view among the middle and upper classes in Peru of those with fewer economic and social resources as particularly dangerous and prone to crime—and therefore needing to be excluded from areas populated by middle- and upper-class Peruvian families.

Gated communities are far from unique to Peru. They reflect a self-perception of vulnerability tied to, paradoxically, wealth. In Ponce, Puerto Rico, more affluent residents seek to distance themselves from crime and danger through gated communities. Zaire Zenit Dinzey-Flores (2013) notes that the boundaries these communities seek to impose and police are as much about class as they are about race, with darker-skinned Puerto Ricans popularly associated with crime and danger and routinely kept out of more affluent, whiter spaces. In Buenos Aires, the rise in popularity in gates and other forms of security around middle-class homes coincided with the growth of an urban mestizo lower class in the city (Guano 2004). In São Paolo, the middle and upper classes identified the sources of rampant crime in the city as the lower classes and sought to protect themselves through distance, gates, and security systems as a way to physically police and impose social boundaries (Caldeira 1996, 2000). In Lima, middle- and upper-class security and status are similarly marked through distance from those who are seen as not belonging to a privileged social group. Manolo's friend's actions thus reflect a broader global pattern of middle- and upper-class anxieties and insecurities that promote the hiring of private security guards in neighborhoods to keep those deemed undesirable and dangerous out.

Manolo also brought up another point that is common in interviews and conversations with Peruvians abroad: the perception that Lima is particularly dangerous for children who grew up abroad. Without exception, parents I spoke with worried in particular that because their children did not experience the dangers their parents experienced in the 1980s and 1990s in Peru, they are not as street savvy and alert as they should be for life in Lima. Manolo does not consider his daughters to be unusual in what he perceives as their disingenuous approach to life in Lima during visits. Concerns about sons and daughters who do not recognize that cars will not usually stop at crosswalks (or that there are no crosswalks), that children could be mugged on public transportation, and that children are generally not as alert as their parents about their surroundings are common. A few days before a recent visit to Lima in May 2017, as my seven-year-old son and I walked through our neighborhood in the United States, I reminded him that he needed to pay more attention to cars when crossing streets because we were about to be in Lima, to which he automatically replied, "I know, I know, cars don't stop there, I know." As he replied, I thought of Manolo and many other Peruvians and their concerns about their children. I, too, there was no doubt, am among the transnational Peruvian parents whose concerns when visiting Lima include that their children are not used to Lima traffic.

Time to Reminisce: Migration as a Strategy to Reclaim Past Security

For middle- and upper-class Peruvians, particularly those in their fifties and sixties, recollections of their own childhoods present a stark contrast to what they imagine their children and grandchildren will experience in Lima. Repeatedly, women and men assured me that knowing that their children could generally safely walk to the park and on the streets without worrying resulted in a significantly more calm and satisfying family life outside Peru.

Aldo, in his midsixties, left Peru in the mid-1970s. He married a Peruvian woman he met while studying in Europe and now lives in Toronto. He returns to Peru every year to visit for one to two weeks but has no plans to return permanently. Asked about his experience growing up in Lima, Aldo refers to a setting very different from the one Manolo and others referred to in the 1980s, when political violence became one of the main reasons for leaving the country:

> Times have changed, it's something else. The youth that I had in Peru I would love to give to my children, and I can't give it to them, because the freedom we had, I would grab my bike and ride from Miraflores to Lince without any problems, now I can't do it. I lived in high society because my parents were very well off, we lived in a certain neighborhood, went to a private school, we had special things that my children do not have here [in Canada], that I can't offer them. So my youth was very nice, and Peru was fantastic during that time for me as a boy—I'm not speaking as someone who worked then.

For Aldo, as for others I spoke with, migration can be interpreted as part of a strategy to return to the safety and tranquility of their childhoods so that their own children and grandchildren will also experience these.

Aldo grew up in Lima before the political violence of the 1980s. Fernando, now in his midfifties and who arrived in Toronto in 1990 with his wife and two sons, similarly explained that "when we were young we played with friends, in that time it was healthy in Peru. The whole group would go out to play *fulbito* [a variation of soccer] and to ride our bikes. We would return home when my dad arrived home to have dinner all together, and [then] he would tell us 'Go do your homework.'" The idea, romanticized or real, that Peru (more specifically, certain neighborhoods in Lima) "was healthy" yet no longer is contributed to Aldo's and Fernando's decision to relocate outside of Peru. Underscoring generational differences, Aldo's and Fernando's childhoods were not shaped in part by the political violence in the country in the 1980s and 1990s that impacted the childhoods of Manolo and others. Whether they grew up during a period of political violence or earlier, however, all Peruvian parents were especially concerned about how a return to Lima could impact their children and their children's sense of security, as the next section examines.

Everyday Violence, Security, Class, and the Parent-Child Relationship: "It's Part of Life to Be on Alert"

Studies of migration and motherhood suggest that pregnancy and motherhood profoundly affect women's experiences of work, self-identification, beliefs, health, and socialization, as well as their relationships with a partner and family (Erel 2002; Hondagneu-Sotelo and Ávila 2003; Ivry 2010; Moon 2003; Sigad and Eisikovits 2009; Tummala-Narra 2004). Conversations and interviews with mothers and fathers in Lima and abroad point to subtle and explicit ways in which the threat of violence and concerns about security inform parenting and interactions with children, particularly with daughters, against the backdrop of return migration to Lima.

In discussing their daughters' everyday life in Lima, Chabela and Marco observed that their relationships to their daughters have changed since they returned to Peru. For Marco, being the father of two daughters in Lima means he worries about their physical safety more than he did when they lived in the United States. He explains that he is "more overprotective with them here. I try to teach them about the dangers they may encounter here so that they can get used to them." These dangers include being mugged, raped, kidnapped, and sexually harassed on the streets or in public transportation. He tells me that he and his daughters have a good, close relationship but that he regrets that it is defined significantly more by his role as their protector than it was when they lived abroad and he felt he was both protector and friend to them. Chabela also comments that the way she behaves and her relationship with her daughters have changed since their return: "It's as if it's part of life to be on alert [in Lima]. In contrast, when you come from someplace else you are still more trusting. And that's what I tell my daughters, 'You have to be looking, if someone gets on, who is behind you, who is to your side.' I try to teach them that here you can't trust, it's not the calmness of there." Both Chabela and Marco view the threat of everyday violence as a problem, yet for Chabela, having family nearby makes the added risks worth it for them as a family. As studies of Peruvian migration emphasize, family is central to migrants' sense of self (Berg 2015; Carrasco 2010; Paerregaard 2013). In the cases I examine, family is central in decisions both to leave and to return. Chabela feels she still has a role to play not only as a mother but as a confidante to her daughters, although postreturn, the advice she gives them centers on everyday safety significantly more than when they lived in the United States. Because they have daughters, Chabela and Marco worry in particular about sexual harassment and sexual assault on the street and in public transportation.

Hilda, thirty-seven years old, considers her return to Lima from England three years earlier "a mistake" and hopes she and her husband will find jobs abroad in the near future. When I asked her about her reasons for returning to Lima, she explained that she originally planned to stay in Lima just during her maternity leave and until her husband found a job in the United States, where they hoped to relocate next. As in the cases of other Peruvian return migrants I spoke with, for Hilda, the proximity to family and the opportunity for her children to develop deeper family ties were major factors in her decision to return. Because her husband did not find a job in the United States, they decided to extend their time in Lima after her maternity leave. Certain of her family's support, they also decided to have a second child. As we sat on the couch and her youngest daughter played in their small, sparsely decorated apartment, Hilda explained that she and her husband were now actively searching for opportunities to leave again. She and her husband both had jobs in Lima, but the threat of violence and accompanying sense of insecurity she felt in everyday life in her role as a mother had become unbearable.

Hilda's apartment is on a quiet street in Surco, not far from the Parque de la Amistad (Friendship Park), a space widely visited and considered safe and welcoming for families. On weekends, the park's antique train, lake, and play area attract families from throughout the city hoping for a leisurely day of fun. Her return and neighborhood, however, had brought her little peace. For Hilda, returning to Lima after spending several years living and working in England had meant that her past experiences and fears reemerged and informed how she mothers her two young daughters. The year before she left Peru, she was kidnapped. She recognizes that the economic and political situation has improved, yet her fears for herself and for her daughters have stayed with her, and she explains that her fears affect how she and her daughters view the world around them. She comments:

> [They] tell you that Peru is marvelous, but I do not feel safe, and so living here is not worth anything to me because my daughter feels it. Like the other day a car stopped, we couldn't see who was inside, and Carla [daughter] suddenly stopped and said, "You know what, Mamá? I'm afraid. Let's go to the other

side [of the street]." And I told her, "No, don't be afraid. Let's go on the other side of the avenue where there are more cars and people." And so we did. And that would never have happened in England.

Carla, Hilda's eight-year-old daughter, had not experienced any direct threats or forms of violence during her time in Lima, yet she perceived her mother's fear. Hilda regretted that if they moved, her daughters would not grow up in the extended family environment she had hoped they would enjoy and that she would not have the same type of family support she did in Lima. Nonetheless, she felt certain her own experiences as a parent and her relationship with her daughters would improve if they left the country again and she did not feel so concerned about safety issues on a daily basis.

Chabela's, Marco's, and Hilda's general experience of heightened awareness of surroundings and concern for their children's safety on the street were echoed by other parents with whom I spoke. Asked if she and her family would consider returning to Lima to live, Tatiana explained that the level of safety she felt in the medium-sized U.S. town she lived in provided the most important thing for her family: peace of mind. Although she and her husband both missed their families, particularly as their parents grew older and traveling to the United States for visits became more physically difficult for them, they did not plan to return permanently. The family visited extended family in Lima at least once every year, during the children's school holidays, and it was during those visits that Tatiana felt the role of everyday violence and the role of security in her decision most acutely. She perceives "an abysmal difference" in her experiences of everyday security in the United States and Peru. In Lima, she typically has to "tell them to hurry, walk fast, or get in the car, close the window, lock the door" each time they leave the house. She also worries about whether or not their iPhones and tablets will be stolen, because she believes her children are not as careful with them as they would be if they lived in Lima.

As I sit in a large shiny conference room with the varnish and unknown chemicals smell of new furniture still in the air, Piero walks in to greet me. He is wearing a dark gray suit, has carefully styled hair, and within a few minutes lets out a hearty laugh as he begins to tell me about his and his wife's first shock as parents of school-age daughters in Toronto. Like Tatiana, he tells me that for him, the difference in everyday security and threats of violence is an "abysmal difference" in his life in Lima and abroad. He recognizes that no city is 100 percent safe, yet in Toronto, he explains, the places he considers dangerous are significantly fewer than in Lima. During the first week his daughters were in school in Toronto, his then eight-year-old daughter announced to her parents that her class was going on a walking excursion to get pizza. Because of their experiences in Lima, he and his wife "were in a panic. That a little girl of eight would leave school with her friends was inconceivable!" They gave her permission to participate in the trip to the pizzeria two blocks from the school, but they stood and watched from a distance to make sure she left and returned to school unharmed. Unlike her school in Lima, her Canadian school was public and did not have security guards, intercoms, locks on every door, or a gate. He added that in particular during their first year, it was striking to him and his wife that their daughters would leave their bicycles, skateboards, and toys outside the house and no one would steal them, that they did not need an alarm system in the house, and that their cars were not stolen. It was different, but, he continued, they had by now become accustomed to this level of everyday security, and for him, returning to Lima permanently would mean giving up the sense of security that shaped their everyday lives.

Discussing his family's experiences adapting to life in Toronto, Piero also brought up his children's safety. He and his family arrived in the city in the early 2000s, lured by a high-paying job for him. Although the political violence of the 1980s had waned and his main reason to leave Lima was the job offer, his daughters' safety was also an important factor in the family's decision. As he explained, in Lima he had his "daughters in Markham. They had a lot of security." Markham College, a British Peruvian school, is among the most prestigious and expensive schools in Lima. Formerly an all-boys' school, recently the school became coeducational. It markets itself as a school in which "children are secure and happy."[2] In 2016 the one-time entrance fee to ensure access to this happiness and security was $17,500 per child, and tuition is approximately $12,000 per year. Yet the security and protection from everyday violence the school can provide are limited. As Piero explained, in 2002 "they had started to kidnap children because they were just beginning with the laptops, so we the parents were very concerned because the children left with their laptops and were targets." The school had begun to provide a laptop for each of its students, and students left school with these laptops. Once this practice became public knowledge, parents believed their children became more vulnerable to kidnappings and thefts.

Forty-eight-year-old David, a friend of Piero, also lived in Toronto and similarly told me that he and his wife decided to move to Toronto in 2000 in large part for the sake of their two sons: they no longer wanted "the insecurity of having our children on the streets, that they can rob them, kidnap them." Fernando, also in Toronto, similarly explained that they stayed abroad "for the children's safety" and future. In the twenty-four years he has lived in Toronto, his car and now the cars belonging to his children have never been burglarized. In contrast, in Lima his family had something stolen every year, and the year they emigrated his wife's car was stripped. When she left her office job one afternoon, she was surprised to find that the car she drove to work and that had been parked outside her office building was suddenly stripped of "tires and wheels, lights, windows, seats." This event also influenced their decision to leave.

Children's safety and parents' reduced stress because they do not have to worry as much about safety became, for many, important reasons for not returning to Peru to live. In her discussion of her adaptation to life in her medium-sized town in the United States, Tatiana explained that during her first two years there she would continue to hide her purse under the car seat when she drove and lock all doors at every stop. She insisted that fewer concerns about everyday security resulted in significantly less stress in her life as a parent and that because of this she believed it was best for her family to stay in the United States. Similarly, forty-nine-year-old Arturo in Toronto explained that for him, his wife, and their two children, "security is the first point we consider, and that makes us doubt" the possibility of a permanent return. For him, providing his family with *una tranquilidad espectacular* (a spectacular calmness) in Toronto makes his role as a parent less stressful.

The experiences of Chabela, Marco, Hilda, Tatiana, Fernando, Piero, David, and Arturo underscore the prevalence of everyday insecurity in their lives in Lima and the impact this has on their decisions as parents. They also remind us that class positioning informs experiences of fear and that middle- and upper-class status provides particular lenses through which to perceive danger and the origins of danger. As an upper-class Peruvian, for example, Piero had access to a prestigious school in Lima, a neighborhood with security guards, and a house with alarms and ample domestic help. For the majority of Peruvians, these items are luxuries that they cannot access regardless of how much and how hard they work. Tatiana, who attended a similarly prestigious girls' school in Lima, and her husband, who attended another prestigious school, similarly had access to private forms of neighborhood and home security to which most Peruvians do not have access. They also had the cultural capital, educational background, and foreign-language skills most Peruvians do not have. And it is precisely the privileged spaces they inhabit in Lima that people I spoke with were convinced made them especially vulnerable to kidnappings, thefts, and other crimes. In this sense, the experiences examined this far echo more global middle- and upper-class anxieties that have led to a rise in gated communities and neighborhoods as a way to create distance from the lower classes, who are typically seen as more prone to violence and crime and therefore as a threat to wealthier groups.

Although many parents spoke of their fears and concerns for their children's safety, their children did not necessarily see the threat of violence and concerns over security and the decision to return in the same light. I met María José at a conference in Lima after a presentation I gave on Peruvian return migration. She explained she had recently returned to Lima after living in the United States for over a decade. Like Hilda's daughter, María José's fears were partly based on her mother's experience of being kidnapped. When María José was ten years old, her mother was kidnapped. The mother returned home physically unharmed, yet this experience had an enormous impact on María José's sense of personal safety and overall views of security. Her fear deepened when, soon after the kidnapping, her mother was mugged, and "they took off all her jewelry, they tried to take the car, and they pointed their gun at us [children]." The mother's kidnapping experience had largely contributed to the family's decision to migrate to the United States, where they overstayed their visa to avoid returning to Peru. María José's family is unique among the Peruvians I interviewed—although certainly not among Peruvians as a group—in that they overstayed their visa. In their concerns about violence and everyday security as motivation to leave and stay abroad, they were far from alone.[3]

Now in her midtwenties, María José returned to Lima to enroll in a local university as part of an exchange program with her U.S. university and to reconnect with her extended family. She was the first in her immediate family to visit Lima in many years, although her mother planned to return to Lima once she retired in about ten years. María José arrived full of fear and anxieties about possible dangers, but after living in Lima for a few months she became convinced that violence and crime in the city were not so different from those she experienced growing up in another large city in the United States, in California. Her most frightening personal safety moment had occurred in California, not in Lima, when she was mugged at gunpoint. When she informed the university in Lima that she would be living with her extended family in a neighborhood close to the university in the district of San Miguel instead of with a host family in a wealthier, more distant neighborhood, she received a letter from the program notifying her that they were concerned about her safety because the neighborhood she was staying in was dangerous.

Her extended family did not live in one of the more traditional middle-class neighborhoods in which study abroad programs regularly place students but considered themselves to live in a safe area. Middle- and upper-class perceptions of danger inform these official programs and further reinforce particular class-based perceptions of safety and danger in the city, marking some areas as out of bounds for outsiders. While out and about in different neighborhoods in Lima, German anthropologist Anna Katharina Skornia noted that she limited herself to doing one interview per day because of the long distances between neighborhoods and because "walking on the streets alone, as an unaccompanied woman who was easily identified as an outsider, was also stressful in terms of security" (2015, 71). As an outsider, she had surely heard general pronouncements about how some neighborhoods are safer than others, and her statement suggests that she had internalized these warnings about safety. These statements are strikingly similar to the middle- and upper-class discourses of safety Gandolfo (2009) calls upon in her own writing on her visits to Lima and that Peruvian migrants I spoke with repeated. The additional qualifier that she is particularly vulnerable as an "unaccompanied woman" is echoed in María José's family demands as well, as discussed below, and underscores the association of perceived vulnerability in particular with women.

Before migrating to the United States, María José had attended a *colegio pituco* (stuck-up school) at which she was the only student who did not live in a more traditional middle- and upper-class neighborhood. Her family's home in a traditionally more lower-class residential area went against hegemonic discourses of safety and danger for *gente decente* (decent people) and reveals the central ways in which class and perceptions of danger are imbricated in everyday life. And although the neighborhood as a whole was not deemed dangerous by her family, her gender and having lived outside Peru for so many years did mark her as particularly vulnerable in their eyes. Each time she went out, the family insisted that one of her older (male) cousins accompany her, and when this was not possible they insisted that she avoid public transportation and instead only hire private taxis, which were safe—something other women return migrants also repeatedly heard from their families in neighborhood across the city.

The social and economic standing of Peruvians I interviewed in Lima and abroad facilitated their migration and international travel in ways that those without those socioeconomic resources cannot count on. In her study of Andean Peruvian migration to the United States, Berg reminds us that in the "post-9/11 political and racial economy, it is virtually impossible for low-income racialized Peruvians from the Andean provinces or from Lima's many shantytowns to obtain a foreign visa via official means" (2015, 73). Unlike the Peruvians Berg interviewed, Peruvians I interviewed for this project generally had the cultural and economic means to leave Peru legally and without obstacles. They also, as many repeatedly discussed, had the economic and legal means to return to Lima for regular visits with their children. Thus, for many of the people I interviewed, the distance to Peru from their current home was regularly bridged through visits and through regular communication with Skype, other social media, and the phone.

During these visits, it was not uncommon for migrants to enjoy time at the beach and to spend time at the Club Regatas in Lima or its beach outside of Lima. Founded in 1875, the Regatas charges a one-time joining fee of over $50,000 in addition to the monthly membership fee. Entrance into the club can be a lengthy process, as each car with guests must stop by the entry gate and provide the guards not only with their names and the name of the member inviting them but also with proof of identification. As I have waited to get in as a guest on several occasions, I have felt uncomfortable at the scale of surveillance that determines who is allowed in and who stays out. Once inside, members have access to pools, restaurants, play areas, sports centers, massage centers, stores, and many other amenities. Ayumi Takenaka and Karen Pren (2010) argue that the privileged background of some Peruvian migrants provides them with the tools to gain further advantage and, therefore, upon return to Peru, to reinforce and even exacerbate existing hierarchies. In many of the stories with which I became familiar, social capital and economic resources that facilitated migration also reinforced existing class and gender hierarchies upon migrants' return. These hierarchies and middle- and upper-class discourses of fear underscore an imaginary in which the poor are positioned as a threat to be contained and excluded.

Gender, Fear, and Insecurity: Sexual Harassment on the Street

In discussing concerns and anxieties postreturn, migrants did not refer to the political violence that had motivated many of them to leave the country. Instead, they brought up verbal violence, aggressive driving, petty crime, and street harassment. These forms of violence, many repeated to me, had gotten worse in Lima in the years migrants had been away even as economic security had increased and political violence had waned. Experiences and the threat of violence and harassment in public spaces in Lima, which extended families continually warned them about, further worked to undermine autonomy and independence gained abroad, especially for women.[4] These decreased feelings of autonomy in the context of return migration stand in stark contrast to the more common findings of increased autonomy among South American women who emigrate (Pribilsky 2007; Nuñez-Borja and

Stallaert 2013; Mora and Piper 2011), and underscore return migration as a significant site for understanding the negotiation of gender scripts and gender relations.

In recent years, studies of women's experiences of fear in public spaces have brought attention to the gendering of spaces and of fear (Hlavka 2014; Koskela 1999; Phadke 2005, 2012; Wesely and Gaarder 2004). Many of the women return migrants I interviewed experienced heightened feelings of vulnerability to sexual assault on city streets after returning. Men also cited violence and insecurity as an important concern in their everyday lives. The threat of sexual violence, however, did not play the same role in men's narratives of return. Men most often brought up fear of public spaces in connection to their role as fathers of daughters or as husbands, prepared to protect the women in their lives. In some cases, like that of Marco, fathers became more protective of their daughters.

A "shadow of sexual assault" (Ferraro 1996) infuses everyday life and takes on particular significance in the context of Peru, which ranks number one in reported cases of sexual violence in South America (Mujica 2011). In spite of high rates of sexual violence, this type of violence is too often dismissed as not worthy of serious consideration: one recent study noted that prosecutors and forensic doctors continue to dismiss sexual violence, particularly against married women by their spouses (Boesten 2012). The threat of violence and feelings of insecurity numerous women in particular referred to are not unfounded: in a recent national survey, seven out of ten Peruvian women between the ages of eighteen and twenty-nine reported having experienced sexual harassment on the streets during the previous six months. In Lima, the number goes up to nine out of ten women.[5]

In late 2014 and early 2015, a three-minute anti–street harassment campaign ad, "Catcall your mother," produced by the sporting goods company Everlast and featuring Peruvian Olympic volleyball player Natalia Málaga, went viral. It was brought up repeatedly in conversations with family, friends, and acquaintances who identified me with "women's issues" during my visit to Lima. In the video, accessible on YouTube, young men in Lima are depicted harassing women on the streets.[6] The men's mothers, recruited to disguise themselves and walk on the streets near their sons, then confront their sons and chastise them for the nation—and beyond—to see. The men's actions reveal what many have long known: street sexual harassment is painfully common and is practiced with impunity.

In response to successful campaigns and protests against street sexual harassment, in March 2015 Peru became the first country in Latin America to pass a law sanctioning street sexual harassment. The law applies to harassment in streets, parks, and public transportation and includes jail terms of up to twelve years. How and if harassment in public spaces will be impacted by this law remains to be seen. Peru has also been at the forefront of passing other laws, such as laws against domestic violence, yet rates of violence against women—including feminicide—continue to be very high. Women of varying ages, civil statuses, racial, economic, and educational backgrounds, and sexual orientations reported experiencing sexual harassment on the streets to me in spite of the existence of this law. As I walked in Lima in early 2017 in the neighborhood Miraflores, where my grandmother once lived in a house on a street that is now dominated by tall apartment buildings and new construction sites, as much of the city is today, I noticed a new type of sign. Posted on the outside fence of a construction site for yet another apartment building, it read "En esta obra no silbamos a las mujeres y estamos en contra del acoso callejero" (In this worksite we do not whistle at women, and we are against street harassment). This sign would not have been possible before the anti–street harassment campaigns and the changes in the law.

Writing on women's safety in Mumbai, Shilpa Phadke (2012) reminds us that danger and risk are gendered—something feminist and women's movements in Peru have also been calling attention to during the last decade. She finds that men feel safer and have greater access to different areas of the city than women, noting the presence of significantly more threats to women's safety than to men's in both men's and women's narratives of city life. These potential threats lead to the use of gendered safety strategies that inform where, how, and when women move through different parts of the city. In Lima, the narratives of women return migrants consistently highlighted the insecurity and fear associated with some public spaces and the different strategies women employed to protect themselves. These strategies reproduced intersecting gender, race, and class hierarchies of men as protectors and women as in need of protection. They also reinforce stereotypes of working-class and poor men, typically those who are mestizo and indigenous, as particularly dangerous to white middle- and upper-class women, as discussed in the final section of this chapter.

Describing her return, Gandolfo writes that part of her reinsertion into city life in Lima involved knowing that "for a few more days I will be shocked by the men in Lima; like with the birds' cries, I'll be startled when I hear [men] hissing, catcalling, yelling, as they frequently do with women in the streets" (2009, 45–46). These gendered experiences of harassment on the streets were echoed in women's narratives. These experiences are also, although not explicitly stated in the previous quote, classed: my guess is that the men Gandolfo refers to are lower-class men on the streets, not those in her family warning her of these dangers. Forty-year-old Berta, who had recently returned from Spain to live in Lima with her husband and three Spanish-born children, did not feel safe on the streets in Lima. Describing herself as an autonomous, independent woman, she regretted that "as a woman I feel I have lost some of my autonomy" through her return. Berta feels she depends on her husband more in Peru than in Spain because as a woman she feels particularly vulnerable, so she routinely asks her husband to ride with her in taxis, especially at night, something she did not do in Spain.

The street repeatedly appears as a space of potential danger in women's narratives of everyday life as return migrants. Twenty-six-year-old Bárbara has a well-paid, desirable job and a recent-model car, and she lives in a chic neighborhood. In discussing her day-to-day life, however, she explains that she feels "super unsafe. Maybe that's one of the areas in which for me it is very difficult to adapt, that street harassment is constantly present, and there is no respect for women. Not even my father, my cousins, or my grandfathers, I mean from the language used, to the people in the *combis* [small public buses] who touch you.... It's horrible, [I feel] completely unsafe, that anyone can come and touch me, push me, bother me."

Bárbara's experience of being physically and verbally harassed and her perception of the generalized sexism that facilitates these forms of harassment against women were echoed by many. As soon as she completed her university degree in the United States, twenty-three-year-old María returned to Lima to a coveted job, to be close to family, and to feel she was contributing to her community. When we spoke, she was considering leaving Peru again, because "in Lima there is very aggressive harassment, and it's everywhere, you can't escape machismo." For her, strategies for feeling safer included self-policing what she wore and how she walked and constantly being on alert in case someone came too close to her. In addition to advocating self-policing, family and friends reminded and warned women of the potential dangers associated with public spaces. When thirty-eight-year-old Alicia visits family in Lima, her sister repeatedly cautions her about possible dangers she could face. She warns her to avoid walking on the streets too much and encourages her to instead take formal, licensed taxis anywhere she wishes to go during her brief visits.

In case after case, women described themselves as strong and independent and expressed frustration about their own vulnerability and powerlessness in public spaces in which they were perceived as accessible and inferior because they were women. Twenty-four-year-old Marina also discussed with me how she felt "more unsafe here, mostly because here street sexual harassment is super strong." Like María's, Marina's strategies for feeling safe included limiting where she went and carefully considering how she dressed and how she walked. Even with these strategies, however, she believed she would "always feel insecure that someone will think my body belongs to them." In spite of her individual feelings of independence, strength, and what she described as empowerment, the sexist structures that informed everyday life made it impossible for her to feel safe. Marina described being verbally harassed on the streets and groped on public transportation. The most common phenomenon she had encountered since her return was men masturbating near her in public transportation. She had yelled at the men and forced the driver to stop and make them get off the bus on a few occasions, but her actions did not prevent other men from doing the same thing soon after.

In very few instances, return migrants commented that they felt just as safe in Lima as they did anywhere else. Yet even in these cases their experiences also underscore the gendered nature of fear and insecurity. Olivia tells me she does not see any significant differences between her life in Germany and in Peru in the area of safety. In fact, she explains, in Frankfurt she was more concerned about the inebriated men she often ran into on the streets at night than in Lima. She adds, however, that "of course I don't take [unlicensed] taxis on the street [here], I don't go out alone if it's dark, I don't speak with people I don't know in nightclubs"—thereby revealing the very strategies she relies on for safety. When she was younger in Lima, she tells me, on one occasion an older man went up to her on the street and unzipped his pants. More than fear, she explains, she felt shock. Her safety strategies, like those of Marina, María, and other women I met with, reflect heightened vulnerability in Lima due to specific threats they anticipated there.

Among the male return migrants, three men (two university professors and one chef) stated that they had the same security concerns in Lima as they did anywhere else. Unlike other men I interviewed, the men were not involved in intimate relationships or had children when we spoke, and this may have informed their own feelings of security and safety. Without concerns for a partner's or child's, particularly daughter's, safety, they may not have confronted women's experiences of heightened vulnerability as directly.

Gendering Street and Home: Continuums of Violence

Feelings of insecurity on the streets were widespread and mark public spaces as potentially dangerous places for women. In her intimate ethnography of Lima, Gandolfo shares that after being mugged in Lima as she walked home to her house in Miraflores, her father insisted that "it's simply dangerous for me to walk alone" (2009, 149). Repeatedly, women are warned about and experience the streets of Lima as potentially dangerous public spaces. Women's vulnerability to street harassment is not unique to Lima, yet this does not lessen the impact of street harassment on women's lives there.

Migrants routinely commented on the dangers of public spaces, but the possibility of violence is hardly limited to those spaces. In discussing their concerns about violence, safety, and insecurity, two women I spoke with brought up the threat of violence in the home. One woman discussed how the issue of personal safety as a woman was of special importance to her because a family acquaintance had raped her when she was younger. Another woman explained that in addition to the street harassment she regularly experienced, she grew up with the knowledge that her mother had been sexually abused by family members as a child. For these women, as for many women around the world, home and street did not reflect a contrast between safety and danger but the reality of the continuum of violence in women's lives.

Recognition of a continuum of violence in women's lives and the increased vulnerability of some women is also reflected in Fernando's comment that when he visits Lima from Toronto, one thing that troubles him is how domestic servants are treated in the homes of relatives, friends, and acquaintances. He commented that "those poor girls, who knows what they face when they leave, in addition to the sexual abuse [in the houses where they work]." Jelke Boesten (2014) points to the prevalence of sexual abuse against domestic servants as an important theme in late twentieth-century Peruvian literature and as a reflection of reality. In these cases, violence in the home—often sexual in nature—is part of a continuum of violence women are vulnerable to and that spills over into public spaces. In 2017 the Household Workers' Labor Union of the Lima Region (SINTTRAHOL) estimated that about 60 percent of household workers in Lima had experienced sexual abuse in their places of employment (*La República* 2017).

The gendered reality of everyday violence and in particular of sexual violence in Peru has been garnering increasing national and international attention as organizations and individuals continue to protest the threat of violence and insecurity women confront daily. On August 13, 2016, individuals, families, politicians, and even the newly elected president of Peru, Pedro Pablo Kuczynski, participated in the peaceful march "Ni una menos" (Not one less) to bring attention to and reject the continuum of violence against women and the impunity with which it is often met. The march was originally estimated to attract fifty thousand participants, but about half a million people participated in the march downtown to the Palace of Justice.⁷ The cover of the Peruvian newspaper *La República* for the following day was an impressive photograph from above of thousands of participants, with the headline "Never Have So Many Marched in Defense of Women." Outside Peru, Peruvians also gathered in solidarity for the "Ni una menos" march, including in Trafalgar Square in London.

Recent work on Peru by feminist anthropologists has approached violence through multilevel, intersectional lenses to link experiences of violence in the home to institutional, state, and structural violence (Alcalde 2010; Boesten 2010, 2014; Bueno-Hansen 2015; Theidon 2013). Boesten (2014) examines connections between and the meanings of wartime and peacetime sexual violence. She emphasizes that the gendered, race, class, and sexual hierarchies that facilitate both forms of violence are embedded in Peruvian society. During both war and peace, intimate and public forms of violence are widespread, and, as Boesten underscores, the state is complicit in perpetuating ideologies and practices that facilitate violence. Challenging ideas of the home or even small community as safe, Boesten (2014) adds that sexual violence during periods of conflict may also be used to settle preexisting conflicts within a community or may reinforce preexisting misogynous practices within a community.

Kimberly Theidon (2013) similarly challenges ideas about the safety of homes and small communities. She carefully examines violence from 1987 to 2000 and notes that this included violence among community members, sometimes relatives, as she connects these more intimate forms of violence to broader forms of political violence informed in part by race, class, and gender hierarchies. Also writing on the sexual violence inherent in broader forms of violence in the 1980s and 1990s, Pascha Bueno-Hansen (2015) points to intersections of state, structural, institutional, and family violence in the Truth and Reconciliation Commission testimonies of indigenous women. Boesten (2014), Bueno-Hansen (2015), and Theidon (2013) expose the sexual violence the military perpetrated against suspected *senderista* (Shining Path member) women, against civilian women begging for news of their loved ones, and against mothers and daughters in their own homes. All of these remind us of broader patterns of discrimination and violence that make possible systemic violence, particularly sexual violence against women.

In my own work on violence in the lives of women who were mostly migrants from rural areas attempting to survive in or leave abusive intimate relationships in Lima (Alcalde 2010), the intersections of multiple forms of violence—in private and public settings—also stood out across the three dozen life history interviews I conducted. Jimena was one of the women who shared her life story with me. She was twenty-six years old, worked as an elementary school teacher, and had two young children when we met. Jimena called in sick to work sometimes because she was in so much pain or could not hide the bruises. She hid her husband's abuse from her coworkers for fear she would lose her job. The messages she had received her entire life were that home and work were two separate spheres and that she should not bring any "private" problems from home to work. On one occasion, she left the house to walk to the pharmacy to buy pain medication after her husband punched her head repeatedly. On the way to the pharmacy, with her head badly injured, she felt disoriented and became lost. When she looked around, she realized she was by a field with a reputation for being dangerous because men had recently raped women there. She did not remember how she arrived there. Jimena temporarily left her home because of the danger she faced there, yet leaving created additional potential threats to her security and well-being. In this case, as in many others I became familiar with, the violence Jimena suffered at home is directly connected to her exposure to other forms of violence on the streets.

In examining perceptions and experiences of street harassment and violence, the reality of persistent and widespread violence against women in their homes, perpetrated by those close to them in their families and communities, cautions us against simplistic dichotomies in which the home is safe and the street is dangerous, to more carefully consider the class, gender, and racialized assumptions underneath these binaries. Women's experiences across private and public spaces underscore the continuum of violence in women's lives. All women do not share the same vulnerability to different forms of violence, however, and violence against all women does not receive the same amount or type of attention. To conclude this chapter, I turn again to the intersecting roles of class, race, and gender in return migrants' perceptions and experiences of violence and security.

Return and Security: Reproducing Gender, Race, and Class Hierarchies

Middle- and upper-class migrants felt strongly about and deeply connected to a version of Peru in which they continued to have privileged positions. Like many Peruvian migrants, they communicated with friends and family in Peru and elsewhere through social media and Skype. Unlike many Peruvian migrants whose immigration status or economic resources prevented them from regular trips to Peru (Berg 2015; Paerregaard 2014), migrants

I spoke with were able to regularly return to Lima to visit family and for business. During these visits, they enjoyed spending time with family and seeing their children bond with grandparents, aunts and uncles, and cousins, eating out, visiting the Club Regatas, going to the beach, and counting on domestic servants to perform many of the household chores they routinely performed in their own homes abroad. For some migrants, concerns about violence and security influenced their decisions to permanently live outside Peru. Viewed as qualitatively better for their children's well-being, for some, living abroad became an opportunity to enjoy the levels of safety they associated with their own childhoods; for others, it was a way to escape the everyday forms of violence they had experienced in their youth or as adults, particularly in the 1980s. Many remarked that they felt unsafe on the streets and were particularly worried about their children, who were not as aware of potential dangers as they were during visits.

The pull of family, the desire to have children grow up near their extended family, and plans to contribute to their own communities and country informed some migrants' decision to return to Peru to live. In these cases, everyday security and violence were also major concerns. Children who had lived most of their lives abroad had to be taught new safety strategies, parents reconstructed their relationships with their children to prioritize everyday safety, and individuals renegotiated their own relationships with family and their anxieties and fears about public spaces.

That safety is gendered and a major concern for return migrants is communicated through warnings received from family members and acquaintances, personal experiences, and fears expressed by return migrants. Women's increased vulnerability to street sexual harassment is an everyday reality. This reality, approached through an intersectional lens, provides additional insights into the role of gender, race, and class in discussions and experiences of safety and security. The hierarchies of race and class work together with gendered hierarchies that position the home as safe for women and the streets as dangerous and in which poor indigenous and mestiza women domestic servants work for wealthier women. Gendered hierarchies also reveal class structures and the assumed differences that present some masculinities as particularly dangerous—it is working-class and poor men on the streets who are viewed as dangerous.

Phadke (2005, 2013) questions the role of class and caste in the safe home / dangerous street dichotomy in media attention to women's safety in Mumbai. She draws our attention to the persistent coverage of anxieties about violence by strangers in public areas and the parallel silence on violence in the home. She makes visible the role of class by analyzing how the street harassment that receives most media coverage is that perpetrated by lower-class men, typically against middle-class women. She observes that all women are not considered equally worthy of sympathy and that attention to class reveals the naturalization of violence against poorer women and poor men as dangerous. In contrast, upper-class men's sexual violence is rarely given as much attention, and "when lower class, dalit or tribal women are sexually assaulted the media barely covers these attacks and there is little or no public outrage" (Phadke 2013, 50).

Similarly, in Lima, it is lower-class men who are assumed to populate public areas as construction workers, bus drivers, loiterers, and the unemployed. Their presence is what marks these areas as potentially dangerous to middle- and upper-class women in particular. To avoid harassment on public transportation, return migrants discussed driving their own cars, as well as safety strategies that included taking only licensed taxis. The perception of who is exposed to violence and who makes public spaces dangerous, however, is tightly connected to existing class-race-gender hierarchies that privilege whiteness, masculinity, and class and in which those who are poorer—including women—are seen as both naturally dangerous (if men) or unworthy of media attention (if women). The harassment domestic servants experience is rarely discussed in the media or by return migrants. For women with few economic resources, the significantly higher costs of using company taxis or of owning a car, as compared to riding in *combis* and *micros* as forms of public transportation, are not viable options. Individuals are gendered, racialized, and classed in both intimate and public spaces, yet even as we examine spaces routinely marked as dangerous in return migration narratives, we cannot assume that violence is limited to or evenly distributed within these spaces. As I examine in the next chapter, private and public spaces may be particularly insecure for return migrants who identify as gay, lesbian, or bisexual. In these cases, exclusion and insecurity undergird belonging in the context of return.

CHAPTER 4

HETERONORMATIVITY, HOMOPHOBIA, AND HOME

I glance at my watch, take another sip from my overpriced small cup of coffee, and look up again, hoping to recognize Ronaldo among the dozens of people rushing by on the street. Some turn toward my table near the doors of the busy coffeehouse in Miraflores, a traditionally middle- and upper-class neighborhood in Lima. It is getting chilly, and until he arrives I keep stretching the sleeves of my sweater, wishing I could extend the warmth to my cold fingertips. I smile as I slowly begin to get up to greet someone I have convinced myself must be Ronaldo. He is oblivious to my actions and walks past me to greet a small group at the next table. He sits with them. Finally, Ronaldo and I spot each other, both of us searching for someone we haven't met before.

Over the course of the next hour and a half, twenty-eight-year-old Ronaldo tells me about his return. He decided to come back to Lima after several years in the Netherlands. He quietly tells me, between disbelief and disappointment, that on the way home from the airport "the first thing [his parents] told me [was] 'you're going to have your own room, but no sneaking in men into our house!'" For the past three years, Ronaldo has been living with his parents in Lima, relieved to be in the city and family home in which he feels he belongs and for which he longed while away. It is in this home that he has been under threat of losing the affection and approval of those most important to him because of the family's homophobic views. Ronaldo had not expected total acceptance, yet his parents' timing and choice of words the night of his return took him by surprise. As we finish the interview, he glances toward the door. His boyfriend has just entered the coffeehouse, and Ronaldo asks if I would like to meet him.

In Lima, as in other locations, homophobic attitudes and practices in private and public realms are shaped by heterosexism, which contributes to a climate of fear toward and rejection of nonnormative sexualities and presents heterosexuality as natural and superior (Boellstorff 2004). In this chapter I suggest that LGB migrants find themselves in the difficult position of experiencing violence against them—homophobic practices, jokes, silencing, and discrimination—in order to be at home with their families, in their homeland, and within immigrant communities. These forms of violence exclude them even as they are otherwise seemingly incorporated back into their families and communities. Drawing on interviews with gay, lesbian, and bisexual Peruvians and on newspapers, ordinances and bills, and field notes, I underscore how these quotidian technologies of exclusion against LGB migrants can undergird, and even define, belonging in cases of return and in Peruvian immigrant communities.

Writing on citizenship and race in Germany after the fall of the Berlin Wall, Damani Partridge (2012) refers to the process of simultaneous incorporation and exclusion of brown and black citizens in that country as "exclusionary incorporation." Even as black and brown people formally become citizens, Partridge argues, they find that it is increasingly challenging if not impossible to exercise their citizenship fully. In Peru, LGB experiences of migration expose multiple forms of "exclusionary incorporation" and exclusionary belonging both through Peruvian immigrant communities and before and throughout the process of return migration. These experiences further mark home as a site of simultaneous safety and fear and underscore the role of homophobia in some forms of exclusionary cosmopolitanism. In this sense, as this chapter examines, neither emigration nor return migration provides protection from exclusionary incorporation.

Homophobia, Violence, and Exclusion

As in other parts of the world (for India, see Gopinath [2005]), dominant nationalisms in Peru construct the nation as essentially heterosexual. The everyday practices and attitudes through which homosexual behaviors are commonly viewed as falling outside of what is considered to be the limits of belonging—in a home, in a public park, on the streets, in a clinic, or as representatives of a nation—reflect this heteronormative construction of the nation. In the 1990s, when many of the Peruvians I spoke with left Peru, President Fujimori's regime employed homophobic discourses and antigay strategies and violence, and media representation of gay and lesbian Peruvians was largely stereotypical and founded on caricatures (Ruz 2003). Fujimori is popularly known for his *mano dura* (firm hand) against suspected *senderistas*, and the racialized targeting of and violence against those suspected as terrorists or accomplices by his regime are now well documented. The targeting of LGBTQ Peruvians during this period is much less well known and acknowledged, yet it too is an important part of Peru's violent past.

The Peruvian Truth and Reconciliation Commission final report, which is composed of twelve volumes, included only two pages about violence against and the targeting of sexual minorities (Fobear 2014). This invisibility and exclusion in the Truth and Reconciliation report further normalizes heteronormativity in approaches to violence and the acceptability of violence against LGBTQ Peruvians (Fobear 2014). In spite of this relative invisibility, these forms of violence are in practice part of a broader pattern of homophobic violence that has characterized state violence during many wars and conflicts. These include Nazi targeting of homosexuals, Franco's targeting of homosexuals as political enemies, and the Egyptian, Namibian, and Ugandan governments' attacks on those suspected of homosexuality (Fobear 2014).

During the internal conflict between the state and the Maoist-Leninist group the Shining Path and to a lesser extent the Movimiento Revolucionario Túpac Amaru (MRTA, or Túpac Amaru Revolutionary Movement) from the 1980s to 2000, the Peruvian military routinely targeted LGBTQ Peruvians (Amnesty International 1997). During this period the Shining Path and the MRTA also targeted for murder those suspected of homosexuality in the areas they controlled (Amnesty International 1997; Bracamonte 2010). Those included as "undesirable" in the moral codes of the Shining Path and who were therefore vulnerable to extrajudicial killings included homosexual men (Serrano-Amaya 2014). In 1986 the Shining Path killed ten people the group identified as "homosexuals and prostitutes" in Aucayacu, and several people who feared being killed for the same reasons left the area soon after that (Montalvo 2006, cited in Serrano-Amaya 2014). In 1989 the MRTA murdered eight Peruvians they identified as *travestis* (transvestites) in Tarapoto. The following year, the MRTA murdered a young man they identified as homosexual and left his corpse with a message that warned that "this is how faggots die" (Serrano-Amaya 2014). None of these murders are isolated incidents. The incidents mentioned here underscore systemic negative representations and a history of marginalization of and violence against LGBTQ Peruvians by state and nonstate actors as the backdrop and pathway to continued violence and exclusion of LGB Peruvians with whom I spoke.

Even when there is no immediate danger of murder, the everyday familial, social, and professional repercussions of coming out can be grave. In the social environment of the country's internal conflict, it was rare to come out as or be suspected of being homosexual without significant negative personal and professional consequences. The widespread negative views of homosexuality had a significant impact on the well-being of those Peruvians identified as homosexual or suspected of being homosexual: in 1993 the government fired 117 government workers because of their suspected homosexuality. The public was overwhelmingly supportive of these firings (Ruz 2003, 24). In 2009 Interior Minister Mercedes Cabanillas proposed a law to ban homosexual men from joining the police force.[1] This more recent law project further underscores the continued and systemic exclusion of homosexuality from the parameters of acceptable identities within Peruvianness as imagined by the state.

A study in the early 1990s reported that out of sixty gay men surveyed in Lima, only four had come out to their families, and all four had faced rejection (Arboleda 1995, 106, cited in Ruz 2003). More recently, in a national survey, 75 percent of respondents stated that they believed homosexual sex between men or between women was always wrong, and 30 percent considered homosexuality to be a mental illness. In the same survey, over half reported that they would not be accepting of homosexual friends (Sulmont 2005, 35–36).

In the online survey I conducted among Peruvians living abroad, 27 percent viewed homophobia as a problem in Peru, and 26 percent stated it was a problem both in Peru and in the country in which they currently lived but that it was a bigger problem in Peru. Among persons who identified as LGBTQ, 100 percent viewed homophobia as a problem in Peru. In other words, from the standpoint of those directly affected by homophobic societal attitudes, there was no question that they were treated more negatively than those Peruvians identified as heterosexual. And among those who did not select one of the predetermined survey answer choices, there were these telling responses in the open-text spaces: "it doesn't interest me"; "it's not my problem"; "I continue to be homophobic"; and "I don't know, and it doesn't interest me." These responses further reflect indifference to the existence and impact of homophobia on Peruvians' everyday lives. More importantly, they underline indifference ("it doesn't interest me") as a strong form of inaction that facilitates the maintenance of forms of exclusion and the dismissal as unimportant of broader patterns of violence that affect LGBTQ individuals. The impact of these societal attitudes, however, permeates all dimensions of a person's life.

On the one hand, cities have been popularly understood as more welcoming, tolerant spaces for gay and lesbian lifestyles in part because they provide more anonymity and privacy than rural areas (Weston 1998; Valentine and Skelton 2003). On the other hand, heteronormativity and homophobia are central components of the city life to which Peruvians return in Lima and in some immigrant communities. Lima in the second decade of the twenty-first century may not be so different from the Lima of the 1990s. LGBTQ individuals still lack basic rights heterosexual individuals enjoy,[2] and homophobia significantly impacts the lives of LGBTQ people in the city (Cáceres, Talavera, and Mazín Reynoso 2013; Vásquez del Aguila 2012, 2015).

The exclusionary and violent attitudes and behaviors toward those Peruvians identified as homosexual are further reinforced and reflected in prevalent religious-cultural values. The archbishop of Lima, Opus Dei member Juan Luis Cipriani, has repeatedly stated that homosexuality is a sin and an illness. He has even demanded that the country's top university, the Pontifical Catholic University, distribute pamphlets that refer to homosexuality as an illness to be cured (Reding 2010, 298). Perhaps not surprisingly, Cipriani also gained notoriety for rejecting human rights as a concern during the Peruvian government's fight against suspected terrorists (Cáceres, Cueto, and Palomino 2008). In 2017 the head of the Movimiento Misionero Mundial (Global Missionary Movement) in Peru, Rev. Rodolfo González Cruz, was recorded declaring that women caught having sex with women should be killed and that the state has the right to kill those who commit homosexual acts (*El Comercio* 2017).

In early 2017 conservative groups organized to reject the school curriculum announced by the Ministry of Education because it included information on sex education and gender equality. Under the banner "Con mis hijos no te metas" (Don't mess with my children), various religious, conservative groups and individuals have come together to fight against what they deride as a harmful "gender ideology," which they claim seeks to promote immorality and homosexuality. In this scenario, gender equality is perceived as dangerous and linked to immorality, which is then linked to homosexuality. Under the guise of the protection of children, homophobia is advanced, and therefore discrimination—or worse—against LGBTQ identities and individuals is presented not only as justified but as necessary for the well-being of children, families, and the nation. In April 2017 the Peruvian Congress put forth a bill to get rid of consideration of sexual orientation and gender identity as aggravating circumstances in hate crimes (decreto legislativo No 1323).

Peruvian writer, journalist, and talk show host Jaime Bayly has written extensively on the homophobia he experienced growing up bisexual in Lima in a socially conservative, Catholic upper-middle-class family in the 1980s and 1990s in his largely autobiographical novels. In his first novel, *No se lo digas a nadie* (Don't tell anyone), the father tells his son, "This city is too small.... [Y]our lifestyle goes against our morality, the morality of the *familias decentes* [decent families] of Lima" (Bayly 1994, 166, cited in Ruz 2003, 24). Similarly to Bayly, Peruvians I interviewed came from *familias decentes*—a euphemism for established middle- and upper-class families, often claiming white European ancestry—and it was not uncommon for them to face rejection and silencing within their families because of their sexual identity. In the remainder of this chapter, I suggest ways in which attitudes and practices transnationally are manifestations of exclusionary incorporation in Lima and within immigrant communities abroad. I do this as I examine possibilities for LGBTQ activism and advocacy and everyday obstacles those I interviewed who identified as LGB confront both vis-à-vis state representatives and within families.

Facing Violence and Exclusion, Engaging in Resistance

Heteronormativity in Peru facilitates homophobic practices, yet it would be disingenuous to assume that there is little or no resistance to homophobia. In 2013 the Peruvian Congress considered national legislation prohibiting discrimination based on sexual orientation. Although the bill was defeated, with fifty-six representatives voting against and eighteen abstaining, it is also worth noting that twenty-seven representatives voted in favor of the bill (*El Comercio*, 2015c). In 2014 one of the representatives who voted in favor, Carlos Bruce, who had recently come out as gay, introduced another bill in support of civil unions among same-sex couples. That bill also failed. An attempt to reintroduce the bill in March 2015 failed to receive support, with only two voting to reconsider it (*El Comercio* 2015c). As of December 2015, six countries in South America recognize same-sex unions.[3] Peru is not one of these countries.

Against this backdrop of continued difficulties in passing nationwide legislation, protests to make LGBTQ Peruvians visible and to demand rights continue to happen. The state does not have a good track record of dealing with these protests and demands in a peaceful and respectful manner. Even seemingly simple displays of affection may result in violence by the state against LGBTQ citizens. On 13 February 2016, police in riot gear responded to the peaceful annual "Kisses against Homophobia" demonstration in the main plaza in downtown Lima by spraying same-sex couples kissing or holding hands and allies with water and kerosene from armored tanks (*Washington Blade*, 15 February 2016).

The Peruvian government does not collect data on violence and discrimination specifically against LGBTQ people. Instead, it is largely left to civil society organizations and movements to compile information, provide resources, and advocate for LGBTQ rights. According to reports by nonprofit organizations, it is impossible to know how many instances of violence and discrimination based on sexual identity there are each year, since many, if not most, go unreported. Nonetheless, in 2012 organizations documented seven reported murders and twelve assaults motivated by discrimination based on sexual identity (Hernández, Miller, and Schneeweis 2015, 6).[4] Lack of laws and legal protection make such violence less visible than violence toward other groups but not less lethal.

Grassroots activism keeps LGBTQ identities and demands visible. In 2002 activists organized Lima's first Pride Parade. In September 2014 Lima hosted the first Encuentro de Liderazgos Políticos LGBTI de América Latina y El Caribe (Meeting of LGBTI Political Leadership of Latin America and the Caribbean), at which LGBTQ politicians, movement and program leaders, and activists and allies discussed the challenges facing diverse LGBTQ populations in the region. That same year, the 13 Encuentro Feminista Latinoamericano y del Caribe (Feminist Latin American and Caribbean Meeting), held in Lima in November 2014, further made visible the topic of LGBTQ oppression and activism and pushed it into the center of the broader conversation of how to combat gender inequality in the region. At the national level, the Ministry of Women and Social Development's National Plan on Violence against Women 2009–2015 includes and addresses women of all sexual orientations.[5] It specifically identifies homophobia as a form of violence against lesbians.

In May 2013 I sat in a small room in the well-worn offices of the Movimiento Homosexual de Lima (MHOL, or Homosexual Movement of Lima) waiting for the then-president of the group. I had long heard of MHOL, which was founded in 1982 and identifies as the oldest gay-lesbian organization in Latin America, and had contacted the president to request a meeting. MHOL is a volunteer-based organization, and the president had significant demands on her time. Meeting with me about a project not directly connected to MHOL's work was yet one more demand on an already busy schedule. During our meeting, I asked about the group's position on political asylum applications from Peruvians who felt discriminated against to the point they could no longer live in Peru. She acknowledged and discussed the challenges and violence those identified as homosexual may face in Lima and other parts of the country. She also asserted that the solution to being homosexual in Lima was not to leave the country but to join the struggle to make Lima, and the country more broadly, a more inclusive and safe place. This, she explained, was what she and the people she collaborated with daily had been focusing on. At the time of our interview, MOHL did not provide any documentation in the form of letters of support or testimony for political asylum applications.[6] Ronaldo, whom I met a couple of weeks after my meeting at MOHL, similarly opined that "you can live here [as a gay man], there's no need to request political asylum." He then added, "That people want to kill you, rape you, here we don't have those types of problems." Existing statistics compiled by nonprofit groups and cited above, however, contradict this statement. His experience of return further calls attention to nonlethal but still harmful forms of discrimination and exclusion that shape everyday life.

Attention to everyday experiences of discrimination similarly brings to the forefront the role of social hierarchies among gay men. As Ernesto Vásquez del Aguila has carefully detailed, "Peruvian racial and social class hierarchy shapes the perception of who is considered 'gay' and who is considered to be a 'maricón' [faggot]" (2012, 209). White and mestizo middle-class Peruvians, including Ronaldo, tend to be associated with gay identities, while those from lower classes and indigenous backgrounds are more commonly associated with *maricón* identities. In being more commonly identified as *maricón* rather than gay, less affluent men are more vulnerable to discrimination and violence than middle- and upper-class gay men whose class and racial position further protects them from some forms of discrimination relative to poorer gay men.

Safe Spaces without State Protection? Ordinances and Everyday Violence

In spite of ongoing efforts and accomplishments, unlike in some other metropolitan centers in Latin America, in Lima openness toward LGBTQ people should be understood in the context of the absence of national laws and indifference to existing antidiscrimination ordinances, as discussed in this section. In contrast to Rio de Janeiro and Buenos Aires, where "English-language campaigns emphasize the city's appealing gay friendly character" (Kanai 2014, 2), and Bogotá and Mexico City, where openly sexually diverse spaces are recognized (Russo Garrido 2009; Ramírez-Arcos 2013), Lima has no citywide ordinance prohibiting discrimination based on sexual identity. Instead, antidiscrimination ordinances are instituted in some districts while not in others, and the types of discrimination included in these ordinances vary.

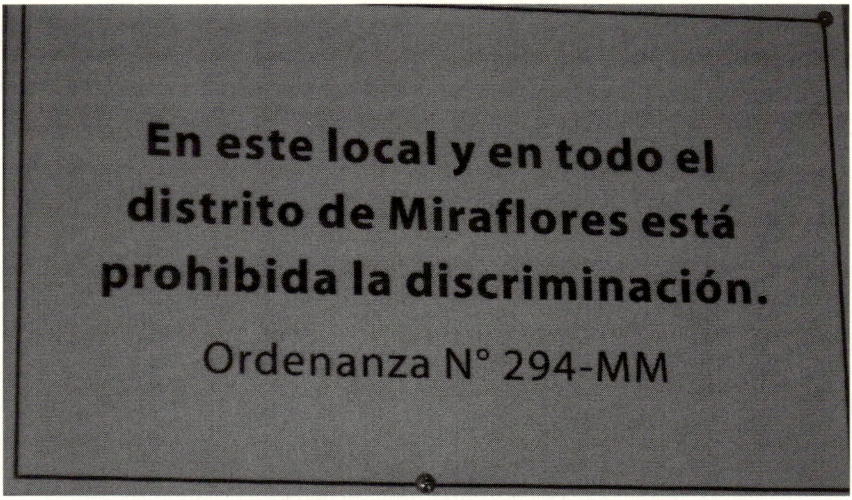

> En este local y en todo el distrito de Miraflores está prohibida la discriminación.
>
> Ordenanza N° 294-MM

Figure 4a: Antidiscrimination ordinance posted outside a supermarket in the Miraflores district.

As of October 2015, sixteen of metropolitan Lima's forty-three districts had passed districtwide ordinances prohibiting discrimination based on sexual identity (*El Comercio* 2015a). While there is little recourse in the majority of districts, where there are ordinances individuals can file formal complaints with municipal governments. Miraflores is one of the sixteen districts with an ordinance against discrimination, including based on sexual orientation.

Founded in 1993, the Park of Love attracts many visitors to Miraflores. The park has at its center *The Kiss*, a large sculpture by Peruvian artist Victor Delfín of a heterosexual couple embracing and kissing. It also has spaces to sit and relax, with many decorated tiles inscribed with poems and quotes about love all around the park. It is known as a popular romantic spot, with a steady stream of tourists and local residents, particularly in the afternoon, when visitors can watch the sun set over the Pacific Ocean from the park.

In November 2015 a *serenazgo* (municipal security officer) approached one couple embracing and kissing in the Park of Love and told the individuals, "Your hormones, control them."[7] There were several other couples similarly showing affection, but the other couples appeared to be, like the statue at the center of the Park of Love, heterosexual. The two men the *serenazgo* harassed used their phones to record the incident, which lasted about five minutes.[8] During that time, the municipal security officer is heard telling

Figure 4b: Park of Love: popular spot for couples above the Pacific Ocean.

them to leave, to control their hormones, and that they are disturbing the peace. In response, one of the men states that they are being discriminated against and harassed, asks if it is because they are a same-sex couple, and declares that they know that the district has an antidiscrimination ordinance and that they are within their rights to be there and express affection to each other. After the incident, the men filed a formal complaint with the municipal government.[9]

Antidiscrimination ordinances are an important tool for sanctioning discrimination, yet they do not guarantee preventative protection from discrimination. In some cases, they are primarily useful in challenging an act of discrimination as it is happening, as in the example of the same-sex couple in the Park of Love. They may also be useful in challenging discrimination after it has occurred, as in the following example. In 2015 a geological engineer went to the Clínica Anglo-Americana (Anglo-American Clinic) to donate blood. The clinic is in the same middle- and upper-class district as the Park of Love. At the clinic, a staff member stopped the woman from donating blood after noting that she had identified as lesbian on the required intake form. The clinic worker stated that she was not suitable to be a blood donor because she was lesbian and proceeded to ask her if her family knew about her homosexuality (*El Comercio* 2015b; *La República* 2015a).[10] The woman who wished to donate blood alerted the media to the treatment she had received.

What happened at the Clínica Anglo-Americana reflects a broader pattern of abuse against LGTBQ Peruvians in the public health sector, which is second only to the national police in terms of discrimination against

LGBTQ persons by a public institution (Jaime 2013, 12). In Lima, transwomen have reported being victims of physical and sexual abuse, arbitrary detention, and kidnapping by *serenazgo* and the national police (Hernández, Miller, and Schneeweis 2015). In the public health sector, discrimination is particularly strong against lesbians (Jaime 2013). More broadly, these forms of discrimination and harassment, including by representatives of municipal governments in districts with antidiscrimination ordinances and at health institutions, underscore the pervasive practice of discrimination against LGTBQ Peruvians.

The project NoTengoMiedo (IAmNotAfraid) draws on efforts to denounce these forms of discrimination and provides a platform for social justice struggles surrounding LGBTQ rights. Started in 2014 by a small collective in Lima, the project's mission is to "promote social justice, liberation and equal access to resources, from a transfeminist and intersectional approach, to the LGBTQI population."[11] One of its projects is "Tell Us Your Story," which invites Peruvians from Lima and other provinces to write a few lines and then send them with a photograph through the twitter hashtag #VisiblesSomosMásFuertes (#VisibleWeAreStronger). By December 2015, the project had collected hundreds of stories. The stories speak of everyday forms of violence and exclusion at the level of family, workplace, and institutions and underline an absence of state protection.

Without statewide protections and guarantees, districtwide ordinances, as well as individual and group activism, become more urgent in fighting against discrimination. Similar to the experience at the Park of Love, one 2015 NoTengoMiedo story by a woman in a same-sex relationship stated that a *serenazgo* harassed her and her partner in Surco, another district with an antidiscrimination ordinance. She writes, "[We were] holding hands, and the *serenazgo* approached us to ask us to leave because we were making the neighbors uncomfortable. I asked him to give me the number of the ordinance rule we were breaking and that if there was none for him to leave us in peace."[12] Similarly to the story in the Park of Love, in this case it is knowledge of existing ordinances that individuals draw on to demand respect and stop discrimination as they go about their daily life in the city.

Outside of the stories collected through the NoTengoMiedo project, there are many other stories of institutional, state, and family as spaces of exclusion for LGBTQ Peruvians. Beyond discrimination by those responsible for protecting citizens, discrimination and exclusion more broadly inform routine everyday behaviors. For Ronaldo, mentioned at the beginning of this chapter, the uneven existence and enforcement of antidiscrimination ordinances across Lima's districts and the pervasive forms of exclusion and discrimination against LGBTQ people in Lima make him feel that in public "to hug my partner, to kiss him, it's impossible to do that because people will stare at you and make fun of you." This is in addition to the vulnerability he feels at home, where his sexuality is the "tacit subject" (Decena 2011) that threatens to disrupt social relations if the agreed-upon silence is ever broken. The cases cited above suggest that being made fun of is only one of several forms of discrimination and exclusion a couple could face in private or public spaces. The stories that follow examine how heterosexism and homophobia shape experiences of migration, including decisions about if and when to return.

Amalia: Peruvian Communities Abroad and the Timing of Return

Some scholars have pointed to migration as a sort of emancipation for LGTBQ persons for whom the childhood home and nuclear family represent heterosexist and gender oppression (Arguelles and Rivero 1993; Fortier 2003; Vásquez del Aguila 2015), while others have also pointed to the ways in which homophobia among immigrant communities promotes marginalization (Decena 2011; Vásquez del Aguila 2015). Both migration as desired emancipation and immigrant communities as perpetuating homophobic practices are reflected in the experiences of Peruvians with whom I spoke. Additionally, in this chapter it is the simultaneous experiences of belonging to and exclusion from the family and larger society that mark narratives of return.

Winter in Toronto means double-digit subzero temperatures and ice and snowstorms that may last for several days. In Lima, invariably overcast winter skies never bring snow, and temperatures rarely fall below 50 degrees Fahrenheit. This contrast in temperatures was one of the main issues *limeños* I met with in Toronto brought up in discussing difficulties adapting to life in their new city. When I arrived in Toronto shortly after the official beginning of spring at the end of March, the remnants of the last snowstorm, which had delayed my flight the night before, were visible on almost every street corner. I walked briskly on recently cleaned sidewalks and around the snow piles, trying to keep warm on my way to meet Amalia at one of the many Tim Hortons restaurants in the area where she had suggested we meet.

Amalia walks in just as I am peeling off the last winter layer and sitting down. As she settles into her chair, she tells me what many other Peruvians repeat: that she enjoys the quality of life and the professional opportunities in Toronto but that this weather is really a problem. As she explains, "Here we have five months of winter, so it depends on your ability to adapt [to the cold]" how well you do in the city. She is soft-spoken, and as we speak and warm up, we move away from discussions about the weather and adapting to the cold and she shares more details of her life.

Amalia and her partner left Lima twenty years earlier largely because of the political violence and broader economic situation of the period. Her decision to leave Peru was also motivated by the homophobic environment in which their lives unfolded in Lima and in which she did not feel safe. She explained that "in Lima, I have felt discriminated against because of my sexual orientation." The more time goes by, the more she realizes that in Lima "your self-esteem is beaten down and you live with feelings of guilt, and that doesn't let you develop your full potential as a person," because "equality does not exist, so you are unprotected." Migration provided Amalia with the space and anonymity she desired to live more openly.

Amalia is quick to connect her own personal acceptance and development to her migratory trajectory: "When you change environment, that is, you move to another country, you don't have that pressure. After some time you begin to accept yourself, mostly when, if you don't have family [around you], you develop your environment, your friends" and can become more comfortable and feel more safe and secure as a lesbian Peruvian. In leaving Peru, she distanced herself from family and social surveillance.

Amalia explains that before moving to Toronto, she and her partner lived outside Peru for several years. Unhappy with both the social climate and professional opportunities in Peru and elsewhere, they moved to Toronto. Their decision to move was tied to their view of Canada as "a country that values diversity a lot, and it's a much freer society, more open [than Peru]." Living in "a country with a social conscience" means she and her partner "do not have the same limitations as same-sex partners in other countries," since in Canada they have "everything anyone could want, legally." In her current home, Amalia and her partner are recognized as having many of the same rights and protections as heterosexual couples.

As we finished our coffee, Amalia lamented that the homophobic sentiments she confronts in Lima during her annual visits are also present within the Peruvian community in Toronto, a city with official multicultural policies and that boasts residents from all over the world. Writing on the sexual imaginaries of Peruvians in New York and Peru, Vásquez del Aguila (2015) also refers to the pressure to conceal sexual identity when becoming actively involved with Peruvian immigrant communities among some Peruvians he interviewed. He examines the cases of men within these Peruvian expat communities who rely on their transnational lives to reinforce and perpetuate gendered expectations about masculine privileges across borders. In one case, one man he interviewed had a "decent" Peruvian wife in the United States and a *novia* (girlfriend) in Lima for short, temporary return trips to Peru. In these cases, the ability to cross borders is key to the reification of heteronormative gendered expectations.

Focusing on gay immigrant Dominican men also in the New York area, Carlos Ulises Decena introduces the concept of *desencuentros*, or "failed encounters," with *dominicanidad* to explain how "though a source of pride and comfort for some informants, expressions of *dominicanidad* were a source of ambivalence and rejection in others" (2011, 72). Amalia similarly negotiated the comforting aspects she associated with home and Peruvian communities with the aspects from which she wished to distance herself. For Amalia, Peruvian immigrant communities have primarily been sources of continued oppression. She explains that in Peru, she was commonly asked the same types of questions by people who barely knew her or who had not seen her in many years: "Whom did you marry? How many children do you have? And if you don't have children, they ask you, 'But why?' and consider it a misfortune." The traditional gender scripts explicitly called upon by these questions reinforce heteronormative, gendered spaces in which women's roles as wife and mother are naturalized and other identities are deemed impossible and even unnatural. In contrast, she explains, in Canada she is not asked these sorts of questions when she meets Canadians. The only time she is asked about these issues, she then adds, is "when you're with Latin Americans here, and they have not lived here long."

Later that same day, I met Davíd, a long-time resident of Toronto who returns to Peru regularly and had not yet decided whether or not he would return to Lima permanently. We spoke about many topics. In discussing his concerns about how things have changed since he arrived in Toronto from Lima over two decades earlier, Davíd brought up that it is proposals to legalize adoption by same-sex couples that concern him currently. He explained, "Homosexuals want us to accept their relationships, and now they want us to accept that they have children. And the government acquiesces, and I think it should be stronger. I left the chaos of [Lima], and if you don't maintain clear rules, the chaos I left behind will also come [here]." For Davíd, homophobia is not something he fears but something he practices. Living in a multicultural, global city provides many educational and economic opportunities for him as an educated, middle-class man and for his family, and he speaks of his appreciation of the openness he has witnessed among Canadians. His own openness is strategically limited to the economic opportunities of the neoliberal marketplace and excludes nonheterosexual identities.

Because of the questions and heteronormative expectations generally embraced by Peruvian communities she has met abroad, Amalia prefers to interact with Peruvian friends in smaller groups, and she avoids participating in larger Peruvian community events and discussions. She felt uncomfortable in these events because of the homophobic comments and questions she encountered: "The groups of Peruvians that there are, here in the communities, I personally do not participate. And I don't participate because I feel uncomfortable many times." In spite of her desire to spend time with other Peruvians, particularly during Peruvian holiday celebrations, the discriminatory and exclusionary attitudes within existing transnational Peruvian spaces make her participation anywhere from uncomfortable to downright painful.

In speaking of her plans for the future, Amalia tells me that her plan is to return to her other home, Lima, after she retires and to do so with her partner. However, she is reminded of the persistence of discrimination and homophobia each time she returns to visit family and sometimes wonders if a permanent return is truly viable. At close to sixty years old, however, she feels much more confident and prepared to return to Peru than she did earlier in her life. At this point, everyone in her family knows that her intimate partner is a woman, and she feels very welcomed: "I am no longer twenty years old. When I was younger the biggest pressure was from my parents, from my mother. My mother passed away, and she detested that about me. [She would ask,] 'Whom will you marry?' The type of questions that are always circulating. As time goes by, those questions pass, no one asks you anymore. . . . It's been many years. One evolves. Before I was really afraid. Now I am not." For Amalia, autonomy from her family and the years of experiences between when she left Peru and this point in her life have resulted in more confidence and knowledge about what she is comfortable experiencing and about her rights. In considering her return to Peru, family pressure to conform to heterosexual standards is no longer a major concern.

For Teresa, her time away from family and age similarly provided some protection from family pressure to conform to heterosexual standards upon her return. Now in her late forties, Teresa sees her time studying and working in France as a "breath of oxygen" that helped her to feel "empowered and stronger." When she and I met at her and her partner's apartment in Lima, she explained that after being away for several years, returning in her late thirties made her realize that "family domination could no longer capture me." Part of freeing herself from homophobic attitudes and family surveillance involved living independently upon her return. Yet even with what she considers to be some necessary distance from her family and a sense of empowerment since her return, she recognizes that her intimate life and sexual identity remain invisible to, or more likely rejected by, many relatives and family friends. For both Amalia and Teresa, planning to return or returning after several years away and at a more mature age provides them with necessary tools with which to protect themselves from the forms of family surveillance and questioning that are particularly oppressive for younger women, who are expected to get married and have children. The timing of return to avoid family surveillance allows for more individual freedom for women who are no longer expected to be concerned about marriage and children by their families in these two cases because of their ages, yet it does not change the overall environment of homophobia in a family or more broadly in the city, as the next section emphasizes.

Return and Homophobia in the Family

When Marina, in her midtwenties, and I met in the new, hip café run by expats she had recommended in Miraflores not far from the Parque Kennedy, it had been a year since her return. After Marina spent four years in the United States studying for her undergraduate degree, her work in Lima now focuses on the social and environmental impact of mining projects. She had originally planned to continue on to graduate school after finishing her undergraduate studies, but as time went by she realized that what she had studied was particularly relevant to Peru. She decided that returning to Peru would be the best way to contribute to a place to which "I owe so much of who I am." Her return was informed by two main factors: her social justice commitment to social change in Peru and her partner. Having maintained a long-distance relationship with her partner for part of the time she was abroad, she welcomed returning as a positive step in their relationship. After a year in Lima she had not yet decided if hers was a temporary or permanent return.

Marina identifies as bisexual, and the homophobia of earlier generations and within her own family is something she refers to as deeply informing her experience of return. Like Ronaldo, Amalia, and Teresa, Marina missed her family profoundly when she was away, yet regular interactions with her extended family now that she has returned remind her of the homophobia that is central to the types of intolerance and discrimination she hopes to challenge: "I've experienced moments during which I love being with my family, and there are moments in which I detest my family. Also because even though my family is super liberal (I believe in a lot of what I believe in because of them), they also have a lot of conservative views, especially about gender, homophobia, that type of thing, and it's been one of the hardest things about returning." Marina is a young woman, and the comfort she had longed for is challenged by the homophobia that is at the center of her family and that more broadly marginalizes her as bisexual in society.

Among return migrants the violence and toxicity of homophobia may be particularly vivid in cases in which the person returns to the family home, as in the earlier case of Ronaldo. For Olivia, who had recently returned to live in Peru after studying in Germany, even before she returned to Lima a primary concern was that "I would return and feel I could not live alone, that I had to live with my parents." Although she initially lived with her parents, she moved into her own apartment within the first few months of returning to Lima after finding a stable, well-paying job. In his research on Latino and Filipino gay men in the United States, Anthony Ocampo (2014, 156) similarly found that within the family, sexual identity "drove a wedge" between the gay (adult) child and his parents, viewed as incongruent to family values, despite the family's appreciation and celebration of multiple other dimensions of their child's life. Living apart from family helped alleviate the effects of these differences in worldviews and lives.

The internalized homophobia within families can reach such levels and intensity that families may take extreme measures to attempt to "cure" gay children. In New Jersey, one Peruvian family pressured their thirty-something son to go to Peru to find a Peruvian wife who would "cure" him of his homosexuality (Vásquez del Aguila 2015). Relying on their social and racial capital, they hoped a poorer, darker, less educated Peruvian woman with less cultural capital would agree to ignore their son's sexual orientation and marry into their family as a form of upward social mobility for her (Vásquez del Aguila 2015). She would gain social capital, and he would demonstrate adherence to the normative, heterosexual imaginary the family desired for him.

Eduarda similarly brought up the persistence of homophobia in the realm of family life. She returned to Peru after studying in the United States. After she earned her doctorate and worked in the United States for close to a decade, the expiration of her visa required her to leave the United States. For her, Lima represented a space in which she had previously felt invisible and "had no rights." After participating in a *plantón* (protest), for LGBTQ rights downtown, she stopped by the place I was staying at for an interview. As we drank coffee in a small room in the house, she discussed how she believed that the LGBTQ population was gaining visibility in Lima and Peru more broadly but that there was still a long, long way to go to gain basic rights. She doubted anything would substantially change for another ten to fifteen years. In spite of her commitment to participate in street protests, within her family she was never asked about her sexual identity. Her siblings had never asked her about her intimate life and whether or not she was dating someone. In contrast, her nieces are more open, and she and they discuss her identity as a lesbian and her dating experiences. The intergenerational changes Eduarda refers to are also present in other narratives.

Soon after I interviewed Marina, I met and interviewed one of her friends. Like Marina, Bárbara had recently returned to Lima. As a bisexual woman in her twenties, she faced similar issues to the ones Marina had spoken about with me.[13] She had become involved with MHOL after returning and believed the movement for LGBTQ rights was "quite strong and has a lot of strong and brave women." In the year since her return, she had experienced several forms of homophobia and felt unsure about whether or not she would stay in Lima permanently. On the streets, she had recently witnessed how when two of her friends kissed and held hands, as many couples do, "a group of men walked by and hit them." To Bárbara, it was clear that the women had been targeted by the men because they were lesbian. Another time, to go home from an LGBTQ protest, Bárbara and some friends took a taxi. When a woman in the back of the taxi kissed her girlfriend, the taxi driver abruptly stopped the car. He demanded that the group pay him and get out of the car. Again, homophobia interrupted and potentially endangered everyday life. She tells me that she knows that there are many brave women who continue to hold hands and kiss in public, yet for her, even walking into the building where MHOL is housed makes her feel fearful about who could be watching her go in and what that person might do to her because of her sexual identity.

Bárbara's feelings of fear, surveillance, and insecurity are also shaped by her interactions with her family. As in the case of other migrants, her family constituted one of the primary reasons for returning to Lima. And as in the case of other LGB migrants with whom I spoke, her family was a significant source of homophobia. When I asked her what she viewed as the biggest challenges of her return, she replied, "In fact, my family and my brother and my aunts know it, but they are silent about it. My father and mother don't accept it, they don't agree with it. My cousins and my friends know about it, but they don't see it as a reality. They see it as something funny, they don't take it seriously, that two women could be together. And I don't talk about it openly, because there is no social acceptance. And in terms of laws, no." The absence of social acceptance, legal protection, and family support made Bárbara's return particularly challenging. Without state acknowledgment of her rights as a bisexual woman, her family's dismissal of her sexual identity as something amusing accentuated the exclusion and marginalization she and others who identify as LGB experience daily.

Like Bárbara and Marina, Lucy is also in her midtwenties and identifies as bisexual. She had returned to Peru approximately two years earlier after years of studying abroad. Lucy had not directly been the target of discrimination, yet she too experienced fear from surveillance and homophobia within her family and in public spaces. On Facebook she is careful to block her relatives from seeing posts related to LGBTQ issues. She is not dating anyone and passes as heterosexual, explaining that "when people meet me everyone thinks I'm hetero. I've met people and they say homophobic things to me. If they only knew." In one case, she spoke with evangelical Christians counterprotesting LGBTQ activists' protest for rights. As they had on other occasions, the people she introduced herself to assumed she was heterosexual and proceeded to make homophobic comments about LGBTQ protesters, unaware that she was one of "them." On the one hand, because Lucy could "pass" as heterosexual, her assumed normative identity protected her from social stigma and the potential dangers associated with being identified as nonheterosexual (Pfeffer 2014). On the other hand, Lucy understood that these privileges and sense of security could be quickly and instantly revoked if the people she was speaking with identified her as bisexual and therefore as outside their realm of acceptance.

Ronaldo's experiences echo and underscore these configurations of family, surveillance, and homophobia. Returning to Lima after several years abroad, he lives with his family and has a boyfriend, but his family refuses to recognize their relationship. He explains that he has to refer to him as "my friend," since to refer to him as "my partner" would be scandalous for his family. He is unable to show affection to his partner for fear of being beaten up or thrown out of the family home. Outside of the home, he is similarly fearful that showing affection could result in insults or worse. Widespread homophobic practices also permeate his professional life. He described how a few years earlier, he had been fired "because a relative told my boss that I was gay, and it was a new job. They called me and told me that they had just called my contacts and that they said I was gay." He added, "The laws here are not clear, they are definitely lacking on the part of the state. We don't have laws that protect us."

In Ronaldo's case, homophobia is not something he can choose to be indifferent to, as many Peruvians in the online survey I referred to earlier did. His family life, his intimate life, his professional success, and his everyday movements in the city are all impacted by the homophobic attitudes and practices of those around him. Ignoring these attitudes and practices has never been a possibility. Ronaldo's sexual identity is the target of his family's strong disapproval and is used against him in other areas of his life. He feels close to his family, yet it is clear to him that "every time there's a problem, they tell me it's because I'm homosexual." In his case, as in other cases, the fluidity of homophobia between private and public realms creates a generalized environment of insecurity and exclusionary incorporation. He feels he belongs, but he is not able to exercise the citizenship rights—including to safety and to protection from discrimination—many middle- and upper-class heterosexual Peruvians can take for granted. He belongs, but safety from discrimination and violence is not part of his sense of belonging.

Rodrigo: Supportive Family and Distancing from LGBTQ Groups and Protests

Unlike other return migrants I spoke with, Rodrigo told me that he had never felt pressured to keep his sexual orientation a secret and that he felt fully supported by his family. Rodrigo is from an upper-middle-class family, had recently returned after several years studying and working abroad, and was in his late twenties at the time of the interview. He emphasized that he understood that there is widespread discrimination against gay and lesbian Peruvians in Lima but that he had never personally experienced that sort of discrimination. As we spoke, the ways in which his upper-middle-class status privilege shielded him from different forms of discrimination and violence through access to and control over safe spaces in Lima in his youth and to travel and migration later in his life became more evident.

Rodrigo does not discuss or make references to his sexual orientation publicly, and the right to marry among those who are the same sex "does not interest me." He avoids involvement in social activism for LGBTQ rights. During the interview he repeatedly expressed disapproval of the public protests in which some who identify as LGBTQ participate. Given his strong feelings on the subject, he explained that he "would never go to one of those marches for gay marriage." When I asked if he felt he could count on the same rights as other Peruvians, he stated that he thinks it is important to be able to inherit "if you've been with someone for forty years" and to adopt children but that people's reactions to LGBTQ people depend on "how you live your life." In response to my confused facial expression, he offered the following response: "There are scandalous people, there are people who are not scandalous, both heterosexual and homosexual. I will feel the same rejection toward a homosexual or heterosexual man who yells and is scandalous." Rodrigo identified the yelling that sometimes accompanied protests as particularly scandalous. He insisted that laws and attitudes toward LGBTQ people would "change little by little" and that this sort of change should not be forced through protests.

It is impossible for me to pinpoint the precise reasons for Rodrigo's beliefs. In interpreting his position, however, I find at least three factors worth considering because they help us see the broader picture not only for

Rodrigo's comments but also for the experiences of other return migrants. First, widespread homonegativity is a part of Catholicism, which is the dominant belief system in Peru.[14] In discussing his disagreement with bringing public attention to LGBTQ rights and demands for marriage, Rodrigo brought up that "you are not going to be able to force religion to marry you." In particular, his comment refers to Catholicism. The archbishop of Lima, Juan Luis Cipriani, described the recent U.S. Supreme Court decision to legalize same-sex marriage as a "tragic decision" and continues to be vocal in his condemnation of homosexuality (*La República* 2015c).

Similarly to other forms of Christianity, Catholicism tends to view sexuality in binary terms of procreation and celibacy. It promotes heterosexual marriage and condemns same-sex identities and behaviors as immoral (Severson, Muñoz-Laboy, and Kaufman 2014). In their study among behaviorally bisexual Catholic Latino men in the United States, Nicolette Severson, Miguel Muñoz-Laboy, and Rebecca Kaufman found that homonegativity was positively correlated with religiosity. Those with high levels of religiosity were more likely to agree with the statement that "it is gay people's fault that they are rejected by society" (2014, 142). Internalized homonegativity, rather than resulting from personal fears, can be shaped by broader societal factors (Berg, Munthe-Kaas, and Ross 2016). Rodrigo did not identify as a religious person, yet his everyday life was saturated with Catholic cultural messages about the unacceptability of homosexuality. He emphasized his family's acceptance of him as a gay man even as he simultaneously excluded from broader social acceptance other gay men whom he viewed as making the individual choice to be scandalous.

A second issue is family support and protection from discrimination and marginalization within the context of a privileged upbringing in an upper-middle-class *familia decente*. Although Rodrigo was in the same age group and shared a middle-class background with Ronaldo, Bárbara, Lucy, and Marina, his perception and experience of familial support were significantly different. Key to Rodrigo's story is that he felt he had been protected from the discrimination others faced through the early and ongoing support and protection of his family. Without feeling the sort of marginalization others referred to in discussing their experiences as LGB Peruvians, he may have found it more difficult to empathize with those who do not have the same levels of support and protection. Third, his responses underline a belief in individual agency over structures and systems of oppression. He believed it was up to individuals to be or not be scandalous—for example, by deciding whether or not to participate in public protests and to yell in public to make demands. He had also recently started his own business and strongly believed it would succeed if he continued to work hard, because of his individual effort. Rodrigo's position vis-à-vis LGBTQ protests relied on his individual experiences rather than the experiences of LGBTQ people as a group and the power of societal structures and institutions of discrimination others had confronted. He was unusual in his condemnation of LGBTQ protests and demands among gay, lesbian, and bisexual Peruvians with whom I spoke but not among Peruvians as a larger population. His emphasis on individualism, hard work, and merit as a way to succeed and to justify his privilege is similarly not unusual among more affluent groups in Peru and the global elite. For example, Shamus Rahman Khan (2011) found that elite students in a U.S. boarding school emphasized merit and hard work in discussing their success. Significantly, he also found that in practice the students' privileged positions were rarely the direct result of individual effort and hard work.

Intersecting Identities, Belonging, Exclusion

Some of the cases in this chapter point to double marginalization—in the family home and city before migration and within immigrant communities abroad, as in Amalia's case in Toronto. All underscore the return context as one in which homophobia permeates everyday life in public settings and often in intimate family ones. For Amalia, the effects of homophobia in her family could be overcome in part through age, by planning to return after retirement, when her social status was higher and she was no longer routinely questioned about plans to marry and have children. Return migrants in their twenties, however, more acutely felt discrimination on the street and pressure to conform to heteronormative standards within their families.

Transnational Peruvians both experienced and contributed to perpetuating exclusionary views regarding LGBTQ Peruvians. In Toronto, Davíd, whose travel and openness to other forms of difference positioned him as cosmopolitan, placed nonheterosexual sexualities outside the realm of tolerance. In Lima, Rodrigo both identified as gay and condemned LGBTQ Peruvians who publicly demanded rights, including the right to marry, thereby also reinforcing existing heteronormative structures that exclude some Peruvians from protection from discrimination. At the iconic Park of Love in Miraflores, two men were harassed by an officer responsible for protecting all citizens in a district with an ordinance that protects residents from homophobic discrimination. In these scenarios, homophobia should not be primarily understood as reflecting interpersonal feelings and individual biases but as being intricately connected to intersecting local and global processes and private and public realms (Murray 2009). Rather than creating cosmopolitan spaces of tolerance, these attitudes reinforce spaces of liminality and rightlessness across borders that challenge inclusive forms of citizenship.

Experiences of homophobia elucidate the role of home in transnational lives as not only a source of safety or fear but also, most significantly, a site of simultaneous safety and fear (Brah 1996) that defines exclusionary incorporation in the Peruvian context. Studies of coming out have mostly focused on white men in the United States and Europe (Seidman 2009, but see Decena 2011 and Vásquez del Aguila 2015 for important exceptions), yet it is also valuable to consider how nonheteronormative identities are negotiated in the context of migration and return migration among populations in other parts of the world. The experiences of migrants who identify as LGB may vary significantly from nonmigrant white LGB US and European experiences due to ties to racial and cultural communities with distinct and varying attitudes toward sexuality (Cantú, Naples, and Vidal-Ortiz 2009; Manalansan 2003; Ocampo 2014; Vásquez del Aguila 2015). Middle- and upper-class status, whiteness, economic resources, and cultural capital facilitate out-migration and return migration and protect individuals from some forms of discrimination. Even in terms of nonheteronormative identities, class and racial privilege allow some men to be identified as gay, while others are given the more negative *maricón* label. These identity categories correspond to different forms and even levels of vulnerability to discrimination and violence in everyday life. Yet, in a broader sense, sexual identity stands out because it is employed societally to render some migrants particularly vulnerable to exclusion and violence both abroad and when they return.

Unlike heterosexual Peruvians who return to Lima, Ronaldo, Marina, Lucy, Bárbara, Teresa, Eduarda, and other LGB individuals must constantly negotiate at least one central aspect of their lives—their sexual orientation—to "belong" in Lima and in their families even as their class and racial privilege protect them from other forms of discrimination. More than other migration narratives, the experiences of LGB individuals challenge simplistic coming-home narratives popularly associated with return migration. Belonging is not a given in returning to Lima, and the negotiation of sexual identity within families, in the workplace, and on the streets underscores fear, violence, and marginalization as everyday technologies of exclusion at the center of homophobic discrimination.

Heteronormativity facilitates exclusion and discrimination against LGBTQ Peruvians and prevents them from feeling safe and secure at home. In the absence of nationwide legislation to guarantee LGBTQ Peruvians the same rights heterosexual citizens enjoy, potential protection from discrimination in Lima comes at the municipal district level. As the experiences examined in this chapter illustrate, these forms of district-level protection are uneven and insufficient. Writing about the position of undocumented Latino immigrants in the popular imagination in the United States, Lisa Marie Cacho (2012) proposes that undocumented Latinos and other minorities are commonly racialized and criminalized and thus relegated to a liminal state of social death in which they have no rights. These liminal spaces of social death, through which some are denied the basic rights attached to personhood, are also reflected in the return migration experiences of Ronaldo, Marina, Eduarda, Teresa, Lucy, and Bárbara. Homophobia, coupled with the absence of nationwide legislation, reinforces spaces of exclusion within families, as well as more broadly within larger spaces, in a society that allows for social death as a characteristic of exclusionary incorporation in the Peruvian context.

Ronaldo's experiences, and those of Amalia, Marina, Lucy, Bárbara, Eduarda, Rodrigo, and other Peruvians I spoke with, underscore the ways in which multiple identities and roles inform return experiences. Writing on personhood and subjectivity, Henrietta Moore reminds us that "individuals are multiply constituted subjects, and they take up multiple subject positions within a range of discourses and social practices. Some of these subject positions will be contradictory and conflicting" (2007, 41). Sexual identity informs Peruvian return migrants' subject positions in significant ways. Without understanding how sexual identity intersects with other identities and practices informed by age, religion, family role, work, and class background, however, we cannot appreciate the complicated on-the-ground experiences of Peruvians on their way to, in, and away from home. Migration and return migration, approached through this intersectional lens, point to a broader, more complicated sense of belonging that includes both security and exclusion, fear and comfort. The conclusion of my meeting with Ronaldo, which opened this chapter, provides a fitting close to this chapter: it further underscores the centrality of interlocking identities in migration trajectories. When I asked him if he planned to leave Peru again, since he now has dual citizenship and the financial means to leave, he replied emphatically, "No. I plan to stay here, because this is my Peru, the food that I love, my friends, and the people, the culture, what I like." His identity and sense of belonging as a gay man are routinely denied and attacked in Lima, yet he feels his other roles as a son, brother, and friend flourish in Lima more so than elsewhere.

CHAPTER 5

THE TASTE OF HOME
Nostalgia, Pride, and the Limits of Inclusion

When I asked Peruvians living outside Peru what they missed most about Peru, the two things they consistently mentioned were their *añoranza*, or "longing," for family and their *añoranza* for Peruvian food. Over and over again, Peruvians who returned to Peru and those living abroad referred to Peruvian dishes as a source of pride and to their consumption as a way to feel and taste home. Ceviche, *lomo saltado*, *ají de gallina*, *causa*, and *papas a la huancaína* were all mentioned as much for how they tasted like home as for how well they represented Peru to the world.[1] In bringing up food, it soon became clear that transnational Peruvians were referring not only to tastes of home but also to particular ways of representing Peru and their place in it to the world.

This chapter looks at the culinary realm as a space through which to also examine the class, racial, and gender hierarchies central to transnational Peruvian lives. On the one hand, the Peruvian gastronomic boom has largely benefited from claims of openness, inclusiveness, and pride in all things Peruvian. On the other hand, the foods and individuals that represent Peru in and that benefit from the gastronomic boom are not typically inclusive. In practice, those included bolster the status of particular groups of Peruvians, including transnational middle- and upper-class Peruvians, while excluding less affluent, rural, and Amazonian indigenous identities. I draw on an online survey, interviews, blogs, restaurant menus, a documentary, scholarship on food and national identity, and field notes from visits to Peruvian restaurants to examine how the gastronomic boom reinforces the privilege that transnational middle- and upper-class Peruvians already experience. In particular, after discussing the role of food as a source of comfort and nostalgia for home for transnational Peruvians, I discuss how the cosmopolitan image of Peruvians coming out of recent nation-branding projects and culinary representations of Peru legitimizes the privileges and high social status middle- and upper-class transnational Peruvians seek to maintain abroad. Rather than unite Peruvians everywhere, even across class differences, as it purports to do, then, the gastronomic boom in practice reinforces social hierarchies in which middle- and upper-class transnational Peruvians are on top—therefore also reflecting the sort of exclusionary cosmopolitanism I argue is central to middle- and upper-class Peruvian transnational lives. In this sense, food becomes a powerful site for the construction of particular brands of Peruvianness in Peru and abroad.

Food as Comfort

Food habits are a significant and long-lasting sensorial practice that help migrants maintain a sense of home and stability in the context of dislocation (Calvo 1982; Mata Codesal 2010; Williams-Forson 2014). Eating habits and preferences from the home country may persist even after the native language is no longer spoken (Valentine 1999). Home-cooked meals with Ghanaian ingredients help Ghanaians in Maryland relieve feelings of nostalgia and taste home (Williams-Forson 2014). In Norway, Filipino women au pairs felt excluded from families for whom they worked and unable to assert their cultural identities precisely because employers denied them the possibility of cooking Filipino food in their homes and demanded that they regularly cook Norwegian food for the family and children (Sollund 2012). For Filipino women working in Hong Kong, Sunday gatherings featuring Filipino dishes allowed women to maintain connections to each other and home and provided the space for more specific comforting practices that included eating with their hands, a practice "less about a refusal to use chopsticks than about enhancing flavour—a practice well known at home" (Law 2001, 276). Among Latinos in the United States, practices surrounding food are an important way of enacting cultural identity and maintaining connections with communities in countries of origin (Mares 2012).

For Marisela, who has lived in a midsize town in the U.S. South for the last twenty years, being away from Peru became easier with time as she created her own family in her new setting and settled on ways to re-create her favorite dishes. Initially, what she missed the most were the familiar tastes of Peruvian food—something her new setting could not provide. Today, her group of friends includes someone who grows and sells *ají amarillo* plants, a key ingredient for many Peruvian dishes. Each summer, she makes sure she purchases a new *plantita* (small plant) to grow, and "that is enough, because with it you can prepare typical foods at home, so I no longer feel that great need as I did before, because it has been less and less little by little." The freshness of this source of *ají amarillo* is preferred over the frozen Goya brand ones available at local markets that cater to Latin American populations—and where local residents can find Inca Kola and other Peruvian food items to include in or accompany homemade Peruvian dishes. She then adds that the food she makes will never be the same as if she were eating it in Lima, her hometown, yet she feels comfortable with that because of the family, professional, and cultural opportunities she enjoys where she currently lives.

The sorts of Peruvian foods Marisela and other migrants have access to in their new homes are key to satisfying not only physical hunger but also a deeper affective longing for home and the soothing of disjunctures between past and present. In the Mexican market in the shopping center just a few blocks away from my house in Lexington, Kentucky, I can buy two-liter bottles of Inca Kola, limes just the size and with just the right flavor for making *limonada*, and the only avocados that come close to the smooth, luscious *paltas* I eat each time I am in Lima. My teenage son, who has spent most of his life in the United States but who was born in Lima, insists we buy an Inca Kola each time we go to the market and has, through our home cooking in Kentucky and our visits to Lima, also developed an affective connection to the foods and tastes from my, and now his, childhood. I can buy limes and avocados at the Trader Joe's even closer to our house, but these do not evoke the same affective and psychological satisfaction as the ones I associate with tastes and smells from my childhood.[2] Like Marisela and many other migrants, for me Peruvian food has been one pathway to comfort and home. It is also intimately tied to family, as it is for many other Peruvians I met and as I discuss in the next section. When I discovered a new Peruvian restaurant, I often included my family in the hopes of sharing with them bits of home, and these shared meals appear throughout the chapter.

Food as Home

Sitting at a Starbucks on a busy street in windy, below-freezing Toronto, I meet Alicia after her workday. While we warm ourselves up by sipping hot tea, she tells me that she has no plans to return to Peru and that she enjoys eating Peruvian food in restaurants because of the "feeling of family, affection" she associates with the food. Kelsey Brain (2014) similarly found that Peruvians in San Francisco prepared and consumed Peruvian food because of childhood memories and nostalgia, because of the food's taste, as a way to foster community building among Peruvians, and to transmit their tastes and cultural identification to their children.

In the online survey I conducted, the two most common items added to the phrase "What I miss most about Peru is _____" were family (mentioned sixty-seven times) and food (mentioned forty-eight times).³ Most commonly, family and food were mentioned in the same answer.⁴ Reflective of the common pattern of mentioning family and food together as what is most missed, one person who wrote "[Peruvian] food" as his answer also wrote in, as if to explain, "My family is already here with me." Another person who only listed "family" as what she missed the most added, "We prepare [Peruvian] food here in our family." The online survey also included a question about what the respondent does to feel connected to Peru while living abroad. In the responses, food appeared among the three most common items: thirty-four people mentioned getting together or communicating with Peruvian friends, twenty-eight mentioned reading *El Comercio* or another Peruvian newspaper, and twenty-two people mentioned eating Peruvian food either at a restaurant or at home as a way to feel connected to Peru.

In the three years since Chabela and her family moved back to Lima, she has faced difficulties in finding a job and a place to live and adapting to everyday life in Lima. Yet, sitting comfortably in her small, sunny living room in her apartment overlooking a park in Surco, a middle-class neighborhood, and getting ready to leave for work, she insists that after living in the United States for almost two decades she relishes every day of being back in Lima. For her, part of the pleasure of returning home is sensory: she particularly enjoys regularly going "to the market or to eat braised and fried pork." Chabela smiles, telling me that "gastronomy is the best of Peru." Chabela's feelings toward food associated with Peru are echoed by Peruvians who plan to return to live in Peru and by those for whom returning is out of the question, as well as by Peruvians with both positive and negative experiences in Peru.

Branding Peruvianness

Feeling connected to Peru might mean reading Peruvian newspapers or being with Peruvian friends or family. According to the nation-branding campaign Marca Perú, being a cultural ambassador is also a good way to stay connected to Peru while teaching others about the country. In the Marca Perú fifteen-minute spot *Peru, Nebraska*, which quickly went viral in 2011, a group of Peruvian celebrities (chefs, singers, musicians, surfers, actors) led by chefs Gastón Acurio and Christian Bravo announce to the small (population: 569) town of Peru in the state of Nebraska that they are there as ambassadors for Peru the country. The first thing a chef is heard telling the town through a megaphone is "You are from Peru! You have the right to eat delicious food!" as we see Peruvian ambassadors entice the town's residents to taste ceviche, *papas a la huancaína, ocopa, anticuchos,* and *picarones* and to combine these with typical drinks such as *chicha morada*, Inca Kola, and *pisco* sours for the adults. That food is the first symbol of Peruvianness announced in this nation-branding campaign is no coincidence.

Peruvian gastronomy had been receiving significant attention as a source of pride—and marketing—for Peru well before Marca Perú's spot. In the 2009 documentary *De ollas y sueños* (also released with the title *Cooking Up Dreams*), featuring famous Peruvian chefs Gastón Acurio and Pedro Miguel Schiaffino, among others, a male voice-over announces that "in the midst of so many differences that you can find in a country, there is a fortunate, unique space where the entire nation feels harmoniously integrated." Peruvian gastronomy continues to be celebrated as this "unique space" of integration and as the space through which to represent *all* of Peru. In reality, Peruvian gastronomy rarely represents all regions and peoples equally and in practice tends to reinforce existing social hierarchies. Peruvian chefs produce dishes embedded in preexisting hierarchies of race, gender, region, and taste for a world that values some differences, presenting them within limits of the safely exotic (and formerly undervalued). As Maria Elena Garcia has aptly observed, the fusion cuisine at the center of the Peruvian gastronomic boom "is an exportable and sophisticated version of what was previously regarded as local and backward" (2013, 511). While Peru is no longer a colony, its internal hierarchies continue to position some groups of people and "their" foods above other people and "their" foods. Once appropriated and transformed by white-mestizo chefs, indigenous foods acquire a higher value while retaining their exotic appeal for a global market.[5]

It is therefore worth noting that the chefs who take on the role of leaders-ambassadors in the Marca Perú spot are men, as this is representative of a broader trend of privileging masculinities in the world of Peruvian gastronomy. While women are also recognized within the culinary world of Peru, it is predominantly well-traveled, middle- and upper-class men who are widely recognized. In this way, gendered hierarchies permeate the Peruvian culinary world just as they permeate other aspects of Peruvian lives. Among the chefs whom Peruvians I spoke with referred to with pride, all were men.[6]

There is little doubt that today many Peruvians see the country as a gastronomic destination and success. According to the World's 50 Best Restaurants 2015 ranking, Peru is home to three of the world's top fifty restaurants, including the top restaurant in Latin America. These three restaurants are in the capital, Lima, which is also home to most of the country's more than fifty culinary schools. The Peruvian Gastronomy Society (Apega) has set as one of its goals to become the world's leading culinary destination by 2021. In October 2015 it came a little closer to this goal: World Travel Awards named Peru as the top culinary destination in South America. Peruvians I met abroad were quick to point to some of these accomplishments.

Marca Perú's *Peru, Nebraska*, video draws on and reinforces the success of the gastronomic boom as it privileges particular forms of being Peruvian. In her critical analysis of the spot, Gisela Canépa (2013) approaches nation branding as a technology of power that legitimizes specific forms of Peruvianness and citizenship. In particular, she suggests that the spot is not about achieving a true representation of Peru; instead, the spot is performatively "designed as a foundational event that gives birth to a new social contract and a new community of Peruvians" (12). These new Peruvians are entrepreneurs for whom consumption of particular cultural repertoires is central. Significantly, they have the economic resources to consume ceviche, *papas a la huancaína*, and other Peruvian symbols regularly and likely at globally recognized establishments—including, for example, at the most exclusive restaurants in Lima.

Elder Cuevas (2016) similarly argues that Marca Perú caters to and legitimizes particular forms of Peruvianness based on economic resources, cultural capital, and consumption of Marca Perú merchandise. Cuevas goes further, arguing that Marca Perú legitimizes colonialist associations between whiteness, happiness, and success and that it is through a focus on whiteness that Marca Perú spots present the fantasy of a homogeneous, united nation. While not all "Peruvian ambassadors" in the *Peru, Nebraska*, spot are white, Cuevas's point of homogenization through whiteness is worth considering. If money whitens, as Cuevas proposes, then the fact that the Peruvian ambassadors are all affluent celebrities certainly reinforces the image of the happy, white, successful Peruvian as representative of all good things Peruvian. It is similarly significant that the Nebraska Peruvians in the spot are largely white. It is also worth noting, as I do shortly in more detail, that the Peruvian chefs in the spot have led largely transnational lives and that several of the other celebrities have also lived outside Peru and have the resources to travel internationally regularly.

The critical characteristics Marca Perú spots promote—entrepreneurship, consumerism, economic resources, whiteness, and comfort with global markets—are well represented among the transnational middle- and upper-class Peruvians I met. Canépa's important point that this new Peruvian is a global citizen who "not necessarily finds himself ascribed to territorial boundaries or to a common historical origin" (2013, 13) is key here. Throughout their migration trajectories, transnational middle- and upper-class Peruvians move from one space to another, potentially creating new homes yet maintaining strong attachments to Peru. These attachments are not necessarily due to a common historical origin. Indeed, among the traditionally more affluent classes in Peru it is common to claim white European ancestry and reject indigenous Peruvian roots. In this sense, we see that it is the specific identities traditionally associated with white, affluent, transnational Peruvians that are reinforced in nation-branding campaigns.

The approach to Peruvian ambassadors as ideally white, successful, and global citizens not necessarily sharing a common historical origin is in line with how, for example, Aldo sees himself. I met Aldo in Toronto. He is tall, white, and slender. He has a successful career and travels to Peru and Europe regularly. And he describes himself as a proud Peruvian. His parents are European and arrived in Peru as migrants in the mid-twentieth century, and they had and raised him and his siblings in Lima. After finishing high school and some university in Peru, Aldo immigrated to Europe to travel and then study. While in Europe studying, he met his Peruvian wife. The couple returned to Peru for a few years and later decided to settle in Toronto and raise their children there. As we spoke of his life in Toronto and regular trips to Peru, he told me that although people who first meet him routinely comment that he looks more German than Peruvian, he feels that he is "as Peruvian as Peru!" Speaking of how he and his wife had encouraged their children's sense of connection to Peru, he explained that all three of his children speak Spanish and that his wife regularly cooked Peruvian food at home when their kids were younger. As they have in other cases in this book, food and language become central markers of Peruvianness among transnational Peruvians.

Aldo and other middle- and upper-class Peruvians easily embody the sort of ambassador Marca Perú and other nation-branding projects promote, and this helps consolidate and legitimize some Peruvians' ties to Peru. Marca Perú's campaign, however, has not been the only campaign to appeal to middle- and upper-class Peruvians' cultural repertoires and self-identification to promote Peruvianness as a brand. Inca Kola, Peru's golden yellow carbonated soft drink, has succeeded as the leading national soft drink—beating out Coca-Cola—in part because it homogenizes local identities by whitening and urbanizing them even as it seeks to represent difference in the global arena through its particular construction of Peruvianness. Its marketing transmits the message that it is possible to be modern, urban, and consumerist and have a unique national identity. The image attached to this modern Peruvian identity, however, largely excludes Peruvians in much of the country (Alcalde 2009).[7]

In Peru, Inca Kola outsold Coca-Cola through marketing that emphasized national identity and its connections to pride in the Inca past, packaged in ways that also spoke to desired modern, urban, consumerist lifestyles (Alcalde 2009).[8] In Inca Kola commercials, urban white-mestizo Peruvians consume traditional Peruvian dishes and affirm Inca Kola's authenticity as

Peruvian and modern.⁹ A subtext of these messages is the definition and presentation of Peruvian as modern through the emphasis on urban settings and whiteness. One commercial in particular has made this emphasis clear. The commercial advertisement *Chullo* (a hand-knit wool or alpaca Andean hat) begins with images of an indigenous rural family in the highlands wearing chullos. The male voice-over explains that although chullos were originally made by Peruvians to protect them from the cold, today "I [the chullo] conquer the world!" The chullo, personified by the male voice-over, announces that after leaving the highlands it went to the coast (i.e., Lima) as images of young white-mestizos playing on a beach appear on the screen. From there the chullo began to travel the world, we are told, as urban settings in Italy, Japan, and France appear, so that ultimately the once indigenous chullo declares, "Today my success is so great that I appear in the most important runways [in Europe]" as we are presented with images of white European models wearing chullos on the front covers of magazines. Whereas in the beginning we see indigenous Peruvians wearing chullos, by the end the chullo is on the head of a young white-mestizo Peruvian and has thus entered the modern world through migration, ready to cross borders and represent a particular brand of Peruvianness (Alcalde 2009), and return victorious.

The gastronomic boom packages and benefits from similar constructions of Peruvianness and mobility. Peruvian ingredients and dishes from the Andes and Amazon are transformed via Lima and at the hands of white-mestizo chefs to present a whitened (largely male) urban version of national identity to the world. It is this version of Peruvianness that is largely celebrated and put on display in Peruvian restaurants outside Peru as well, as the next section discusses. For foreign visitors to Peru in search of "so-called authentic and traditional Andean people and culture" beyond Lima, local entrepreneurship has resulted in tourist packages that may include "experiential" homestays with indigenous families in rural communities (Babb 2011, 71, see in general 71–92) as a way to bring in money and respond to the desire to find indigenous "authenticity" in the spaces often dismissed as backward by *limeños*.

Seen historically, in the Andes "citizenship has been constituted through Spanish heritage, language, and literacy, and administered via European-style legal and educational systems leaving the indigenous majority practically disenfranchised" (Paulson 2006, 657). Now, as Peruvianness is celebrated transnationally, it is also the white-mestizo elite administering the messages via the food, now haute cuisine, served. As Andean and Amazonian ingredients and dishes travel to Lima and then other parts of the globe, they are transformed into a new, more palatable white-mestizo cuisine as they become financially out of reach for the Peruvians who have traditionally produced and consumed them. Men and women food producers, farm workers, and vendors have long been crucial to food production in Peru (Babb 1998), yet they are rarely celebrated in discussions of Peru's gastronomic success.

In Toronto, Amalia, who had been living outside of Peru for over twenty years with her partner, lamented that the homophobic sentiments she and her partner confronted in Lima were also present within the Peruvian community in Toronto, as examined in the previous chapter. Yet when our conversation turned to Peruvian food, she insisted that "gastronomy unites us all." For Amalia, as for many others I spoke with, the topic of food sparked feelings of national pride that many other subjects and experiences could not. Indeed, while racial, gender, and class hierarchies were more clearly identified by those I spoke with in other dimensions of their lives, in referring to Peruvian gastronomy there was little if any mention of how it also could reflect social hierarchies. The message that "food unites us" in this sense seems to have succeeded among the middle- and upper-class Peruvians commonly associated with the success of the gastronomic boom.

Back in Lima, twenty-four-year-old Marina, a white, middle-class woman who had recently returned to Lima to work after studying abroad for several years, similarly explained that she felt proud of Peru and enjoyed Peruvian food. However, she added, "But I don't think it's because we have the best food (that's what people normally identify with Peruvianness) but because it is a rich country in every way, and there is a lot to do and to learn in this country. That's what I think makes me feel more Peruvian: the complexity of our society." Her sense of pride and belonging was tied most concretely to her interests in and work on social justice abroad and in Peru. Her statement reminds us that Peruvian cuisine may provide an easy way to refer to a desired imagined community of Peruvians, yet the reality of everyday life reveals how divisions and hierarchies should not be so easily separated from discussions of food.

The marketing and success of Peruvian cuisine globally relies on its presentation of Peru as exotic and inclusive, and it reflects white-mestizo cultural-racial hierarchies. For the sake of providing a marketable version of Peruvian food, native ingredients and traditional dishes undergo transformations that homogenize a substantial part of the local differences in Peru to present these as haute cuisine produced by chefs who have trained abroad and now become experts on the local. Peruvian cuisine varies by region, with ceviche and other seafood dishes characteristic of the coast; guinea pig, trout, and sometimes alpaca of the Andean highlands; and river fish, other wild animals, and jungle fruits of the Amazon. Once outside national borders, Peruvian restaurants abroad charged with representing "Peruvian cuisine" meld components across regional differences while commonly privileging coastal dishes. How Peruvian dishes are presented in restaurants frequented by transnational Peruvians and what is excluded and changed are topics I turn to shortly. I also provide a brief tour of Peruvian restaurants in and around Munich, Germany, as a way to further understand how Peruvianness is served and represented in a particular setting.

Serving (Cosmopolitan) Peruvianness

Tanta is one of Gastón Acurio's several dozen global restaurants. In Chicago, Tanta promises to "take each guest that walks through our doors on a culinary adventure through Peru. The menu, created by Acurio and Tanta Chicago Chef Jesus Delgado, takes diners on a voyage through Peru via its food. From the Pacific Ocean, through the Andes, to the desert, to the Amazon, Tanta celebrates the diverse landscape and ethnicities that make up Peru's culture."[10] This invitation to experience Peru through its food and the emphasis on the inclusivity of its food (and therefore of Peruvian culture) are also reflected in the documentary *De ollas y sueños*, which features the iconic Peruvian chef, as mentioned earlier. The documentary emphasizes Peruvian gastronomy as "una experiencia deliciosamente integradora" (a deliciously integrating experience) in which "todas las sangres de una nación estan representadas" (all of the races of a nation are represented).

The inclusivity celebrated in the marketing of Peruvian food at Tanta and other restaurants may strike some as surprising, given Peru's history of social and economic inequality, which is partially based on geography, race, and class. Focusing on the gastronomic boom in Peru, Garcia critiques the supposedly cosmopolitan portrayal of tolerance, openness, and collaboration, pointing out that the gastronomic boom "obscures a dark side of continuing marginalization and violence against indigenous and nonhuman bodies in Peru" (2013, 507). With the gastronomic boom, ingredients previously discounted by the *limeño* elite as too exotic and unrefined are now welcomed as exemplifying the country's diversity even as they are distanced from indigenous Peruvian farmers, transformed at the hands of predominantly white and mestizo chefs from prominent and well-to-do families (Matta 2010), and served as Peruvian haute cuisine in expensive restaurants in different parts of the globe. Previously dismissed items such as *aguaymanto*, *chicha de jora*, and *cuy* (guinea pig) gained desired status as socially privileged chefs introduced them to other Peruvians in their milieus through new presentations (Matta 2013). Now a safely and acceptably exotic item that could be proudly consumed and celebrated by Peruvian chefs trained in Europe and the United States, guinea pig, traditionally served whole (with extremities and head visible) in the Andes, has been transformed to appeal to supposedly more cosmopolitan palates through the creation of guinea pig ravioli and other dishes that avoid showing the animal whole. Some differences are avoided in these cosmopolitan settings as outside the limits of the comfortably exotic.

The groups who mainly benefit from the gastronomic boom and the growing pride in Peruvian cuisine by Peruvians transnationally are not the producers of the products used to make the dishes but a smaller group of people that includes mostly male, white, and mestizo upper- and middle-class—often transnational—chefs (Garcia 2013; Matta 2013). Gastón Acurio, for example, comes from a conservative elite family and trained in Europe. According to a poll conducted in 2014, 23 percent of Peruvians claim they would vote for the celebrity chef if he were to run for president.[11] Rafael Osterling is the son of a former senator and similarly trained as a chef in Europe after obtaining a law degree (Matta 2010). Pedro Miguel Schiaffino, among the most renowned Peruvian chefs, is similarly based in Lima and studied in the United States and Europe. The website of his restaurant, Amaz, includes a short bio in which he describes himself as a "cook and researcher of the Amazon."[12] Dishes include "conchas canga con camu camu" (scallops with a sauce made from camu camu, an Amazonian fruit) and a series of Amazonian-inspired dishes. When I visited Lima in 2017, I noted that the restaurant, opened in 2012, continues to be very much in demand and attracts both Peruvians and foreign visitors for whom Amazonian cuisine is still not a familiar component of Peruvian gastronomy. Virgilio Martínez, a white *limeño* chef whose restaurant was named the top restaurant in Latin America in 2014, similarly studied law and then trained at Le Cordon Bleu in London.

If we are to believe that the contemporary rise of Peruvian cuisine in the world is inevitable given its high quality and appeal, as Marca Perú suggests, and if we approach food as a central aspect of home for migrants, it may be a particularly opportune time for Peruvian restaurants abroad. Peruvian chefs have become local celebrities, and large cities outside of Peru may have multiple Peruvian restaurants through which to export and enhance the visibility of particular constructions of Peruvianness. In San Francisco, the appeal of Peruvian food makes it possible for there to be ten Peruvian restaurants in a five-square-mile section of downtown (Brain 2014). Whereas restaurants that opened before the mid-1990s catered primarily to Peruvians, the ones that have opened since the late 1990s catered more to non-Peruvians. This coincides with a broader trend in the United States of ethnic cuisine becoming more accepted in the mainstream by the mid-1990s and restaurant menus actively promoting a multicultural atmosphere even when appealing to mostly North Americans (Gvion and Trostler 2008).

In Santiago, Chile, two Peruvian brothers successfully opened four Peruvian restaurants. Whereas the restaurants in Chile can attract a large number of Peruvians (Paerregaard 2014), the significantly lower Peruvian population in Germany makes it impossible to rely only or even mostly on Peruvians for a restaurant to stay open. Peruvians comprise the largest immigrant population in Chile, constituting approximately 2.5 percent of the country's population and making it possible for Peruvian restaurants and other food businesses to thrive precisely because they play an important role in the integration and settlement of Peruvians in Chile by providing pathways for migrants to display visible connections to their national identity (Imilan 2015, 227–228). In Barcelona, one of the Peruvian restaurants Karsten Paerregaard visited during his fieldwork on Peruvian migrants relied on Spanish customers during the workweek, but on Sunday "the usual customers stay away," and the restaurant "attracts many Peruvians who use their days off to enjoy a moment in the company of their fellow countrymen" while enjoying flavors from home (2014, 169). The larger Peruvian population in Spain and particularly in Barcelona creates a higher demand for Peruvian products, so the owner is able to buy all the Peruvian ingredients she needs in the city where she lives (Paerregaard 2014).

Arturo, a longtime Toronto resident, suggested that there were no good Peruvian restaurants in the metropolitan area. Commenting on a specific Peruvian restaurant in the city, he told me that he had heard other Peruvians complaining about the quality of the food and size of the portions there, adding that particularly in recent times Peruvians increasingly consider themselves to be experts on food and have become very *quisquillosos* (picky, finicky) when it comes to national dishes. This heightened sense of what is and is not legitimate and what should and can represent Peru coincides with the gastronomic boom and was also evident in Munich, as the next section discusses.

A Tour of Comfort, Status, and the Exotic around Munich

Sitting on the terrace of a restaurant by the train station in Pasing, a wealthy Munich suburb, I wait for two women I hope to interview to arrive. I have been introduced to one of them via email through a mutual acquaintance across multiple national borders, yet in the back-and-forth emails and calls we neglected to tell each other anything about our appearance so we could recognize one another when we met. Will they arrive *hora peruana* (Peruvian time) or *hora alemana* (German time)? In case it is *hora peruana*, I am prepared to answer a few emails on my phone as I wait. I also try to look up their pictures online, realizing that perhaps one of them is already at the restaurant. There is no online picture, and I begin to more carefully notice people walking out of the train station in case I recognize a Peruvian textile purse, familiar Peruvian silver earrings or necklace, or some other Peruvian marker that might indicate this could be the person.

It is not long until Catia arrives. A few minutes later, María joins us. It is a cool summer morning, and the sun has not yet come out. I felt particularly proud that morning that I had been in enough cafés and restaurants by that point to confidently ask the waitress for a cappuccino and water "ohne Kohlensaure, bitte" (without bubbles, please). I am ready to learn about Catia's and María's moves from Peru to Germany and their experiences learning German and living in Germany as adults. Before we continue, María asks the waitress for a table inside. With the sun still hiding behind the clouds and a cool breeze, María is worried she might get sick from an *airecito* (little breeze) if we stay outside too long. This is beginning to feel more and more like a conversation we could be having in Lima.

Inside, the conversation soon turns to María's sons, who Catia informed me a few minutes earlier moved to Germany as teenagers and now owned the best-known Peruvian restaurant in the city. Before we say good-bye, we make plans to be in touch again before I leave, and María invites me to visit her sons' restaurant. Before my visit to the restaurant, a friend and my family accompanied me to another well-known Peruvian culinary destination: the Inti Raymi festival in celebration of the sun god and winter solstice in Peru.

In Peru, the annual Inti Raymi festival in Cuzco attracts hundreds of thousands of visitors from the country and abroad for a week-long celebration that culminates on June 24 with a reenactment at Sacsayhuamán. In Munich, hundreds gathered to celebrate the festival, which the Peruvian community there first organized in 2009 for a one-day event. The gathering included not only a reenactment ceremony—including the Inca's speech to the sun god in Quechua—on the stage but also performances by Andean bands from the region, dances, and plenty of food. Over a dozen stalls provided numerous offerings. Small stalls sold *alfajores de maicena* (cornstarch sandwich cookies), *picarones* (fried sweet potato doughnuts), *papas a la huancaína* (potatoes with cream sauce), ceviche, *cordero* (lamb), *pisco* sours, and several other treats. In spite of ominous dark clouds followed by spells of rain, minutes after the stall selling *picarones* opened for business a long line—including members of my family—formed. After purchasing one or usually several food items, families—most often German-Peruvian families—enjoyed the festival, the music, and the food under a large covered area with picnic tables. The event was a vast, diverse event of Peruvians, other Latin Americans, and Germans.

Figures 5a, 5b, 5c: The Inti Raymi festival in Munich attracts Peruvians, other Latin Americans, and Germans from the area.

I made a reservation for María's sons' restaurant for a few days after the festival. In contrast to the Inti Raymi festival, where Peruvians and Germans of all backgrounds met in a single (large) space, María's sons' restaurant catered to a more middle- and upper-class clientele, including transnational Peruvians. María had encouraged me to state I was a friend of hers when I called and suggested which table to request to have a good view of the whole restaurant, noting that the restaurant was often fully booked. Now in its sixth year, the restaurant was also highly recommended by other Peruvians I met, and Yelp reviews hinted at great flavor in small but beautifully presented portions. I had my first warm *papas a la huancaína* on a hot summer evening in this beautifully lit, busy Peruvian restaurant in a trendy neighborhood near one of the main universities in Munich. After commenting on the smooth, flavorful *huancaína* sauce, I asked María, who was sitting at a large nearby table with her sons (the owners) and their extended family, about the warm *papas a la huancaína*, a dish traditionally served cold. Local residents, she explained, did not like to eat cold potatoes, so the chef had decided to adapt the dish to the German palate and serve the dish lukewarm. It had become one of the most popular appetizers on the menu.

For Peruvian restaurants to survive and thrive in locations with small Peruvian and Latin American populations, appealing to local tastes is vital. In appealing to non-Peruvian palates and adapting to new settings, recipes may undergo changes as chefs and owners negotiate how to represent Peru in the context of local preferences and available ingredients. Not all dishes, however, are deemed adaptable, and some simply should not be adapted, according to some Peruvians. Peru's signature coastal dish, ceviche, is the restaurant's most popular dish and was not similarly adapted to local tastes. The restaurant owners went to great lengths to serve ceviche as closely as possible to how it would be served in Peru. Beautifully plated and made with *rocoto* (Peruvian hot pepper) and perfectly sliced onions, with caramelized sweet potatoes and Peruvian corn on the side, and *cancha* (toasted corn) carefully placed in white ceramic serving spoons, this dish and others reflected a specific image of Peru the restaurant wished to transmit to local residents: that found in upscale restaurants in Lima.

In presenting Peruvianness through specific foods, menus and restaurants also make visible, and invisible, parts and populations of Peru. In cookbooks, the choice of what recipes and regional specialties to include and exclude tells readers "what is appropriate and what is not. They tell us what is French or Italian or Provençal or Tuscan, and what is not," providing messages about what is worthy of representing a national cuisine (Ferguson 2010, 107).

Similarly, in menus, what is and is not included tells us what is privileged and what is being erased or excluded in particular representations of Peru.

At approximately twenty euros, the ceviche costs significantly more than the weekend ceviche served at smaller, more modest neighborhood corner restaurants. It is well within the economic reach of affluent Peruvians, whereas the price is not within reach of poorer Peruvians. Rather than having ceviche for lunch, as is typically done in Peru, the dinner-only opening hours of the restaurant created an evening market for ceviche in this German city.

Customers' economic resources, together with the desire to taste something "exotic" among local residents and the nostalgia for home and home flavors among Peruvians who can afford to eat there, ensure the restaurant stayed busy most evenings. In marketing its Peruvian cuisine as both exotic and authentic, food preparation, ingredients, and décor may also contribute to a restaurant's success. A few minutes after I arrived at the restaurant, after speaking with the bartender about the numerous Peruvian drinks he regularly prepares—including his famous *pisco* sour—I am also introduced to the chef. He is young, quiet, and eager to return to the kitchen during this busy evening. María proudly tells me that he won one of the competitions in

Figures 5d, 5e, 5f: Variations on a theme: ceviche in Germany. 5d: *Ceviche clásico* at an upscale restaurant in Munich.

Figures 5d, 5e, 5f (*continued*): 5e: *Ceviche mixto* at the Inti Raymi festival in Munich. 5f: *Ceviche clásico* at a restaurant in Nuremberg.

Mistura, the biggest annual food festival in Latin America, which is held in Lima. He has been working as the head chef for six months since winning a separate competition sponsored by the restaurant to fill the spot of head chef, a competition that takes place every four years. Mistura, as a path to being head chef at the restaurant, is a significant factor given how well recognized the festival is among middle- and upper-class Peruvians. Having a chef who successfully passed through Mistura further cements its high status transnationally.

To comply with German law, the restaurant offers Peruvian chefs four-year contracts, with the first six months as a trial period. After the contract ends, the chef must return to Peru. The change in chefs means the menu changes slightly with each new chef, but as María insists, the restaurant's signature dishes remain the same, and the priority is continuously on fresh, authentic Peruvian ingredients. Significantly, the authenticity and appropriateness of offerings for global palates are determined by transnational Peruvians. The bartender adds that a few years ago, when the previous chef complained that the avocados the restaurant received were not adequate for the Peruvian dishes on the menu, María found a way to import avocados directly from Peru. The restaurant now proudly serves only Peruvian avocados.

The restaurant also constructs and presents Peruvianness to both locals and Peruvians through the choice of paint colors and wall decorations. Its décor works to proclaim openness to all things Peruvian and an orientation toward global markets and global palates. The country's three regions are mainly represented in the colors on the walls of the sitting areas: dark yellow to represent the sun and coast, warm brown earth tones to represent the highlands, and wood-brown tones to represent the jungle. A small statue of the Virgin Mary is also near the middle of the restaurant to represent Peru's and the family's Catholic background. Further legitimizing the restaurant's status as representative of Peru are the framed photographs near the restrooms. Next to framed newspaper reviews of the restaurant there are autographed pictures of Eva Ayllón, a well-known Afro-Peruvian singer who has visited the restaurant on several occasions. There are also photographs of Claudio Pizarro, the Peruvian soccer star who played for FC Bayern Munich for nine seasons.[13] Known as the top foreign scorer in the history of German soccer, he is well known and admired in both Peru and Germany. María tells my son, a soccer fan intently staring at the photographs, that Pizarro is a regular at the restaurant. With that comment, my son's excitement about connections between Peru and Germany became more palpable, and we are ready to return to our table to order our little piece of Peru in Germany. The menu, however, is decidedly coastal. There are no Amazonian dishes, and the highlands dishes there have been transformed first to Lima tastes and then to those of restaurant-goers in Munich. Like Marca Peru, the restaurant appeals to a broad, united, yet diverse sense of Peruvianness through décor, but its offerings reinforce particular coastal, Lima tastes as represented by middle-class transnational Peruvians, Peru's preferred ambassadors vis-à-vis nation-branding efforts.

The balance between promoting Peruvian cuisine as exotic and promoting it as comfort food is also central to two nearby restaurants, with one seeking to appeal to more affluent customers and the other to a broader, more diverse clientele. In Nuremberg, about two hours from Munich, the only Peruvian restaurant in the city sits on a slope at the foot of one of the city's main tourist attractions, the Nuremberg Castle, and its façade and menu are visible to tourists and local residents walking down to the main plaza. Open only in the evenings, it too transmits a more upscale feel than most casual restaurants that serve ceviche and *lomo saltado*—the restaurant's top dishes—in Peru. Like the restaurant in Munich, its target customers are the global middle and upper classes. And like the Munich restaurant, as a Peruvian restaurant it overrepresents the coast (through dish offerings) and highlands (through décor) while excluding the largely indigenous Amazon.

I arrived just as it opened for the evening, and over the course of the next hour and a half, with instrumental Andean music playing in the background, my sons and I enjoyed ceviche, *trio de causas* (mashed potato dish), and freshly made *chicha morada* (a sweet, blue corn drink). I observed about a dozen small groups of tourists walk down the hill, comment on the menu outside, and continue to walk to the main plaza. Unlike us, they had come to Nuremberg mainly for the castle, and this small, seemingly exotic (from the comments we overheard) restaurant was not on their itinerary.

The chef, whom I spoke with during our meal, is also the owner and moved to Germany from Peru over a decade before to attend university. Five years ago, he opened the restaurant and now worked there every day. He explained that in spite of the gastronomic boom in Peru, in Germany Peruvian food is still considered exotic and unfamiliar by many and that this works against its popularity in midsize cities in the region. Nuremberg's population is about one-third that of Munich. The two versions of the menu, one in German and the other in English, underscore that Germans and English-speaking tourists—not Latin Americans and, more specifically, Peruvians—are the restaurant's primary customers, given the area's small Latin American population. Peruvians also visit the restaurant, but, the chef adds, only occasionally, and when they do it is not unusual for them to complain. Peruvians comment on the size of the portions and the price, since these differ significantly from the more generous portions of lunch-time ceviche, *lomo saltado*, and other typical Peruvian dishes available at casual neighborhood restaurants in Peru. Echoing what many other Peruvians in Canada, the United States, and those who had returned to Peru mentioned, the chef also expressed that when it comes to food, many Peruvians consider themselves experts and are eager to offer critiques.

The restaurant in particular appeals to Germans who have visited Peru or the Andes and for whom Andean cuisine may be both exotic and known. On some occasions, it is these customers, as well as Peruvians, who request *cuy*, which is traditionally eaten in the Andes. The chef tells me he has refused these requests each time because of the difficulties of finding *cuys* raised for meat and not for pets in Germany and to avoid scrutiny from animal rights groups. What appeals as potentially exotic, however, also keeps other customers away. As I comment on how I've seen several tourists stop to read the menu outside, he tells me he once heard a little boy tell his father outside the restaurant that he didn't want to eat in the restaurant, as the father read the menu, because he didn't want to have to eat guinea pig. He adds, again, that *cuy* has never even appeared on his menu.

Unlike in the case of the Munich restaurant discussed previously, difficulties in regular access to Peruvian ingredients for the restaurant owner in Nuremberg have led to several adaptations over the years. Unable to ensure a regular or affordable stream of Peruvian ingredients for the restaurant, the chef-owner now uses Thai chili peppers instead of Peruvian *rocoto* for the very tasty ceviche he prepares, and he serves the ceviche without Peruvian corn or Peruvian sweet potatoes. The *causa rellena*, a potato dish traditionally made with a yellow potato—one of Peru's hundreds of varieties of potatoes—is also made with a different potato more easily accessible in Germany.[14] At the end of the meal, when I asked for the *picarones* listed on the menu, the Peruvian-style freshly fried sweet potato doughnuts typically served warm with *chancaca* (piloncillo, or cone sugar) syrup, I was sad to learn that these were not available that evening because there would not be enough customers to warrant making the dough that night. Just a few minutes earlier, the chef had mentioned that he used to include even more items on the menu but that each year he pruned it down to the most popular ones because of the lack of demand for many others. I wondered if *picarones* would disappear in the menu's next incarnation. By the time I paid the check, a large party of ten customers in their twenties, the one reservation that evening, had arrived and were already asking questions about unfamiliar dishes.

Back in Munich, the appeal of Peruvian food as exotic in a city with a small population of Peruvians is precisely what led the owner-chef of another small restaurant that also doubles as a food market to advertise itself as serving "exotische Kuche aus Lateinamerika" (exotic Latin American cuisine) rather than exclusively Peruvian cuisine.[15] The owner did not follow the Marca Perú strategy of appealing to an upscale middle- and upper-class global elite. She preferred to cater to a younger, less affluent clientele with the broader appeal of "Latin American" food. In this case, the owner was not a professional chef, and rather than appeal to the prestige of having a

Mistura-tested chef, her venue had more of a vibe of a friendly neighborhood *bodega* or neighborhood restaurant that serves the cheaper plates of ceviche Peruvians spoke of nostalgically (but she did not serve ceviche). The owner, a woman of Brazilian-Peruvian descent who spent several months in South America learning cooking techniques and recipes before opening her business about three years ago, sells jars of Peruvian chilies—*aji panca* and *aji amarillo*—as well as Inca Kola and bags of dried potato. Bottles of *pisco*, Peruvian hard liquor, and cans of the beer Cristal also line the shelves, making it possible to create a full "authentic" Peruvian meal for those so inclined. It should also not go without notice that the restaurant that is most widely positively regarded in this setting is the one with a Mistura association, and the one with the least prestige—but perhaps the most diverse clientele—is the one owned and run by a woman without professional chef accreditations.

Unlike the two exclusively Peruvian restaurants described above, even as Peruvian ingredients and dishes play a central role in this business, the owner markets the products and restaurant more broadly as Latin American to attract a larger clientele. Whereas the first two dinner-hours-only restaurants catered to a well-heeled clientele interested in the latest gastronomic trends, the third restaurant appealed more to those looking for comfort and more generally ethnic food. The market shelves and the price of restaurant dishes here, combined with its lunch opening hours, create a more casual atmosphere than in the two other restaurants I visited in the area. Rather than appeal to a middle- and upper-class identity with award-winning chefs, dinner-only hours, and carefully orchestrated dish presentations, this restaurant provides comfort-inspiring meals that customers with fewer economic resources can also access more regularly.

Sitting down to eat with my husband and our two sons, as we chatted with the owner standing behind the counter just a few feet away from our table, we first enjoyed the ubiquitous *papas a la huancaína*, also served warm here. Whether called Machu Picchu, Nazca, or another name that exalts the country's cultural heritage and top tourist attractions, Peruvian restaurants—in Barcelona, Santiago, Lima, Munich, and elsewhere—consistently offer *papas a la huancaína*. The placement of *papas a la huancaína* at the top of the menu marks it as an entry point into Peruvian flavors.[16] After the *papas*, we feasted on *escabeche* (a dish made with fish and onions) and a portion of *salchipapas* (freshly cut fries and hot dogs) at our younger son's request. Freshly squeezed *limonada*, *chicha morada* (purple corn sweet drink), Inca Kola, and some *arroz con leche* (rice pudding) rounded off our meal. Exotic to some of the restaurants' customers, these were appealing to us precisely because we view them as comfort foods. For the many young tourists—particularly North American ones, the owner tells us—and Germans who frequent the restaurant, these flavors are unfamiliar, yet the low lunch prices, location, and appeal of the exotic guarantee a steady stream of customers.

Tasting and (Re)Producing Some Forms of Peruvianness

When Peruvian writer Gustavo Rodríguez was asked by the newspaper *El Comercio* why he decided to have a chef as the main character in his novel *Cocinero en su tinta* (Chef in his ink), he responded that he could have just as easily have made him a photographer or a painter. However, it seemed particularly interesting to Rodríguez to make the character a chef in the Peruvian setting, "where what is most talked about has to do with food" (*El Comercio* 2012). Asked about his own food preferences, Rodríguez explained that to him Peruvian food was good but not necessarily the best in the world—something those who had watched Marca Perú's *Peru, Nebraska*, spot just a few months before the interview came out might find to be a problematic, if not unpatriotic, view. He then added, as if to make his appreciation of Peruvian food clear and avoid offending anyone's national pride, "It's enough pride (for me) to know it is among the five or six best cuisines of the world" (*El Comercio* 2012).

Sitting in a café inside a bookstore on Yonge Street near snowy downtown Toronto, Arturo chuckled as he told me that recently a coworker whom he would not have guessed had ever traveled outside of North America had asked him where he was from after detecting Arturo's accent. When Arturo replied that he was from Peru, his coworker commented that he had heard that the food was particularly good there. Arturo was both surprised and pleased that his coworker recognized Peruvian food as a world-renowned cuisine. Similarly to Rodríguez's own attitudes toward Peruvian food, however, Arturo enjoys eating traditional Peruvian dishes but tells me that to him, "it's not true that Peruvian food is the best in the world. It is very good, but others are very good as well, and in Peru we say that it is the second in the world, after the French." That it is globally recognized, however, is an important factor for him, as for Rodríguez, even if being considered the best is not. This recognition of high status, significantly, has been consistently associated with the racial-class identities of middle- and upper-class Peruvians. The better Peruvian gastronomy is considered, one could argue, the more the status of middle- and upper-class Peruvians benefits, and the more they are perceived as the rightful ambassadors or representatives of Peru.

Food is a source of comfort and pride and provides a way for Peruvians to speak of and express their identity and feel connected to Peru. It also, as I have suggested, allows them to construct particular forms of Peruvianness that privilege and reinforce the high status of middle- and upper-class transnational Peruvians. The centrality of food in Peruvians' discussions of what they miss most about Peru and feel most proud of gains new significance when we critically examine how this "unique space where the entire nation feels harmoniously integrated" (*De ollas y sueños* documentary) is also founded on hierarchies of national identity and belonging. These hierarchies within the gastronomic boom and its representation of Peruvianness go beyond individual feelings of nostalgia and pride and appropriate elements of excluded indigenous Peruvian identities to privilege urban white middle- and upper-class identities. Whether it is through Marca Perú spots, Inca Kola commercials, or the choice of dishes to include or exclude in Peruvian restaurants outside Peru, the images of Peru that emerge consistently privilege the cosmopolitan, urban, white-mestizo identities associated with the transnational Peruvians I interviewed.

CONCLUSION

Persistent Hierarchies and Transnational Lives

Every so often, particularly around Peruvian holidays, the phrase "salí del Perú pero el Perú jamás saldrá de mi corazón" (I left Peru, but Peru will never leave my heart) makes the rounds on social media among Peruvians. The phrase is typically accompanied by images of Peruvian food, the Peruvian flag, or Machu Picchu. Red and white, the colors of the Peruvian flag, tend to appear somewhere in these images even when the flag does not. The phrase and images come up regularly, yet the sentiments behind them may vary significantly. What is at stake in different constructions of home, of Peru, and of Peruvians? More specifically, what and how do the lens of imagined, rejected, or physical return and an intersectional approach to transnational Peruvian lives contribute to our understanding of home, Peruvian identities, and transnational lives?

In speaking with Peruvians, and as the previous chapter emphasized, food emerges as a central way of connecting to and defining national identity. In Lima, Chabela named Peruvian gastronomy as what she felt most proud of about Peru. Many other Peruvians abroad and in Lima agreed with her view. In Toronto, Alicia explained that in her view "all socialization takes place in family get-togethers where there is food, everything is food. When I go to Lima . . . it's always about food." Among transnational Peruvians, it is clear that a focus on food serves as a pathway to multilayered images of home. References to food bring up not only certain flavors and smells associated with home but also family as central to home. Family is the main reason Peruvians provided for leaving Peru during particularly insecure times, for staying abroad, and for returning to Peru. Food and family, however, are only partial and superficial answers to how home is constructed and what is at stake in constructions of home. Even within culinary and family realms, as the chapters in this book underscore, middle- and upper-class Peruvians' transnational experiences include associations with Peru that are reflective of race-gender-class hierarchies. Return provides a way to understand what transnational Peruvians desire, reject, or feel ambivalent about in constructions of Peruvianness, home, and belonging. At stake in constructions of home, Peru, and Peruvians is the persistence as well as possibilities for change of various social hierarchies and forms of power rooted in exclusions that shape Peruvians' lives across borders. These hierarchies, I have suggested, inform the lives of Peruvians of diverse class backgrounds both in Peru and abroad.

Whether in Munich, Toronto, Lima, or elsewhere, Peruvian lives are embedded in familiar and unfamiliar configurations of power. Abroad, middle- and upper-class Peruvians may find themselves "othered" for the first time—as Latino/a, as someone with an accent, or as a noncitizen. They will likely also find that the everyday privileges of middle- and upper-class life they had become accustomed to are not as easily available to them outside of Lima and that their class status may not be as apparent to others in their new communities as it is to them. Yet all interviewees referred to and welcomed the increased sense of personal and family security they experienced outside of Peru in comparison to in Lima. Outside of Peru, a few were able to explore openly gay lifestyles for the first time. Several spoke of becoming particularly conscious of the fluidity of their own identities across borders. In cases in this book, over and over again, social hierarchies appear as central to processes of belonging and exclusion.

As a way to understand Peruvian middle- and upper-class transnational experiences, I have suggested that cosmopolitanism cannot be divorced from existing racial-gender-class hierarchies in social spaces. I have introduced exclusionary cosmopolitanism as a concept that underscores tolerance as an ideological orientation (see Ahmed et al. 2003; Nussbaum 1994; Hannerz 1996) yet that, significantly, is characterized by on-the-ground exclusionary practices (see Glick-Schiller, Darieva, and Gruner-Domic 2011; Hiebert 2002). While it cannot and does not pretend to cover all circumstances, exclusionary cosmopolitanism presents a productive framework for approaching middle- and upper-class transnational Peruvian lives. Negotiations of identities and behaviors stretch and challenge existing structures of power. In identifying the resulting limits of inclusion among individuals from groups that have traditionally held significant social power in Peru, we can develop a realistic, multilayered, fluid image of power structures at work in constructions of Peruvianness and how these are reinforced, adapted, and challenged.

My approach to cosmopolitanism centers on the transnational reproduction of privilege and power based on social hierarchies founded on Peruvian histories and contexts. The reproduction of privilege, I argue, can take place even in cases in which transnational Peruvians also experience discrimination or marginalization as migrants. To assert their own belonging, I show through numerous examples and analyses, middle- and upper-class Peruvians exclude those they view as inferior because of race, class, or sexual identity. I propose the concept of exclusionary cosmopolitanism to describe claims of tolerance and accompanying—often exclusionary—social practices. It is this rich tension between proclaiming openness and the pragmatic reliance on Peruvian-based local hierarchies of race, class, and sexual identity to assert (high) status that I propose is at the center of exclusionary cosmopolitanism.

The forms of exclusionary belonging I have identified and examined rely on local configurations of power based on the politics of class, race, gender, and sexual identity in Peru. In tracing how social hierarchies are performed across borders in everyday lives, this multisited study finds that belonging is routinely expressed at least in part by identifying what is outside the realm of inclusion: which city areas to visit and avoid; what types of people or identities to engage with, relate to, and shun; and which foods to celebrate and reject. In negotiating what is and is not within the limits of inclusion in daily interactions, transnational middle- and upper-class Peruvians both directly experience and engage in subtle and more direct policing of borders of belonging that have long privileged the status quo.

Among transnational Peruvians, exclusionary cosmopolitanism takes many forms. Sitting in the warm, sunny apartment he shares with his wife and children, forty-four-year-old Marco confides in me that as a self-identified open, tolerant individual he regrets that he has again embraced racist attitudes since his return. He feels particularly annoyed at this realization because he has personally experienced discrimination as a Latino migrant in the United States. As I noted at the beginning of the book, he insists that his views are a direct reaction to the actions of poorer indigenous Peruvian migrants and *cholos* in Lima who "urinate on the streets, throw bottles on the streets, they insult you, take the gun out, they go in to rob." In Marco's view, the everyday insecurity he and his family experience is largely the result of the behaviors and attitudes of Peruvians who refuse to, or cannot, belong to the more educated, cosmopolitan world with which he and his white, middle-class family identify. He considers himself open, and, most significantly and paradoxically, this openness must be carefully protected from those who simply cannot belong to this open world. It would be disingenuous to approach this form of cosmopolitanism without also critically considering the embedded and long-standing racial-class hierarchies in Marco's middle-class lifestyle in Lima that inform his views of "others."

Social hierarchies tend to benefit middle- and upper-class Peruvians in Lima by privileging their racial, class, and geographic background vis-à-vis other Peruvians—even in the realm of gastronomy. Racist and sexist power structures have long been recognized by Peruvian scholars as central to inequalities in Peru (i.e., Francke 1990). Colonial legacies have provided the foundation for persistent efforts to naturalize socially constructed hierarchies of intersections of race, class, and place of origin. Today in Lima, diversity rarely translates into egalitarianism among different groups. The city of ten million—currently the second largest city in the Americas by some counts—is a popular destination for Peruvians from throughout the country and visitors from around the world. As a city it might well be "the place, above all, of living with others" (Laurier and Philo 2006, 193), yet it is a city in which everyday life occurs against the backdrop of segregation, discrimination, and social inequalities. These social hierarchies accompany Peruvians on their transnational journeys.

Visitors to Lima will find information in popular guidebooks such as the Lonely Planet series and travel advice websites such as TripAdvisor that direct them to wealthier neighborhoods and away from poorer, periurban areas. The city's traditionally wealthiest neighborhoods, including La Molina, Monterrico, Miraflores, Surco, and San Isidro, boast green areas, gated spaces, and numerous *guachimanes* (privately employed security guards). It was from their homes in these neighborhoods that Peruvians I interviewed commonly traveled abroad. By contrast, poorer neighborhoods cannot afford the necessary irrigation systems and services required for green areas in a city located in one of the driest desert areas in the world. The possibilities for employing private security guards are also lower in poorer neighborhoods, and infrastructure such as roads and paved sidewalks may be noticeably incomplete or absent. Wealthier neighborhoods are common destinations for poorer Peruvians who work as household workers, while poorer neighborhoods are rarely visited by the upper- and middle-class Peruvians I interviewed.

The persistence of hierarchies examined in this book is reflective of what Aníbal Quijano (2000) has referred to as the "coloniality of power" and Marisol de la Cadena (1998) has previously pointed to as Peru's historically "silent racism." Racism exists and intersects with other social structures of inequality in Lima, even as middle-class and upper-class Peruvians deny or feel ambivalent about the existence of racism in Peru (Oboler 2005). Here, inasmuch as they are manifested in Lima, as well as outside Peru's borders, I have examined ways in which hierarchies are both embraced and challenged by middle- and upper-class transnational Peruvians.

Hierarchies are palpable in how public spaces are deemed particularly dangerous for middle- and upper-class women return migrants. The threat and experiences of street sexual harassment undermine autonomy gained abroad, especially for women, as families and individuals themselves reinforce restrictive spatial mobility for women in the name of safety. Fathers and mothers may in particular exert more control over their daughters' movements in the name of safety. Young women and men in their twenties also referred to greater expectations of adherence to conservative gender norms and surveillance by extended families in Lima. In regard to class and race, women are warned of men's ongoing street sexual harassment in particular because it is men racialized as violent (poor, working-class, indigenous, internal migrants) who are viewed as particularly dangerous to white and mestiza, urban middle- and upper-class *limeñas*. Hierarchies are visible in how nonheteronormative sexual identities are marginalized, rejected, and resisted in private and public spaces—whether it's a return migrant simultaneously welcomed as a son and marginalized and silenced as a gay man by his family or a gay or lesbian couple harassed by private security guards or the municipal police on the street or in a public park. Hierarchies are discernible in the choice and presentation of foods deemed appropriate for global palates and markets and included in or excluded from Peruvian restaurant menus.

In reflecting both privilege and discrimination, Olivia's experiences underscore the multilayered and intersecting identities of transnational Peruvians both within and outside of Peru and how these are informed by societal hierarchies. When she was a child her family briefly moved from Lima to Cuzco. After returning to Lima her parents enrolled her in an elite school. One day her next-door neighbor in Lima, also a young girl at the school, yelled at her to "go back to Cuzco," calling her a *chola*, a *cuzqueña*. Olivia vividly remembers that moment in detail more than twenty years later and explains that she felt more discriminated against in that moment than she ever felt during her years in Germany, where she described being treated unfairly at times as a foreigner.

In Peru, the moment of discrimination Olivia experienced is a widespread reality for rural-to-urban migrant poor indigenous women. As I discuss in chapters 1 and 2, in many wealthy *limeño* homes in return for precarious, low-paid employment, intracountry migrant women work as live-in domestic servants and provide the labor that keeps households clean, ready for guests, and stocked with prepared foods daily. Their labor is a marker of status in middle- and upper-class households.[1] Women's gender, class, and racial "otherness" as rural-to-urban migrants from predominantly indigenous areas to mestizo and white middle- and upper-class households mark them as exploitable and disposable.

Although not marked as disposable in the same way as rural-to-urban migrants in Peru, Peruvians I spoke with pointed to their own experiences of marginalization after leaving Lima. These experiences tended to fall into two categories: discrimination based on the projection of a homogenized, racialized Latino identity onto them, and discrimination based on their perceived accents. Both resulted in being categorized as "other," in contrast to their unmarked, privileged status as middle- and upper-class Peruvians in Lima. Additionally, outside Peru some Peruvians engaged in employment that they would not have accepted in Lima because it would have lowered their social status. Even without these markers of Peruvian middle- and upper-class status—private schools, particular types of employment, relying on domestic servants for household labor—abroad, migrants held on to their self-identification as middle and upper class as they renegotiated configurations of power in their new settings.

Renegotiating their social identities and social roles could also lead to critical reflections about and efforts to transform existing unequal structures and behaviors. The discomfort some Peruvians expressed about the treatment of household workers, for example, is perhaps best represented by Manolo. Contemplating his life in Munich, his upper-class upbringing in Lima, and his role as the father of two German Peruvian daughters, Manolo lamented that as a young man in Lima he had uncritically embraced racism and sexism. In his position as a middle-aged man living in Germany who regularly visited family and friends in Lima, he now rejected the very behaviors and attitudes toward household workers he had practiced in his family home as a young man. To varying degrees, in particular among the twenty-something-year-old return migrants I met and interviewed, the questioning and rejection of racist, homophobic, and gendered-biased attitudes and behaviors point to the recognition of unearned benefits and the break from traditional middle- and upper-class exclusionary social hierarchies by some. These fissures in structures of power are worth noting because they reflect the roles of those who have traditionally held power not only in reinforcing but also in holding the potential to forge new challenges to persistent structures that uphold the status quo.

Migration tends to shake individuals out of their comfort zones, presenting—if not forcing—new forms of interactions and encounters with unfamiliar identities. If it follows that intergroup contact reduces prejudice (Allport 1954), then we could safely assume that transnational migration decreases preexisting biases against varied forms of "otherness" regarding class, gender, and sexuality. Although this is certainly the case for some, the experiences discussed in previous chapters illustrate that this is not a safe assumption. To claim openness and tolerance does not negate including exclusionary practices rooted in racial, gender, and class hierarchies that privilege some identities over others in worldviews and practices. That these hierarchies are continuously directly and indirectly referred to speaks to their significance in Peruvian lives. The endurance of questions about where (what district) in Lima one is from and what school one attended in first-time encounters among middle- and upper-class Peruvians, for example, brings to the forefront the performance and practice of spatial, racialized hierarchies from the first interaction with other Peruvians beyond Peru's physical borders.

Critically examining belonging among transnational middle- and upper-class Peruvians moves us farther away from flattened, static, binary images of Peruvians as rich versus poor, empowered versus oppressed, migrant versus nonmigrant, and included versus excluded. To approach belonging intersectionally is to engage with identities, practices, and ideas that are rich and multilayered. Attention to intersections in social identities foregrounds incongruities and contradictions of belonging: a middle-class gay return migrant who claims home in the context of his family's and Lima's palpable homophobia and resulting silencing of his identity as a gay man, a young heterosexual woman who insists that her boyfriend's father is open and tolerant even as she makes visible his routine racist comments and condemns racist behaviors in others, a young gay man who privileges his individual experience of family acceptance and wealth to reject LGBTQ public demands for basic rights in Lima.

In the contemporary world, from my vantage point as I write this in 2017 in the United States, it is particularly urgent to recognize and critically examine exclusionary practices in our societies. While racism in the United States and in Peru certainly has different histories and dynamics, it is worth noting that just as in the United States, American identity is still implicitly understood as white (Omi and Winant 2015), among transnational Peruvians, belonging is commonly constructed against the backdrop of social hierarchies that prioritize whiteness in the context of Peru. Heteronormativity, class, and racialized geographies result in additional dimensions through which to include and exclude. It is the rich tensions resulting from claims to openness and practices grounded in material conditions and power relations associated with long-standing social hierarchies that remind us to push our analysis away from simplistic binaries.

The examples in this book relate to Peru, yet the approach to exclusionary cosmopolitanism could also be applied to relations of power and forms of exclusion more broadly. As I have suggested, claims of belonging commonly invite forms of exclusion that may be framed in binary terms but in practice reflect multiple identity intersections. Exclusionary cosmopolitanism, in this sense, cautions us against equating sentiments of tolerance and openness with inclusive practices even as it recognizes some spaces of ongoing negotiation and possibilities for transformation. For example, in the United States in 2010, Mexican American studies was banned in Arizona schools. Proponents of excluding Mexican American studies from school curriculum argued that it was a necessary move "to protect a multicultural, tolerant, and inclusive America from exclusionary, separatist, or racist groups" (Cisneros 2013, 75). In other words, discrimination and exclusion were justified in the name of openness.[2] I have also examined elsewhere how in the United States millennials in the U.S. South have employed color-blind rhetoric to paradoxically justify excluding Latino immigrants from the realms of belonging to a color-blind, egalitarian, tolerant society. Some who self-identified as open and postracial associated Latinos with illegality and spoke of those they identified as "illegal," or undocumented, as somehow not worthy of the same rights as others and as deserving of exclusion from protection from discrimination and some forms of violence (Alcalde 2016). Such justifications for exclusion are founded on encounters with unfamiliar or undervalued identities and set boundaries on inclusiveness in the name of tolerance.

At stake in constructions of home, Peruvianness, and belonging is protection from discrimination and from multiple forms of violence that are tolerated against those who are perceived as outside the realms of belonging in and out of Peru. Engaging with multiple intersecting identities among middle- and upper-class Peruvians in varied settings emphasizes that to belong often means to exclude, as well as to be excluded; that to position oneself above others in racial-gender-class hierarchies in one space does not mean to be free from discrimination in another space; and that to be discriminated against does not prevent one from feeling one belongs. In Peru, among transnational Peruvians and, more broadly, in the contemporary world, privilege, exclusion, and power are at stake in constructions of belonging—to a group, to a community, to one or more nations.

NOTES

INTRODUCTION

1. "Déjame que te cuente, limeña. Déjame que te diga la gloria, del ensueño que evoca la memoria, del viejo puente, del río y la alameda."

2. Throughout the book, I employ terms such as "immigrant communities" and "immigrant population" in referring to existing studies of particular communities. In referring to Peruvians outside Peru who participated in this study, I opt for "migrant" instead of "immigrant." Like Patricia Zavella, I find the term "migrant" preferable because it helps "evoke the ambiguities and indeterminacies that are involved in the process of migration" and underscores that "migration is not necessarily linear but processual and contingent upon changing circumstances" (2011, xiii–xiv).

3. Gloria Anzaldúa (1987) also pointed to processes of belonging and nonbelonging as central to home in her analysis of the marginal spaces of the borderlands, and this topic has also since been extensively analyzed by Chicana feminists (i.e., Blackwell 2016; Hurtado 1998; Saldivar-Hull 2000).

4. In this case, Takeyuki Tsuda's (2003) differentiation between home and homeland may be particularly useful. Writing on Brazilians of Japanese descent who migrate to the ancestral home of Japan, Tsuda proposes that homeland (the place where one is from and to which one feels an emotional attachment) and home (the place where one lives and that feels familiar and secure) may result in significantly different feelings and practices of belonging, as well as in vastly different treatment by those living in each place. In these cases, home and homeland interact in migrant lived experiences as meanings attached to each are created not in isolation but in reference to one another so that "the transnational is embedded in the local" (Decena 2011, 209).

5. The public Facebook page of Peruanos en el Extranjero is https://www.facebook.com/peruanosenelextranjero/?fref=nf and was accessed on February 2, 2016. The original post is from May 19, 2015.

6. The themes of migration, gender, exclusion, and insecurity, as well as several others that I trace in these chapters, arose from a particular set of methods and

approaches to Peruvian transnational experiences and my discussions with Peruvians in Peru and abroad.

7. Outside of anthropology, there is also an emerging interest in approaching and analyzing South American middle classes in studies of national identity, including historian Rebekah Pite's 2013 *Creating a Common Table in Twentieth-Century Argentina* and sociologist Sebastián Carassai's 2014 *The Argentine Silent Majority: Middle-Classes, Politics, Violence, and Memory in the Seventies.*

8. In my work, I have previously focused on poor and working-class Peruvians in Peru (Alcalde 2006, 2010) and labor migrants in the United States (Alcalde 2007, 2009, 2011).

9. In the United States, at 16 percent of the national population, Latinos are the largest and fastest-growing minority group (U.S. Census Bureau 2011).

10. Yet as the Peruvian economy continued to improve, in 2010 the rate of Peruvians leaving Peru decreased by approximately 5 percent (IOM 2012).

11. Migrants' connections to home and their plans and decisions to return may also be mediated by remittances. Among Peruvian migrants in Argentina, Chile, Japan, Spain, and the United States, the pressures and obligations associated with remittances impact intimate and familial relationships across national borders and shape migrants' sense of connection to home communities and families in Peru (Paerregaard 2014). On the one hand, remittances reinforce familial and affective bonds. On the other hand, remittances allow migrants to exert power and control over family members and communities in Peru through pledges to cover educational, household, or medical expenses for family members, donations to or sponsorship of community events, and investments (Paerregaard 2014). On a more practical level, remittances may allow migrants to guarantee that they or their children will have a house and social network to return to during temporary visits or permanent returns.

12. Peruvian migration includes individuals from all regions and from across the socioeconomic spectrum (Berg 2010). Both political and economic crises have resulted in increases in migration (Altamirano 1996). Unlike other Latin American migrants who typically migrate abroad directly from rural areas, the majority of migrants come from urban areas (Paerregaard 2014). Peruvians most commonly migrate to urban areas in-country before migrating abroad. This makes internal migration to Lima a common first step to international migration. The educational levels of Peruvian migrants tends to be high in the context of Latin American migration. For example, in 2009 "53 percent of persons in the U.S. born in Peru had some college education, about the same rate as in the U.S. generally (52 percent) and much greater than among those born in Mexico (14 percent), the Dominican Republic (28 percent), Ecuador (37 percent), or Colombia (46 percent)" (Takenaka and Pren 2010, 179). One study suggests that both men and women migrants tend to be married, with singles representing less than one-fifth of all migrants (Durand 2010), while another study finds that 20 percent of Peruvian women who migrate are married at the time of migration (UNFPA 2012).

13. Over the last decade, the three most popular destinations (in order of popularity) have been the United States, Argentina, and Spain (Escriva, Santa Cruz, and Bermudez 2010). In 2007 the Peruvian population reached 120,300 in Spain and 70,800 in Italy (Takenaka, Paerregaard, and Berg 2010, 6). In Argentina (home to approximately 100,000 Peruvians) and Chile (home to approximately 62,000 Peruvians), women and men from Peru's poorer areas seek employment, and work as domestic servants is common among Peruvians (Takenaka, Paerregaard, and Berg 2010). According to a recent study, Chile is on its way to becoming the most common destination for Peruvians (UNFPA 2012).

14. In 2014 there were approximately 450,000 Peruvian immigrants in the United States. The other four South American countries with high numbers of immigrants in the United States are Colombia, Ecuador, Brazil, and Guyana (Zong and Batalova 2016).

15. Juan Velasco was president from 1968 to 1975; Alan García's presidencies were from 1985 to 1990 and 2006 to 2011; and Alberto Fujimori was president from 1990 to 2000.

16. During this period but to a lesser extent, the Movimiento Revolucionario Túpac Amaru (MRTA, the Túpac Amaru Revolutionary Movement) also played a role in the political violence and conflicts.

17. During Peru's internal conflict between the early 1980s and 2000, approximately seventy thousand people were killed. Most were indigenous and from rural areas. Additionally, the Truth and Reconciliation Commission documented over five hundred cases of rape during wartime. None of the documented cases have resulted in trials. The majority of sexual violence was perpetrated by the armed forces (Boesten 2014). Preexisting hierarchies of race, class, language, gender, and location informed soldiers' decisions about which women to rape or kill (Boesten 2014). These preexisting racial, gender, and class ideologies create a hierarchy of women largely based on broader racial-ethnic hierarchies that did not disappear with the relative end of the internal conflict, as is discussed throughout the following chapters.

18. In much of my earlier work on Peru, I focused on how gendered violence in heterosexual relationships intersects with institutional and structural violence in the lives of predominantly poor indigenous and mestiza women who migrated from other parts of the country to Lima (Alcalde 2006, 2007, 2010). In that research, which relied primarily on fieldwork and life history interviews, the themes of mobility and migration, multidimensional identities, and resistance to marginalization cross-cut distinct life narratives. My interest in migration and the multidimensionality and fluidity of identities deepened as I embarked on new research on the experiences of Latin American immigrants in the United States. Continuing to develop my interests in gender, migration, and violence, as well as nonviolence, across borders, I expanded my research to include the construction and everyday practices of masculinities among Latino men in the United States (Alcalde 2011, 2014). I also regularly returned to Peru for research and for family. This book is one way to bring together

my long-standing and expanding research interests and work on gender, migration, intersectional identities, violence and exclusion, and Peru.

19. The survey results were central to developing interview questions for Peruvians in Canada, Germany, and the United States.

20. As with the interviews, the majority identified as white (58 percent) or mestizo (40 percent). Survey respondents, like interviewees, were predominantly from Lima and reported high levels of education. Peruvians who completed the survey had been living outside Peru anywhere from two to fifty years.

21. Open-ended survey questions included "What is the best thing about living outside of Peru?"; "What is the worst thing about living outside of Peru?"; "What symbols, objects, or other factors do you associate with Peruvianness?"; "What are your main reasons for returning / not returning to live in Peru?"; "What I miss most about Peru is . . ."; "Do you think your ideas about how women and men should behave have changed now that you do not live in Peru? If yes, in what ways?"

22. Neighborhoods I visited in Lima during my previous research had included those in San Juan de Lurigancho, San Juan de Miraflores, Carabayllo, Comas, Independencia, and Villa María del Triunfo. These were precisely the districts those I interviewed for this project avoided as dangerous or simply unimportant to their everyday lives when in Lima.

CHAPTER 1. PRIVILEGE, RACIALIZATION, AND EXCLUSIONARY COSMOPOLITANISM IN TRANSNATIONAL TRAJECTORIES

1. My use of the term *Othering* here draws on the work of Edward Said (1978), who underscores that the exoticization of the Other should be approached as essentialized perceptions grounded in specific cultural, social, political, and historical imaginaries; on Chandra Talpade Mohanty's (2003) critique of the Other as a homogeneous entity seen as inferior or in need of saving; and on Gayatri Chakravorty Spivak's (1988) analysis of the essentializing and disempowering forces behind Othering.

2. Return visits are also generally easier to accomplish within Peru, as is ensuring that remittances arrive at their destination.

3. There are significant differences between internal and international migration. It is also worth examining intersections among internal and international mobilities. Both internal and international migration may inform migrants' sense of belonging and exclusion and sometimes result in changes to how migrants view themselves, their position in society, and the position and value of those around them. Both, in effect, have the potential to disturb or reinforce social hierarchies and the racialized, classed, and gendered discourses that support social hierarchies and shape cosmopolitanism among middle- and upper-class transnational Peruvians.

4. For example, while international migrants make up less than 3 percent of the global population, the number of internal migrants in China alone is likely to surpass the total for international migrants globally (King and Skeldon 2010).

5. Richard King and Robert Skeldon, in their discussion of the separate treatment of internal and international migration in research, succinctly explain that "this dichotomisation seems to have been influenced by several factors, including different data sources, different disciplinary backgrounds of researchers, different analytical techniques, and different research agendas that reflect different policy concerns and funding sources" (2010, 1620).

6. Internationally, upper-class Peruvians made up the majority of emigrants until the 1950s. By the 1980s, Peruvian international migrants came from all socioeconomic classes. Yet even before the rise in accessibility of international migration, in-country mobility constituted a common strategy for family well-being and progress. Middle- and upper-class migrants tend to identify as white and mestizo and have more access to international migration, and internal migrants are more likely to be poorer and indigenous. In part because of its greater affordability, the majority of migrants move within rather than away from their country of origin (King and Skeldon 2010), and this is also the case in Peru.

7. Linguistic and cultural barriers affect both Peruvians who leave the country and those who move within Peru. In Lima, Andean migrants who speak Quechua and other indigenous languages are routinely discriminated against by local residents, potential and current employers, and state institutions. Even those who speak Spanish commonly experience discrimination because their accent, clothing, mannerisms, or behaviors are associated with indigenous rural areas by local residents. In the realm of health services, migrants settling in newer periurban settlements may have a particularly difficult time gaining access to needed resources. Outside Peru, international migrants may have difficulty gaining access to resources and employment also because of their language skills, even when they meet all legal regulations for employment. Additionally, stereotypes—including those of Latinos in the United States—can inform how local residents perceive and interact with Peruvian migrants.

8. In examining his experiences as a Haitian immigrant in the United States, Georges Fouron similarly explains that during trips to Haiti his fluid identity and experiences did not fit into the common view among his friends and family of "life in the United States as bountiful. Whenever you leave home, people think that you have money" (Glick-Schiller and Fouron 2001, 81) and that it may be challenging to explain the adjustments, changes, and forms of marginalization migrants experience transnationally.

9. There was, however, as is examined in other chapters, significant discussion and anxiety surrounding sexism and street harassment.

10. In the online survey—discussed in the introduction—I employed in part as a preliminary exploration of Peruvians' migration experiences and return migration plans, 57 percent identified as white and 39 percent as mestizo/a. Only about one-fourth opined that racism affected her or his life in Peru.

11. She does not want to relinquish her Peruvian citizenship, which is required if she acquires German citizenship—yet she has lived in Germany for well over a decade and speaks fluent German.

12. Among the white Peruvians I interviewed in Munich, none had experienced this sort of surveillance when entering or leaving the country with their German Peruvian children.

13. Chilean president Michelle Bachelet, for example, was imprisoned and tortured during Pinochet's military dictatorship. She originally left Chile in 1975 with her mother and sought refuge in Australia. Soon after, she immigrated to Berlin and studied German and medicine at Humboldt University there before returning to Chile.

14. The only time she had felt personally discriminated against was on one occasion when a store clerk made fun of her pronunciation of the items she was purchasing. In retrospect, she felt it had been absurd for her to feel offended, given her privileged status as a white, well-educated Latin American, when well-off migrants from other immigrant groups had significantly more difficult experiences.

15. Language barriers magnified experiences of downward mobility that accompanied various difficulties in attempts to have Peruvian degrees validated in Germany. Without recognition of prior educational and professional accomplishments and with limited ways of communicating, migrants could experience marginalization and exclusion on multiple levels.

16. Reflecting on his earlier behaviors and his life now, he explains that he feels more content without relying on domestic servants to do the cleaning and cooking. He and his wife find working full-time and rearing children challenging, but they also believe it is particularly important to directly teach their daughters about working together to maintain the household and to learn to do and respect different types of work.

17. This campaign received significant media attention. Domestic servants, as well as journalists, human rights activists, students, and many other NGO members, participated. One of the two main national newspapers, *La República*, headlined the story "Maids Will Enter the Beaches in Asia" (http://larepublica.pe/10-01-2007/empleadas-ingresaran-playas-de-asia).

18. Reflecting on his life in Munich, Manolo explains that initially he tried to maintain distance from Peruvians because he wanted to learn German and socialize with Germans. Based on his previous experience living abroad, he believed Peruvian communities tended to isolate themselves from the rest of society. Because he wanted to learn more about the world outside Peru, he also decided to travel to other places during vacations instead of returning to Peru during his first seven years abroad.

19. Anthony is additionally frustrated because, having striven to distance himself from his past in the Peruvian highlands through his migration to the United States, a cousin's unexpected visit from Peru threatens to bring Peru back to him. He believed his cousin needed to become "more white and less *cholo*" (*The Peruvian Notebooks*, 179) yet could not find a way to explain this to the newly arrived cousin.

CHAPTER 2. GENDERING RETURN

1. Neoclassical approaches to migration emphasize wage differentials between sending and receiving countries and present return migration as the result of an individual's failed migration experience. Structural approaches emphasize the situ-

ational and contextual issues that must also be considered to understand individual or familial decision to return. Transnational and social network approaches emphasize an individual's linkages to multiple locations as a way to understand the experience of migration and return migration. Small-scale qualitative approaches underscore the complex ways in which migrants negotiate belonging upon returning to their community of origin (De Bree, Davids, and de Haas 2010). Rather than focus on return migration theories or types, I am interested here in examining the intersection of migrants' multiple identities as these inform decisions to return or not return permanently and as these impact everyday life for those who return.

2. Based on interviews with men from the middle and lower classes, Norma Fuller (2002) further identifies three different configurations of masculinity in the Peruvian context: the natural, the domestic, and the outside or public. Natural masculinity refers to men's genitalia, (hetero)sexuality, and physical strength, all three of which are understood by men and women as innate and foundational to being a man. The domestic construction of masculinity prioritizes family, marriage, and fatherhood. The outside or public form of masculinity emphasizes men's activities in the world outside the home and is associated with virility, politics, competition, rivalry, and seduction. Men may identify with different forms of masculinity at different stages of their life.

3. Whereas immigration laws and the legal immigration status of women I interviewed in Canada and the United States made it possible for those women to seek employment, for Peruvian women who migrated to Germany with their German spouse the situation was significantly different.

4. As of January 2016, the German government's *Kindergeld* (allowance for children) consisted of monthly benefits of between 190 and 221 euros per child. Families are eligible to receive *Kindergeld* until the child is eighteen years old. Parents also qualify for *Elterngeld* for the first twelve to fourteen months of a child's life. The *Elterngeld* can be a maximum of 1,800 euros per month or 67 percent of the parent's income before the child's birth.

CHAPTER 3. GENDERING EVERYDAY VIOLENCE AND *SEGURIDAD* ACROSS SPACES

1. Manolo's concerns about security for his children were also echoed in the concerns expressed by Peruvians elsewhere who completed the online survey.

2. This quote is from the "About" section of the Markham College website, accessed in January 2016, http://www.markham.edu.pe/about.cfm.

3. María José had only recently legalized her immigration status, which allowed her to return to Peru and then to the United States without fear of deportation. Since the family overstayed their tourist visa, they lived in the United States for many years as undocumented immigrants.

4. For some women, the challenges and dangers they associated with driving in Lima were so great that they decided to avoid driving and relied on taxis or their spouses instead.

5. Estudio del IOP PUCP, en coordinación con el "Observatorio Virtual de Acoso Sexual Callejero," http://www.scribd.com/doc/129336700/Boletin-Acoso-Sexual-Callejero-IOP-Marzo-2013-OK.

6. "Sílbale a tu madre," or "Catcall Your Mother," had received over six million views by December 2015. It is available at https://www.youtube.com/watch?v=RDpaX_KhWSk.

7. Facebook posts and newspaper coverage of the march showed diverse organizations and groups of people from all over the country participating. Some of the newspaper coverage included articles in *El Comercio* (http://elcomercio.pe/sociedad/lima/niunamenos-todo-lo-que-necesitas-saber-sobre-marcha-manana-noticia-1923768), *RPP Noticias* (http://rpp.pe/politica/actualidad/ni-una-menos-sigue-en-vivo-la-marcha-que-se-realizara-en-lima-noticia-986942), and the *Guardian* (https://www.theguardian.com/global-development/2016/aug/13/women-peru-protest-rising-tide-murder-sexual-crime).

CHAPTER 4. HETERONORMATIVITY, HOMOPHOBIA, AND HOME

1. Cabanillas argued that homosexuality tainted the police's image and honor as a way to discipline and penalize those suspected of homosexual behaviors. In addition to prohibiting any gay or lesbian Peruvians from joining the police force, the bill stated that those identified as homosexual and already in the police force could be expelled.

2. In 1973 the American Psychiatric Association and in 1990 the World Health Organization stopped categorizing homosexuality as a pathology.

3. These countries are Argentina, Brazil, Colombia, Chile, Ecuador, and Uruguay.

4. Murders of transpeople are similarly underreported. On May 31, 2016, a fourteen-year-old transgirl was murdered in Trujillo. As in other murders of transpeople, the motivation appeared to be her gender identity. See http://sinetiquetas.org/2016/05/31/peru-asesinan-a-una-chica-trans-de-4-balazos-en-trujillo/.

5. The full text of the "Plan nacional contra la violencia hacia la mujer 2009–2015" is available at http://www.unfpa.org.pe/mgenero/PDF/MIMDES-PNCVM-2009-2015.pdf.

6. In April 2014 the president of MHOL I interviewed resigned. It is not clear from available literature if the organization's position on political asylum cases has changed since then.

7. A *serenazgo* is a municipal-level security officer whose specific duties may vary by district in Lima. In general, *serenazgos* monitor compliance with safety and districtwide regulations and ordinances, provide citizens with information, and may assist in redirecting traffic.

8. The video, as published by the news journal *Peru21*, is available at http://peru21.pe/actualidad/miraflores-serenazgo-hostigo-pareja-gay-besarse-parque-amor-video-2232644.

9. One of the men was a university student and MHOL activist at the time.

10. In practice, the clinic should have been using a generic form introduced in 2012, which no longer included homosexuality as a high risk behavior for blood donors (*El Comercio* 2015b).

11. The website for the project NoTengoMiedo is http://www.notengomiedo.pe/.

12. This story, as shared publicly on the NoTengoMiedo website, is available at http://www.notengomiedo.pe/alba-paula-aguero.

13. At the time of the interview, Bárbara was in a same-sex relationship.

14. Homonegativity refers to the negative attitudinal and behavioral reactions to homosexuality.

CHAPTER 5. THE TASTE OF HOME

1. Ceviche is raw fish cured in lime juice, typically served with onions, spicy rocoto pepper, corn, and sweet potato. *Lomo saltado* is a sliced beef, onions, and sliced potatoes dish served with rice. *Ají de gallina* is a creamy chicken stew also served with rice. *Causa rellena* is a mashed-potato dish served cold, usually in layers, and *papas a la huancaína* are potatoes in a rich, creamy sauce, typically served with black olives and hard-boiled egg.

2. I can now also buy an *aji amarillo* sauce at our local Kroger's and even *pisco* for *pisco* sours at Trader Joe's. I can also buy a candy bar similar to my childhood favorite, Sublime, in my town, yet this usually does not make the conflict over who gets to eat the last Sublime bought in Peru in my house any easier. I am not alone in relishing the fact that these Peruvian foods have reached so many global and local markets and are accessible to many Peruvians worldwide.

3. Respondents could include as many items as they wished in the open text box for the survey question. Other less frequent answers included "the beach / the ocean" (mentioned by eleven people); "music" (mentioned by six people); "what I had gained professionally / in professional status" (mentioned by two people), which points to the possibility of professional downward mobility in those cases; "people's warmth" (la calidez de la gente) (mentioned by two people); "my neighborhood" (mentioned by two people); and "my own house" (mentioned by one person), which may also point to economic downward mobility as a result of migration.

4. The only other item that came close to being mentioned as many times was friends, mentioned twenty-seven times.

5. This process whereby products and dishes of the Andes and Amazon that were historically undervalued by the upper classes are taken from their origins to benefit coastal, white-mestizo elites who more easily cross national borders can be understood as a form of "cultural food colonialism" (Heldke 2003). This form of colonialism is akin to the conquering attitudes of earlier Europeans who "discovered" and translated so-called exotic items, peoples, and behaviors for markets and tastes of self-identified cosmopolitan Europeans at the time. For Lisa Heldke, it refers to the common appropriation of and attraction to cuisines deemed exotic by middle- and upper-class, often white, individuals. The foods considered exotic are typically

from formerly colonized populations in the Global South. In this sense, then, the exclusionary cosmopolitanism discussed in previous chapters is present here too in the tension between relying on and being open to important resources associated with Peruvian identities historically viewed as backward and excluding those same forms of Peruvianness from realms of belonging. In the case of gastronomy, undervalued preparations of certain ingredients may be excluded, while techniques and presentations that appeal to more privileged groups may be included in representations of Peru to consumers within and beyond Peru.

6. To better understand the gendered hierarchies on which Peruvian gastronomy thrives transnationally, it is useful to at least briefly examine and refer to the gendered workings of the culinary world. Women play important roles in Peruvian cuisine, yet there are very few women executive chefs. I am not aware of any scholarly publications on the gendering of professional kitchens in Peru. Deborah Harris and Patti Giuffre (2010, 2015) have done research on this phenomenon in the United States, and their general findings can enhance our understanding of the role of gender in the global culinary world and in Peru. Their work underscores that women are still viewed as curiosities in the male-dominated culinary world and are much less likely to reach the highest ranks in the professional kitchen. Women are less likely than men to be promoted to executive chef, the highest position and one that encompasses management of the kitchen and staff and creative control over dishes. In the United States in 2013 in the culinary industry, only 20 percent of chefs and head cooks were women; the percentage of women in the culinary industry was only higher in the pastry department (Harris and Giuffre 2015). Among the top fifteen U.S. restaurant groups, women held just 6 percent of executive chef positions (Harris and Giuffre 2015, 3). Interviews with women chefs pointed to difficulties in balancing a career as a chef with responsibilities as primary caretaker of children (Harris and Giuffre 2010). Harris and Giuffre (2015) also underscore that within the masculinized space of the professional kitchen, sexualized banter is commonly employed by members of the kitchen team as a way of earning acceptance, making these spaces particularly challenging for women.

Within this context of gendered dynamics and inequality within the culinary world, in a 2015 interview Peruvian chef Virgilio Martínez was asked if he believed Peru "will be the breakthrough country to have a female chef at the forefront." According to Martínez, who replied that he hoped this would be the case for Peru, women chefs "can work as well and sometimes better than men," but they tend to seek less attention, including media attention, than male chefs. Those without access to the prestigious, and expensive, culinary schools attended by Peru's most well known chefs, however, may also find they do not share the widely applauded (by the media and others) characteristics of those chefs and even question their own inclusion in the same category as those chefs.

Teresa Izquierdo, an Afro-Peruvian woman from Lima from a working-class background, is nationally renowned for her cooking and made a name for herself before the gastronomic boom and Peruvian cuisine went global. Explaining that she does not consider herself a chef even if others refer to her as one, she stated, "I am a cook. Of whatever level you want, but I am not a chef. I put a hat on and I'm a chef? No, sir. We have to recognize everything those persons [who are chefs] have studied. And, that, one should respect" (Algunos grandes chefs peruanos 2017). In this case, the privileged status of the urban white-mestizo elite and access to foreign culinary schools are evident and emphasized as factors to be recognized and respected by others. If it is primarily elite men who are recognized as representing Peruvianness transnationally as chefs, however, those Peruvians who do not fit the profile can more easily be made invisible in the representation of Peruvianness.

As in the U.S. culinary world, it is only in the pastry department that we tend to find a higher percentage of women in positions of power. Two of these Peruvian pastry chefs are Astrid Gutsche and María José Jordan. Astrid Gutsche is head pastry chef at the Lima restaurant Astrid y Gastón, which is consistently included in Latin America's fifty best restaurants list and was the top restaurant on that list most recently in 2014. Born in Germany and having lived in Peru for almost twenty years, she is well known for her desserts. She is also married to celebrity chef Gastón Acurio, whom she met in culinary school in Paris, where she trained as both a chef and a pastry chef. In discussing her work with London Chocolovers in 2015, she explains, "I've had to pull back more because of my family, but that's fine. Gastón can have the limelight" (London Chocolovers 2015). These experiences reflect the challenges for women of balancing both caring for small children and working as a chef, underscored by Harris and Giuffre (2015), as well as the media attention given to, or sought by, male chefs in comparison to women chefs. In 2015 María José Jordan, the twenty-four-year-old pastry chef at the highly ranked Amaz restaurant, was selected as the best young chef in Latin America and the Caribbean and competed in the S.Pellegrino Young Chef International Competition. Before starting her work at Amaz, she had trained in Peru, Canada, and the United States, as is the common trajectory of prominent chefs central to the gastronomic boom. In these cases, migration as middle or upper class facilitates success in the culinary world and provides spaces in which to represent specific constructions of Peruvianness.

7. Introduced into the Peruvian market in 1935, today Inca Kola holds the honor of being the only national cola to outsell Coca-Cola in its own territory. This did not change even after 1999, when Coca-Cola bought half of the Inca Kola Corporation and approximately one-third of the parent company, the José R. Lindley Corporation. In spite of Inca Kola's venture with Coca-Cola, the drink's advertisements continued to assert Inca Kola's national flavor.

8. The connections between Inca Kola and Peruvianness have become so common that one Peruvian described the sense of identity of Peruvians living in Japan as "outside we are a bottle of sake and inside us there is Inca Kola" (Takenaka 1997, 94).

9. The commercials discussed here, from Alcalde (2009), appeared in 2005 and 2006 and are available at http://www.incakola.com. pe/spottv.htm and http://www.edimovie.net/demos/incakola/spots.html.

10. This text comes from the restaurant's website, visited in November 2015 and available at http://www.tantachicago.com/.

11. This news was widely reported. Only 16 percent reported that they did not know who he was. Available at http://rpp.pe/politica/actualidad/un-23-votaria-por-gaston-acurio-si-postula-a-la-presidencia-segun-sondeo-noticia-670152.

12. Full text and short biography available at http://www.amaz.com.pe/pedromiguel.php.

13. In July 2015 Claudio Pizarro announced he would be leaving Bayern Munich.

14. In the United States, Peruvian *papa amarilla* is commonly substituted with Yukon gold potato in Peruvian dishes.

15. The success of the gastronomic boom has been accompanied by the opening of more restaurants, broader distribution of Peruvian products, and media attention to Peru as a culinary destination. It has also made access to Peruvian food easier for many Peruvians outside of Peru even as some Peruvian restaurants cater specifically to the more affluent middle- and upper-class Peruvians and their global counterparts.

16. For those unfamiliar with particular cuisines, the position of a dish in a restaurant menu consistently lets customers know at what point in the meal it should be consumed so that even when something appears exotic, the menu provides a familiar meal structure for its consumption (Gvion and Trostler 2008).

CONCLUSION

1. On the first day of 2017, a headline in *La República*, a popular newspaper, announced that "in Lima more than 30% of household workers are still in a position of semi-slavery." In the article, the secretary general of the Household Workers' Labor Union of the Lima Region (SINTTRAHOL) explained that, like other household workers from rural areas, she had been discriminated against, exploited, given inferior and smaller quantities of food than the family for which she worked, and forced to use a uniform to be marked as a servant in public areas.

2. In August 2017 a federal judge ruled that the ban had been unconstitutional, noting that it was based on racism and on discriminatory practices to gain political favor.

BIBLIOGRAPHY

Agadjanian, Victor, Evgina Gorina, and Cecilia Menjivar. 2014. "Economic Incorporation, Civil Inclusion, and Social Ties: Plans to Return Home among Central Asian Migrant Women in Moscow, Russia." *International Migration Review* 48 (3): 577–603.

Ahmed, Sara. 2004. *The Cultural Politics of Emotion*. New York: Routledge.

Ahmed, Sara, Claudia Castañeda, Anne-Marie Fortier, and Mimi Sheller, eds. 2003. *Uprootings/Regroundings: Questions of Home and Migration*. Oxford: Berg.

Alcalde, M. Cristina. 2006. "The Roles of Migration and Class in Women's Attempts to Escape Violence in Lima, Peru." *Latin American Perspectives* 33 (6): 147–164.

———. 2007. "'Why Would You Marry a Serrana?': Women's Experiences of Identity-Based Violence in the Intimacy of Their Homes in Lima." *Journal of Latin American and Caribbean Anthropology* 12 (1): 1–24.

———. 2009. "Between Incas and Indians: Inca Kola and Race in the Construction of a Peruvian-Global Modernity." *Journal of Consumer Culture* 9 (31): 31–54.

———. 2010. *The Woman in the Violence: Gender, Poverty, and Resistance in Peru*. Nashville: Vanderbilt University Press.

———. 2011. "Masculinities in Motion: Latino Men and Violence in Kentucky." *Men and Masculinities* 14 (4): 450–469.

———. 2014. "An Intersectional Approach to Latino Anti-violence Engagement." *Culture, Society & Masculinities* 6 (1): 35–51.

———. 2015. "Transformative Journeys: The Impact of First-Time Motherhood on Mexican Women's Migration Experiences in the U.S. South." *Chicana/Latina Studies* 14 (2): 64–101.

———. 2016. "Racializing Undocumented Immigrants in the Age of Colorblindness: Millennials' Views from Kentucky." *Latino Studies* 14 (2): 234–257.

Algunos grandes chefs peruanos. 2017. "Teresa Izquierdo." Blog. http://comidaperuana.about.com/od/Chefsperuanos/tp/Algunos-Grandes-Chefs-Peruanos.htm.

Allport, Gordon. 1954. *The Nature of Prejudice*. Reading: Addison-Wesley.

Altamirano, Teófilo. 1996. *Migración el fenómeno del siglo: Peruanos en Europa, Japón y Australia*. Lima: Fondo Editorial Pontificia Universidad Católica del Perú.

———. 2000. "Los peruanos en el exterior y su revinculación con el Perú: Comunidades peruanas en el exterior; situación y perspectivas." http://www4.congreso.gob.pe/historico/cip/materiales/imigra/Peruanos_exterior_revinculacion.pdf.

———. 2010. *Migration, Remittances and Development in Times of Crisis*. Lima: UNFPA.

Amit, Vered. 2007. "Structures and Dispositions of Travel and Movement." In *Going First Class? New Approaches to Privileged Travel and Movement*, edited by Vered Amit, 1–14. New York: Berghahn Books.

Amnesty International. 1997. *Breaking the Silence: Human Rights Violations Based on Sexual Orientation*. London: Amnesty International.

Anderson, Benedict. 1999. *Imagined Communities*. London: Verso.

Anderson, Jeanine. 2007. "Economías del cuidado colapsadas: ¿A quien le tendría que preocupar?" In *Nuevas migraciones latinoamericanas a Europa: Balances y desafíos*, edited by Isabel Yepez del Catillo and Gioconda Herrera, 507–530. Quito: FLACSO.

Andits, Petra. 2015. "Rethinking Home, Belonging, and the Potentials of Transnationalism: Australian Hungarians after the Fall of the Berlin Wall." *Ethos* 43 (4): 313–331.

Anthias, Floya. 2013. "Hierarchies of Social Location, Class and Intersectionality: Towards a Translocational Frame." *International Sociology* 28 (1): 121–138.

Antiporta, Daniel, Liam Smeeth, Robert H. Gilman, and J. Jaime Miranda. 2015. "Length of Urban Residence and Obesity among Within-Country Rural-to-Urban Andean Migrants." *Public Health Nutrition* 19 (7): 1270–1278.

Anzaldúa, Gloria. 1987. *Borderlands / La Frontera: The New Mestiza*. San Francisco: Spinsters / Aunt Lute.

Appadurai, Arjun. 1996. *Modernity at Large: Cultural Dimensions of Globalization*. Minneapolis: University of Minnesota Press.

Appiah, Kwame Anthony. 1996. "Cosmopolitan Patriots." In *For Love of Country: Debating the Limits of Patriotism*, edited by M. C. Nussbaum and J. Cohen, 21–29. Boston: Beacon Press.

———. 2007. *Cosmopolitanism: Ethics in a World of Strangers*. New York: W. W. Norton & Company.

Arana, Marie. 2002. *American Chica: Two Worlds, One Childhood*. Toronto: Dial Press.

———. 2010. *Lima Nights: A Novel*. Toronto: Dial Press.

Arguelles, Lourdes, and Anne M. Rivero. 1993. "Gender / Sexual Orientation Violence and Transnational Migration: Conversations with Some Latinas We Think We Know." *Urban Anthropology* 22 (3/4): 259–275.

Armony, Martha Barriga, and Daniel Schugurensky. 2004. "Citizenship Learning and Political Participation: The Experience Of Latin American Immigrants in Canada." *Canadian Journal of Latin American and Caribbean Studies* 29 (57): 17–38.

Babb, Florence. 1998. *Between Field and Cooking Pot: The Political Economy of Marketwomen in Peru*. Austin: University of Texas Press.

———. 2011. *The Tourism Encounter: Fashioning Latin American Nations and Histories*. Stanford, CA: Stanford University Press.
Bahkru, Tanya. 2008. "Negotiating and Navigating the Rough Terrain of Transnational Feminist Research." *Journal of International Women's Studies* 10 (2): 198–216.
Berg, Rigmor, Heather M. Munthe-Kaas, and Michael W. Ross. 2016. "Internalized Homonegativity: A Systematic Mapping Review of Empirical Research." *Journal of Homosexuality* 63 (4): 541–558.
Berg, Ulla. 2010. "El Quinto Suyo: Contemporary Nation-Building and the Political Economy of Emigration in Peru." *Latin American Perspectives* 37 (5): 121–136.
———. 2015. *Mobile Selves: Race, Migration, and Belonging in Peru and the U.S.* New York: New York University Press.
Biao, Xiang, Brenda S. A. Yeoh, and Mika Toyota, eds. 2013. *Return: Nationalizing Transnational Mobility in Asia*. Durham, NC: Duke University Press.
Blackwell, Maylei. 2016. *Chicana Power! Contested Histories of Feminism in the Chicano Movement*. Austin: University of Texas Press.
Boehm, Deborah. 2012. *Intimate Migrations: Gender, Family, Illegality among Transnational Mexicans*. New York: New York University Press.
———. 2016. *Returned: Going and Coming in an Age of Deportation*. Berkeley: University of California Press.
Boellstorff, Tom. 2004. "The Emergence of Political Homophobia in Indonesia: Masculinity and National Belonging." *Ethnos* 69 (4): 465–486.
Boesten, Jelke. 2010. *Intersecting Inequalities: Women and Social Policy in Peru, 1990–2000*. Philadelphia: Penn State University Press.
———. 2012. "The State and Violence against Women in Peru." *Social Politics* 19 (3): 361–383.
———. 2014. *Sexual Violence during War and Peace: Gender, Power, and Post-conflict Justice in Peru*. New York: Palgrave Macmillan.
Bonnerjee, Jayani. 2013. "Invisible Belonging: Anglo-Indian Identity in Multicultural Toronto." *Journal of Intercultural Studies* 34 (4): 431–442.
Bracamonte, Jorge. 2010. "Self-Portrait." In *Urgency Required: Gay and Lesbian Rights Are Human Rights*, edited by Ireen Dubel and André Hielkema, 215–217. The Netherlands: HIVOS.
Brah, Avtar. 1996. *Cartographies of Diaspora: Contesting Identities*. New York: Routledge.
Brain, Kelsey. 2014. "The Transnational Networks of Cultural Commodities: Peruvian Food in San Francisco." *Yearbook of the Association of Pacific Coast Geographers* 76:82–101.
Bruce, Jorge. 2007. *Nos habíamos choleado tanto: Psicoanálisis y racismo*. Lima: Universidad de San Martín de Porres.
Bueno-Hansen, Pascha. 2015. *Feminist and Human Rights Struggles in Peru: Decolonizing Transitional Justice*. Chicago: University of Chicago Press.
Cáceres, Carlos, Marcos Cueto, and Nancy Palomino. 2008. "Sexual and Reproductive Rights Policies in Peru: Unveiling False Paradoxes." In *SexPolitics: Reports*

from the Frontlines, Sexuality Policy Watch, edited by Richard Parker, Rosalind Petchesky, and Robert Sember, 127–166. http://www.sxpolitics.org/frontlines/home/index.php.

Cáceres, Carlos, Victor Talavera, and Rafael Mazín Reynoso. 2013. "Diversidad sexual, salud, y ciudadanía." *Revista peruana de medicina experimental y salúd pública* 30 (4): 698–704.

Cacho, Lisa Marie. 2012. *Social Death: Racialized Rightlessness and the Criminalization of the Unprotected*. New York: New York University Press.

Caldeira, Teresa. 1996. "Building Up Walls: The New Pattern of Spatial Segregation in São Paulo." *International Social Science Journal* 147: 559–572.

———. 2001. *City of Walls: Crime, Segregation, and Citizenship in São Paulo*. Berkeley: University of California Press.

Calhoun, Craig. 2002. "The Class Consciousness of Frequent Travellers: Towards a Critique of Actually Existing Cosmopolitanism." In *Conceiving Cosmopolitanism—Theory, Context, Practice*, edited by S. Vertovec and R. Cohen, 86–109. Oxford: Oxford University Press.

———. 2008. "Cosmopolitanism in the Modern Social Imaginary." *Daedalus* 137 (3): 105–114.

Callirgos, Juan Carlos. 1993. *El racismo: La cuestión del otro (y de uno)*. Lima: Desco.

Calvo, Manuel. 1982. "Migration et alimentation." *Social Science Information* 21: 383–446.

Canépa, Gisela. 2013. "Nation Branding: The Re-foundation of Community, Citizenship and the State in the Contexts of Neoliberalism in Perú." *Medien Journal* 37 (3): 7–18.

Cantú, Lionel, and Eithne Luibheid, eds. 2005. *Queer Migrations: Sexuality, U.S. Citizenship, and Border Crossings*. Minneapolis: University of Minnesota Press.

Cantú, Lionel, Nancy Naples, and S. Vidal-Ortiz. 2009. *The Sexuality of Migration*. New York: New York University Press.

Carassai, Sebastián. 2014. *The Argentine Silent Majority: Middle-Classes, Politics, Violence, and Memory in the Seventies*. Durham, NC: Duke University Press.

Carling, Jorgen, and Marta Bivand Erdal. 2014. "Return Migration and Transnationalism: How Are the Two Connected?" *International Migration* 52 (6): 1–11.

Carrasco, L. N. 2010. "Transnational Family Life among Peruvian Migrants in Chile: Multiple Commitments and the Role of Social Remittances." *Journal of Comparative Family Studies* 41 (2): 187–204.

Chakravarty, Debjani, and Elena Frank. 2013. "Abstracting Academic Feminist Aspirations: What Do Doctoral Dissertation Abstracts (1995–2010) Say about an Emergent Interdisciplinary Field?" *Feminist Formations* 25 (3): 57–78.

Chang, Grace. 2000. *Disposable Domestics: Immigrant Women Workers in the Global Economy*. Boston: South End Press.

Chavez, Leo. 2008. *The Latino Threat: Constructing Immigrants, Citizens, and the Nation*. Stanford, CA: Stanford University Press.

Cisneros, J. David. 2013. "The Son of a Black Man from Kenya and a White Woman from Kansas: Immigration and Racial Neoliberalism in the Age of Obama." In *American Identity in the Age of Obama*, edited by A. Barreto and R. O'Bryant, 70–99. New York: Routledge.

Coles, Anne, and Anne-Marie Fechter. 2008. *Gender and Family among Transnational Professionals*. New York: Routledge.

Collins, Dana. 2012. "Performing Location and Dignity in a Transnational Feminist and Queer Study of Manila's Gay Life." *Feminist Formations* 24 (1): 49–72.

Collins, Patricia Hill. 1998. *Fighting Words: Black Women and the Search for Justice*. Minneapolis: University of Minnesota Press.

Constable, Nicole. 1997. *Maid to Order in Hong Kong: Stories of Filipina Workers*. Ithaca, NY: Cornell University Press.

———. 1999. "At Home but Not at Home: Filipina Narratives of Ambivalent Returns." *Cultural Anthropology* 14 (2): 203–228.

Contreras, Ricardo, and David Griffith. 2012. "Managing Migration, Managing Motherhood: The Moral Economy of Gendered Migration." *International Migration* 50 (4): 51–66.

Conway, Dennis. 2005. "Transnationalism and Return: 'Home' as an Enduring Fixture and 'Anchor.'" In *Experiences of Return: Caribbean Perspectives*, edited by Robert Potter, Dennis Conway, and Joan Phillips, 263–283. London: Ashgate.

Conway, Dennis, and Robert Potter. 2009. *Return Migration of the Next Generations: 21st Century Transnational Mobility*. Burlington, VT: Ashgate.

Costa, Gino, and Rachel Neild. 2007. "La reforma policial en Perú." *Revista latinoamericana de seguridad ciudadana* 2:112–126.

Crenshaw, Kimberlé. 1991. "Mapping the Margins: Intersectionality, Identity Politics, and Violence against Women of Color." *Stanford Law Review* 43 (6): 1241–1299.

Cuevas, Elder. 2016. "Marca Perú: ¿Una nación en construcción?" *Contratexto* 25:95–120.

Davis, Kathy, and Lorraine Nencel. 2011. "Border Skirmishes and the Question of Belonging: An Authoethnographic Account of Everyday Exclusion in Multicultural Society." *Ethnicities* 11 (4): 467–488.

De Bree, June, Tine Davids, and Hein de Haas. 2010. "Post-return Experiences and Transnational Belonging of Return Migrants: A Dutch-Moroccan Case Study." *Global Networks* 10 (4): 489–509.

Decena, Carlos Ulises. 2011. *Tacit Subjects: Belonging and Same-Sex Desire among Dominican Immigrant Men*. Durham, NC: Duke University Press.

De la Cadena, Marisol. 1998. "Silent Racism and Intellectual Superiority in Peru." *Bulletin of Latin American Research* 17 (2): 143–164.

———. 2000. *Indigenous Mestizos: The Politics of Race and Culture in Cuzco, Peru*. Durham, NC: Duke University Press.

Dickey, Sarah. 2000. "Permeable Homes: Domestic Service, Household Space, and the Vulnerability of Class Boundaries in Urban India." *American Ethnologist* 27 (2): 462–469.

Dinzey-Flores, Zaire Zenit. 2013. "Communities for the Rich and Poor." *Contexts* 12 (4): 24–29.

Domingo, Andreu, Albert Sabater, and Richard Verdugo, eds. 2015. *Demographic Analysis of Latin American Immigrants in Spain: From Boom to Bust*. New York: Springer.

Dreby, Joanna. 2006. "Honor and Virtue: Mexican Parenting in the Transnational Context." *Gender & Society* 20:32–59.

Dreby, Joanna, and Leah Schmalzbauer. 2013. "The Relational Contexts of Migration: Mexican Women in New Destination Sites." *Sociological Forum* 28 (1): 1–26.

Durand, Jorge. 2010. "The Peruvian Diaspora: Portrait of a Migratory Process." *Latin American Perspectives* 37 (5): 12–28.

Ehrenreich, Barbara, and Arlie Russell Hochschild, eds. 2003. *Global Woman: Nannies, Maids, and Sex Workers in the New Economy*. New York: Metropolitan Books.

El Comercio. 2012. "Gustavo Rodríguez: 'Es una exageración decir que mi libro habla sobre el boom gastronómico en el Perú.'" 7 February, http://elcomercio.pe/luces/arte/polemica-comida-peruana-gustavo-rodriguez-preocupado-su-libro-noticia-1371088?ref=flujo_tags_345765&ft=nota_1&e=titulo.

———. 2015a. "Cercado de Lima y 26 distritos no sancionan discriminación." 24 October, http://elcomercio.pe/lima/sucesos/cercado-lima-y-26-distritos-no-sancionan-discriminacion-noticia-1850547.

———. 2015b. "Mujer no pudo donar sangre por ser lesbiana: Esto dice la ley." 8 July, http://elcomercio.pe/lima/ciudad/mujer-no-pudo-donar-sangre-lesbiana-esto-dice-ley-noticia-1824317.

———. 2015c. "Unión civil fue archivada definitivamente por este Congreso." 14 April, http://elcomercio.pe/politica/congreso/union-civil-fue-archivada-definitivamente-este-congreso-noticia-1804160.

———. 2017. "Aparece nuevo audio de pastor con discurso homofóbico." 3 May, http://elcomercio.pe/sociedad/lima/aparece-nuevo-audio-pastor-discurso-homofobico-noticia-1988457.

Erel, Umut. 2002. "Reconceptualizing Motherhood: Experiences of Migrant Women from Turkey Living in Germany." In *The Transnational Family: New European Frontiers and Global Networks*, edited by Deborah Bryceson and Ulla Vuorela, 127–146. Oxford: Berg.

———. 2011. "Complex Belongings: Racialization and Migration in a Small English City." *Ethnic and Racial Studies* 34 (2): 2048–2068.

Escrivá, Angeles, Ursula Santa Cruz, and Anastasia Bermúdez. 2010. "Migration, Gender, and Politics: The 2006 Peruvian Elections Abroad." *Latin American Perspectives* 37 (5): 106–120.

Esses, Victoria, Stelian Medianu, and Andrea Lawson. 2013. "Uncertainty, Threat, and the Role of the Media in Promoting the Dehumanization of Immigrants and Refugees." *Journal of Social Issues* 69 (3): 518–536.

Ewig, Christina. 2010. *Second-Wave Neoliberalism Gender, Race, and Health Sector Reform in Peru*. University Park: Penn State University Press.

Falcón, Sylvanna M. 2016. *Power Interrupted: Antiracist and Feminist Activism inside the United Nations*. Seattle: University of Washington Press.

Fallov, Mia Arp, Anja Jorgensen, and Lisbeth Knudsen. 2013. "Mobile Forms of Belonging." *Mobilities* 8 (4): 467–486.

Farahani, Fataneh. 2013. "Racializing Masculinities in Different Diasporic Spaces: Iranian-Born Men's Navigation of Race, Masculinities, and the Politics of Difference." In *Rethinking Transnational Men: Beyond, between, and within Nations*, edited by Jeff Hearn, Marina Blagijevic, and Katherine Harrison, 147–162. New York: Routledge.

———. 2015. "Home and Homelessness and Everything In Between: A Route from One Uncomfortable Zone to Another." *European Journal of Women's Studies* 22 (2): 241–247.

Ferguson, Priscilla Parkhurst. 2010. "Culinary Nationalism." *Gastronomica* 10 (1): 102–109.

Ferraro, Kathleen. 1996. "The Dance of Dependency: A Genealogy of Domestic Violence Discourse." *Hypatia* 11 (4): 77–91.

Ferrer, Ana, Garnett Picot, and William Craig Riddell. 2014. "New Directions in Immigration Policy: Canada's Evolving Approach to the Selection of Economic Immigrants." *International Migration Review* 48 (3): 846–867.

Fobear, Katherine. 2014. "Queering Truth Commissions." *Journal of Human Rights Practice* 6 (1): 51–68.

Foner, Nancy. 1986. "Race and Color: Jamaican Migrants in New York and London." *International Migration Review* 19:708–727.

Fortier, Anne-Marie. 2003. "Making Home: Queer Migrations and Motions of Attachment." In *Uprootings/Regroundings: Questions of Home and Migration*, edited by Sara Ahmed, Claudia Castañeda, Anne-Marie Fortier, and Mimi Sheller, 115–136. Oxford: Berg.

Francke, Marfil. 1990. "Género, clase, etnia: La trenza de la dominación." In *Tiempos de ira y amor*, edited by Carlos Ivan Degregori and Marfil Francke, 79–106. Lima: DESCO.

Fuller, Norma. 2002. "El papel de las clases medias en la producción de la identidad nacional." In *Interculturalidad política: Desafíos y posibilidades*, edited by Norma Fuller, 419–440. Lima: Pontificia Universidad Católica del Perú.

Galarza, Francisco, Liuba Kogan, and Gustavo Yamada. 2012. "Detectando discriminación racial y sexual en el mercado laboral en Lima." In *Discriminación en el Perú: Exploraciones en el estado, la empresa, y el mercado laboral*, edited by F. Galarza, 103–135. Lima: Universidad del Pacífico.

Gandolfo, Daniella. 2009. *The City at Its Limits: Taboo, Transgression, and Urban Renewal in Lima*. Chicago: University of Chicago Press.

Garcés, Alejandro. 2015. *Migración peruana en Santiago: Prácticas, espacios, y economías*. Santiago: RiL Editores.

Garcia, Maria Elena. 2005. *Making Indigenous Citizens: Identity, Development, and Multicultural Activism in Peru*. Stanford, CA: Stanford University Press.

———. 2013. "The Taste of Conquest: Colonialism, Cosmopolitics, and the Dark Side of Peru's Gastronomic Boom." *Journal of Latin American and Caribbean Anthropology* 18 (3): 505–524.

Getrich, Christina. 2013. "'Too Bad I'm Not an Obvious Citizen': The Effects of Racialized US Immigration Enforcement Practices on Second-Generation Mexican Youth." *Latino Studies* 11 (4): 462–482.

Glick-Schiller, Nina. 2015a. "Explanatory Frameworks in Transnational Migration Studies: The Missing Multi-scalar Global Perspective." *Ethnic and Racial Studies* 38 (13: 2275–2282.

———. 2015b. "Whose Cosmopolitanism? And Whose Humanity?" In *Whose Cosmopolitanism? Critical Perspectives, Relationalities, and Discontents*, edited by Nina Glick-Schiller and A. Irving, 31–33. New York: Berghahn Books.

Glick-Schiller, Nina, and Cristina Szanton Blanc. 1994. *Nations Unbound: Transnational Projects, Postcolonial Predicaments, and Deterritorialized Nation-States.* New York: Routledge.

Glick-Schiller, Nina, Tsypylma Darieva, and Sandra Gruner-Domic. 2011. "Defining Cosmopolitan Sociability in a Transnational Age: An Introduction." *Ethnic and Racial Studies* 34 (3): 399–418.

Glick-Schiller, Nina, and Georges Eugène Fouron. 2001. *Georges Woke Up Laughing: Long-Distance Nationalism and the Search for Home.* Durham, NC: Duke University Press.

Glick-Schiller, Nina, and Andrew Irving, eds. 2015. *Whose Cosmopolitanism? Critical Perspectives, Relationalities and Discontents.* New York: Berghahn Press.

Gmelch, George. 2004. "West Indian Migrants and Their Rediscovery of Barbados." In *Coming Home? Refugees, Migrants, and Those Who Stayed Behind*, edited by Lynnellyn D. Long and Ellen Oxfeld, 206–223. Philadelphia: University of Pennsylvania Press.

Golash-Boza, Tanya. 2010. "Had They Been Polite and Civilized, None of This Would Have Happened: Discourses of Race and Racism in Multicultural Lima." *Latin American and Caribbean Ethnic Studies* 5 (3): 317–330.

———. 2012. *Immigration Nation: Raids, Detentions, and Deportations in Post-9/11 America.* Boulder, CO: Paradigm Publishers.

Golte, Jurgen, and Doris León Gabriel. 2011. *Polifacéticos: Jóvenes limeños del siglo XXI.* Lima: Instituto de Estudios Peruanos.

Gopinath, Gayatri. 2005. *Impossible Desires: Queer Diasporas and South Asian Public Cultures.* Durham, NC: Duke University Press.

Greene, Shane. 2007. "Entre lo indio, lo negro, y lo incaico: The Spatial Hierarchies of Difference behind Peru's Multicultural Curtain." *Journal of Latin American and Caribbean Anthropology* 12 (2): 441–474.

Grewal, Inderpal. 1996. *Home and Harem: Nation, Gender, Empire and the Cultures of Travel.* Durham, NC: Duke University Press.

———. 2006. "'Security Moms' in the Early Twentieth-Century United States: The Gender of Security in Neoliberalism." *Women's Studies Quarterly* 34 (1–2): 25–39.

Gruner-Domic, Sandra. 2011. "Transnational Lifestyles as a New Form of Cosmopolitan Social Identification? Latin American Women in German Urban Spaces." *Ethnic and Racial Studies* 34 (3): 471–489.

Guano, Emanuela. 2004. "The Denial of Citizenship: 'Barbaric' Buenos Aires and the Middle-Class Imaginary." *City & Society* 16 (1): 69–97.

Gvion, Liora, and Naomi Trostler. 2008. "From Spaghetti and Meatballs through Hawaiian Pizza to Sushi: The Changing Nature of Ethnicity in American Restaurants." *Journal of Popular Culture* 41 (6): 950–975.

Hallett, Miranda Cady. 2012. "'Better than White Trash': Work Ethic, *Latinidad* and Whiteness in Rural Arkansas." *Latino Studies* 10 (1/2): 81–106.

Hannerz, Ulf. 1996. *Transnational Connections: Cultures, People, Places*. London: Routledge.

Hansen, Peter. 2008. "Circumcising Migration: Gendering Return Migration among Somalilanders." *Journal of Ethnic and Migration Studies* 34 (7): 1109–1125.

Harris, Deborah, and Patti Giuffre. 2010. "'The Price You Pay': How Female Professional Chefs Negotiate Work and Family." *Gender Issues* 27:27–52.

———. 2015. *Taking the Heat: Women Chefs and Gender Inequality in the Professional Kitchen*. New Brunswick, NJ: Rutgers University Press.

Hartman, Todd, Benjamin Newman, and C. Scott Bell. 2014. "Decoding Prejudice toward Hispanics: Group Cues and Public Reactions to Threatening Immigrant Behavior." *Political Behavior* 36:143–163.

Heldke, Lisa. 2003. *Exotic Appetites: Ruminations of a Food Adventurer*. New York: Routledge.

Hernández, Ana Cristina, Kellea Miller, and Irene Schneeweis. 2015. *Peru LGBTI: Landscape Analysis of Political, Economic and Social Conditions*. New York: Astraea Lesbian Foundation for Justice.

Hernández, Berenice. 2007. "¡Pues para Europa! La migración latinoamericana a Alemania—desde una mirada de género." In *Nuevas migraciones latinoamericanas a Europa: Balances y desafíos,* edited by Isabel Yépez del Castillo and Gioconda Herrera. Barcelona: OBREAL.

Hiebert, Daniel. 2002. "Cosmopolitanism at the Local Level: The Development of Transnational Neighborhoods." In *Conceiving Cosmopolitanism: Theory, Context and Practice,* edited by Steven Vertovec and Robin Cohen, 209–223. Oxford: Oxford University Press.

Hirsch, Jennifer. 1999. "En el norte la mujer manda: Gender, Generation, and Geography in a Mexican Transnational Community." *American Behavioral Scientist* 42 (9): 1332–1349.

———. 2003. *A Courtship after Marriage: Sexuality and Love in Mexican Transnational Families*. Berkeley: University of California Press.

Hitlan, Robert T., Kimberly Carrillo, Michael A. Zárate, and Shelley N. Aikman. 2007. "Attitudes toward Immigrant Groups and the September 11 Terrorist Attacks." *Peace and Conflict* 13:135–152.

Hlavka, Heather. 2014. "Normalizing Sexual Violence: Young Women Account for Harassment and Abuse." *Gender & Society* 28 (3): 337–358.

Hondagneu-Sotelo, Pierette. 2001. *Doméstica: Immigrant Workers Cleaning and Caring in the Shadows of Affluence*. Berkeley: University of California Press.

Hondagneu-Sotelo, Pierette, and Arlene Avila. 1997. "I'm Here but I'm There: The Meaning of Latina Transnational Motherhood." *Gender and Society* 11 (5): 548–571.

Hondagneu-Sotelo, Pierrette, and Ernestine Avila. 2003. "'I'm Here but I'm There': The Meanings of Latina Transnational Motherhood." In *Gender and US Immigration: Contemporary Trends*, edited by Pierrette Hondageneu-Sotelo, 317–340. Berkeley: University of California Press.

hooks, bell. 1989. *Talking Back: Thinking Feminist, Thinking Black*. New York: South End Press.

Huber, Ludwig, and Leonor Lamas. 2017. *Deconstruyendo el rombo: Consideraciones sobre la nueva clase media en el Perú*. Lima: Instituto de Estudios Peruanos.

Hurtado, Aída. 1998. "*Sitios y lenguas*: Chicanas Theorize Feminisms." *Hypatia* 13 (2): 134–161.

Hurtado, Aída, and Mrinal Sinha. 2008. More Than Men: Latino Feminist Masculinities and Intersectionality." *Sex Roles* 59 (5): 337–349.

Ibarra, María de la Luz. 2000. "Mexican Immigrant Women and the New Domestic Labor." *Human Organization* 59 (4): 452–464.

Imilan, Walter A. 2015. "Performing National Identity through Peruvian Food Migration in Santiago de Chile." *Fennia* 193: 2, 227–241.

Ivry, Tsipy. 2010. *Embodying Culture: Pregnancy in Japan and Israel*. New Brunswick, NJ: Rutgers University Press.

Jaime, Martin. 2013. *Diversidad sexual, discriminación y pobreza frente al acceso a la salud pública: Demandas de la comunidad TLGBI en Bolivia, Colombia, Ecuador y Perú*. Buenos Aires: CLACSO.

Jaramillo, Fidel, and Omar Zambrano. 2013. "La clase media en Perú: Cuantificación y evolución reciente." Technical Note IDB-TN 550. Lima: Banco Interamericano del Desarrollo.

Kanai, J. Miguel. 2014. "Whither Queer World Cities? Homo-entrepreneurialism and Beyond." *Geoforum* 56:1–5.

Khan, Shamus Rahman. 2011. *Privilege: The Making of an Adolescent Elite at St. Paul's School*. Princeton, NJ: Princeton University Press.

Khan, Shamus, and Colin Jerolmack. 2013. "Saying Meritocracy and Doing Privilege." *Sociological Quarterly* 54 (1): 9–19.

King, Richard, and Robert Skeldon. 2010. "'Mind the Gap!': Integrating Approaches to Internal and International Migration." *Journal of Ethnic and Migration Studies* 36 (10): 1619–1646.

Kitch, Sally, and Mary Margaret Fonow. 2012. "Analyzing Women's Studies Dissertations: Methodologies, Epistemologies, and Field Formation." *Signs* 38 (1): 99–126.

Kofman, Eleonore, and Parvati Raghuram. 2015. *Migration, Minorities and Citizenship: Gendered Migrations and Global Social Reproduction*. New York: Palgrave Macmillan.

Kogan, Liuba. 1998. "Relaciones de género en las familias de sectores altos en Lima." *Debates en sociología* 23/24: 191–208.

Kokotovic, Misha. 2007. *The Colonial Divide in Peruvian Narrative: Social Conflict and Transculturation.* Portland: Sussex Academic Press.

Koskela, Hille. 1999. "'Gendered Exclusions': Women's Fear of Violence and Changing Relations to Space." *Geografiska Annaler* 81B (2): 111–124.

Kuntsman, Adi. 2009. "The Currency of Victimhood in Uncanny Homes: Queer Immigrants' Claims for Home and Belonging through Anti-homophobic Organising." *Journal of Ethnic and Migration Studies* 35 (1): 133–149.

La República. 2005. "La reja de la discordia." 13 May, http://larepublica.pe/13-05-2005/la-reja-de-la-discordia.

———. 2013. "Congreso rechazó que la orientación sexual sea un agravante de discriminación." 5 July, http://elcomercio.pe/politica/gobierno/congreso-rechazo-que-orientacion-sexual-sea-agravante—discriminacion-noticia-1599663.

———. 2015a. "Clínica no permitió a una mujer donar sangre por ser lesbian." 8 July, http://larepublica.pe/sociedad/13655-clinica-no-permitio-una-mujer-donar-sangre-por-ser-lesbiana.

———. 2015b. "Habla el muro que separa a Pamplona Alta de Casuarinas." 11 October, http://larepublica.pe/impresa/sociedad/709468-habla-el-muro.

———. 2015c. "Matrimonio gay: Humala considera que 'cada país tiene su propia realidad.'" 27 June, http://larepublica.pe/politica/11139-matrimonio-gay-humala-considera-que-cada-pais-tiene-su-propia-realidad-video

———. 2017. "En Lima más del 30% de trabajadoras del hogar todavía está en una situación de semiesclavitud." 1 January, http://larepublica.pe/impresa/domingo/835623-en-lima-mas-del-30-de-trabajadoras-del-hogar-todavia-esta-en-una-situacion-de-semiesclavitud.

Laurier, Eric, and Chris Philo. 2006. "Cold Shoulders and Napkins Handed: Gestures of Responsibility." *Transactions of the Institute of British Geographers* 31:193–207.

Law, Lisa. 2001. "Home Cooking: Filipino Women and Geographies of the Senses in Hong Kong." *Ecumene* 8 (3): 264–283.

Leinaweaver, Jessaca. 2013. *Adoptive Migration: Raising Latinos in Spain.* Durham, NC: Duke University Press.

Li, Fabiana. 2015. *Unearthing Conflict: Corporate Mining, Activism, and Expertise in Peru.* Durham, NC: Duke University Press.

Local.de. 2014. "Germany's Safest and Most Dangerous Cities." June 4, http://www.thelocal.de/20140604/germanys-most-dangerous-and-safest-cities-crime-rates.

London Chocolovers. 2015. "Interview with Astrid Gutsche." https://londonchocolovers.wordpress.com/2015/02/27/astrid-gutsche-head-pastry-chef-at-astrid-y-gaston-lima-peru/.

Long, Lynnellyn D., and Ellen Oxfeld. 2004. *Coming Home? Refugees, Migrants, and Those Who Stayed Behind.* Philadelphia: University of Pennsylvania Press.

López Villanes, Noam. 2014. "Inseguridad y percepción de seguridad en Lima, Perú." *Cuadernos de investigación* 10. Lima: PUCP, Instituto de Opinión Pública.

Lu, Lingyu, and Sean Nicholson-Crotty. 2010. "Reassessing the Impact of Hispanic Stereotypes on White Americans' Immigration Preferences." *Social Science Quarterly* 91 (5): 1313–1328.

Lutz, Helma. 2011. *The New Maids: Transnational Women and the Care Economy.* London: Zed Books.

Mahler, Sarah, Mayurakshi Chaudhuri, and Vrushali Patil. 2015. "Scaling Intersectionality: Advancing Feminist Analysis of Transnational Families." *Sex Roles* 73:100–112.

Mahler, Sarah J., and Patricia R. Pessar. 2006. "Gender Matters: Ethnographers Bring Gender from the Periphery toward the Core of Migration Studies." *International Migration Review* 40:27–63.

Mallett, Shelley. 2004. "Understanding Home: A Critical Review of the Literature." *Sociological Review* 52 (1): 62–89.

Manalansan, Martin. 2003. *Global Divas*. New York: New York University Press.

———. 2006. "Queer Intersections: Sexuality and Gender in Migration Studies." *International Migration Review* 40 (1): 224–249.

Mares, Teresa. 2012. "Tracing Immigrant Identity through the Plate and the Palate." *Latino Studies* 10:334–354.

Markowitz, F., and A. H. Stefansson, eds. 2004. *Homecomings: Unsettling Paths of Return*. Lanham, MD: Lexington Books.

Marquadt, Kairos M. 2012. "Participatory Security: Citizen Security, Participation, and the Inequities of Citizenship in Urban Peru." *Bulletin of Latin American Research* 31 (2): 174–189.

Masseroni, Susana, and Susana Sauane. 2002. "Psychic and Somatic Vulnerability among Professional Women in Argentina as a Result of the Precarization of Labor Linked during the Socioeconomic Crisis." *Journal of Developing Societies* 18 (2/3): 59–80.

Mata Codesal, Diana. 2010. "Eating Abroad, Remembering (at) Home: Three Foodscapes of Ecuadorian Migration in New York, London, and Santander." *Anthropology of Food* 7: 1–14.

Matta, Raul. 2010. "'Indian' Eating in Renowned Restaurants in Lima (Peru): Elite Chefs and Birth of a Native 'Cuisine Fusion.'" *Anthropology of Food* 7:65–92.

———. 2012. "Cocinando una nación de consumidores: El Perú como marca global." *Consensus* 17 (1): 49–60.

———. 2013. "Valuing Native Eating: The Modern Roots of Peruvian Food Heritage." *Anthropology of Food* S8: 1–15.

———. 2014. "República gastronómica y país de cocineros: Comida, política, medios y una nueva idea de nación para el Perú." *Revista colombiana de antropología* 50 (2): 9–13, http://www.scielo.org.co/scielo.php?script=sci_arttext&pid=S0486-65252014000200002&lng=en&nrm=iso.

McKay, Deirdre. 2005. "Migration and the Sensuous Geographies of Re-emplacement in the Philippines." *Journal of Intercultural Studies* 26 (1/2): 75–91.

Mendoza, Zoila. 2008. *Creating Our Own: Folklore, Performance, and Identity in Cuzco, Peru*. Durham, NC: Duke University Press.

Menjívar, Cecilia. 2011. *Enduring Violence: Ladina Women's Lives in Guatemala.* Berkeley: University of California Press.
Minh-ha, Trinh T. 1989. *Woman, Native, Other: Writing Postcoloniality and Feminism.* Bloomington: Indiana University Press.
Ministerio de la Mujer y Desarollo Social. N.d. Plan nacional contra la violencia hacia la mujer 2009–2015. http://www.unfpa.org. pe/mgenero/PDF/MIMDES-PNCVM-2009-2015.pdf.
Mintz, Sidney. 1960. *Worker in the Cane: A Puerto Rican Life History.* New Haven, CT: Yale University Press.
Mohanty, Chandra Talpade. 2003. "'Under Western Eyes' Revisited: Feminist Solidarity through Anticapitalist Struggles." *Signs* 28 (2): 499–535.
Molina, Carmen Exposito. 2012. "¿Qué es eso de la interseccionalidad? Aproximación al tratamiento de la diversidad desde la perspectiva de género en España." *Investigaciones feministas* 3:203–222.
Moon, S. 2003. "Immigration and Mothering: Case Studies from Two Generations of Korean Immigrant Women." *Gender & Society* 17:840–861.
Moore, Henrietta. 2007. *The Subject of Anthropology: Gender, Symbolism Psychoanalysis.* Cambridge: Polity Press.
Mora, Claudia, and Nicola Piper. 2011. "Notions of Rights and Entitlements among Peruvian Female Workers in Chile." *Diversities* 13 (1): 5–18.
Moraga, Cherríe, and Gloria Anzaldúa. 1981. *This Bridge Called My Back: Writings by Radical Women of Color.* Watertown: Persephone Press.
Mújica, Jaris. 2011. *Violaciones sexuales en el Perú 2000–2009.* Lima: Promsex.
Muñoz, Braulio. 2006. *The Peruvian Notebooks.* Tucson: University of Arizona Press.
Murray, David A. B., ed. 2009. *Homophobias: Lust and Loathing across Time and Space.* Durham, NC: Duke University Press.
———. 2014. "The Challenge of Home for Sexual Orientation and Gendered Identity Refugees in Toronto." *Journal of Canadian Studies* 48 (1): 132–152.
Nader, Laura. 1969. "Up the Anthropologist: Perspectives Gained from Studying Up." In *Reinventing Anthropology*, edited by Dell Hymes, 284–311. New York: Pantheon.
Napolitano, Valentina. 2015. *Migrant Hearts and the Atlantic Return: Transnationalism and the Roman Catholic Church.* New York: Fordham University Press.
Nencel, Lorraine. 2010. "'Que viva la minifalda!': Secretaries, Miniskirts and Daily Practices of Sexuality in the Public Sector in Lima." *Gender, Work and Organization* 17 (1): 69–90.
Ní Laoire, Caitriona. 2008. "Complicating Host-Newcomer Dualisms: Irish Return Migrants as Home-Comers or Newcomers?" *Translocations* 4 (1): 35–50.
Nowicka, Magdalena, and Anna Cieslik. 2014. "Beyond Methodological Nationalism in Insider Research with Migrants." *Migration Studies* (2) 1: 1–15.
Nugent, David. 1994. "Building the State, Making the Nation: The Bases and Limits of State Centralization in 'Modern' Peru." *American Anthropologist* 96 (2): 333–369.
Núñez-Borja, Carmen, and Christiane Stallaert. 2013. "Mujeres andinas en Bruselas: Género y colonialidad del poder." *Anuario Americanista Europeo* 11: 31–50.

Nuñez Carrasco, Lorena. 2010. "Transnational Family Life among Peruvian Migrants in Chile: Multiple Commitments and the Role of Social Remittances." *Journal of Comparative Family Studies* 41 (2): 187–204.

Nunura, Juan, and Edgar Flores. 2001. *El empleo en el Perú: 1990–2000*. Lima: Ministerio de Trabajo y Promoción Social.

Nussbaum, Martha C. 1994. "Patriotism and Cosmopolitanism." *Boston Review* 19 (5): 3–16.

Oboler, Suzanne. 2005. "The Foreignness of Racism: Pride and Prejudice among Peru's Limeños in the 1990s." In *Neither Enemies nor Friends: Latinos, Blacks, Afro-Latinos*, edited by Anani Dzidzienyo and Suzanne Oboler, 75–100. New York: Palgrave Press.

Ocampo, Anthony. 2014. "The Gay Second Generation: Sexual Identity and Family Relations of Filipino and Latino Gay Men." *Journal of Ethnic and Migration Studies* 40 (1): 155–173.

Oeppen, C. 2013. "A Stranger at 'Home': Interactions between Transnational Return Visits and Integration for Afghan-American Professionals." *Global Networks* 13 (2): 261–278.

Ohna, Ingrid, Randi Kaarhus, and Joyce Kinabo. 2012. "No Meal without Ugali? Social Significance of Food and Consumption in a Tanzanian Village." *Culture, Agriculture, Food and Environment* 34 (1): 3–14.

OIM (Organización Internacional para las Migraciones) / INEI (Instituto Nacional de Estadísticas e Informática). 2009. *Migración internacional en las familias peruanas y perfil del peruano retornante*. Lima: OIM.

———. 2010. *Perú: Estadísticas de la emigración internacional de peruanos e inmigración de extranjeros, 1990–2009*. Lima: OIM.

———. 2012. *Perfil migratorio del Perú 2012*. Lima: OIM.

Olwig, Karen Fog. 2007. "Privileged Travelers? Migration Narratives in Families of Middle-Class Caribbean Background." In *Going First Class? New Approaches to Privileged Travel and Movement*, edited by Vered Amit, 87–102. New York: Berghahn Books.

Omi, M., and H. Winant. 2015. *Racial Formation in the United States*. New York: Routledge.

Ong, Aihwa. 1999. *Flexible Citizenship*. Durham, NC: Duke University Press.

Orlove, Benjamin. 1993. "Putting Race in Its Place: Order in Colonial and Postcolonial Peruvian Geography." *Social Research: An International Quarterly* 60 (2): 301–336.

Paerregaard, Karsten. 2008. *Peruvians Dispersed: A Global Ethnography of Migration*. Lanham, MD: Lexington Press.

———. 2014. *Return to Sender: The Moral Economy of Peru's Migrant Remittances*. Washington, DC, and Berkeley: Woodrow Wilson Center Press and University of California Press.

———. 2015. "The Resilience of Migrant Money: How Gender, Generation and Class Shape Family Remittances in Peruvian Migration." *Global Networks* 15 (4): 503–518.

Parker, David. 1997. "Discursos, identidades y la invención histórica de la clase media peruana." *Debates en sociología* 22:99–112.
Parreñas, Rhacel. 2001. *Servants of Globalization: Women, Migration, and Domestic Work*. Stanford, CA: Stanford University Press.
Partridge, Damani J. 2012. *Hypersexuality and Headscarves: Race, Sex, and Citizenship in the New Germany*. Bloomington: Indiana University Press.
Paulson, Susan. 2006. "Body, Nation, and Consubstantiation in Bolivian Ritual Meals." *American Ethnologist* 33 (4): 650–664.
Pellegrini Calderón, Alessandra. 2016. *Beyond Indigeneity: Coca Growing and the Emergence of a New Middle Class in Bolivia*. Tucson: University of Arizona Press.
Pereyra, Omar. 2015. *Contemporary Middle Class in Latin America: A Study of San Felipe*. Lanham, MD: Lexington Books.
Perez, Ramona Lee. 2014. "Las fronteras del sabor: Taste as Consciousness, Kinship, and Space in the Mexico-U.S. Borderlands." *Journal of Latin American and Caribbean Anthropology* 19 (2): 310–330.
Perreault, Samuel. 2013. "Police-Reported Crime Statistics in Canada, 2012." *Juristat* 85-002-x.
Peru21. 2015. "Miraflores: Serenazgo hostigó a pareja gay por besarse en Parque del Amor." November 21, http://peru21.pe/actualidad/miraflores-serenazgo-hostigo-pareja-gay-besarse-parque-amor-video-2232644.
Pfeffer, Carla A. 2014. "'I Don't Like Passing as a Straight Woman': Queer Negotiations of Identity and Social Group Membership." *American Journal of Sociology* 120 (1): 1–44.
Phadke, Shilpa. 2005. "'You Can Be Lonely in a Crowd': The Production of Safety in Mumbai." *Indian Journal of Gender Studies* 12 (1): 41–62.
———. 2012. "Gendered Usage of Public Spaces: A Case Study of Mumbai." In *The Fear That Stalks: Gender-Based Violence in Public Spaces*, edited by Sara Pilot and Laura Prabhu, 51–80. New Delhi: Zubaan.
———. 2013. "Unfriendly Bodies, Hostile Cities: Reflections on Loitering and Gendered Public Space." *Economic and Political Weekly* 48 (39): 50–59.
Phillips, Joan, and Robert B. Potter. 2009. "Questions of Friendship and Degrees of Transnationality among Second-Generation Return Migrants to Barbados." *Journal of Ethnic and Migration Studies* 35 (4): 669–688.
Pite, Rebekah. 2013. *Creating a Common Table in Twentieth-Century Argentina: Doña Petrona, Women, and Food*. Chapel Hill: University of North Carolina Press.
Portes, Alejandro, Luis E. Guarnizo, and Patricia Landolt. 1999. "The Study of Transnationalism: Pitfalls and Promise of an Emergent Research Field." *Ethnic and Racial Studies* 22 (2): 217–237.
Portocarrero, Gonzalo. 1993. *Racismo y mestizaje*. Lima: Sur Casa de Estudios del Socialismo.
Powell, Stephen J., and Paola A. Chavarro. 2008. "Toward a Vibrant Peruvian Middle Class: Effects of the Peru–United States Free Trade Agreement on Labor Rights, Biodiversity, and Indigenous Populations." *Florida Journal of International Law*, http://scholarship.law.ufl.edu/facultypub/127.

Pribilsky, Jason. 2007. *La Chulla Vida: Gender, Migration, and the Family in Andean Ecuador and New York City*. Syracuse, NY: Syracuse University Press.
Quijano, Aníbal. 1980. *Dominación y cultura: Lo cholo y el conflicto cultural en el Perú*. Lima: Mosca Azul Editores.
———. 2000. "Coloniality of Power, Eurocentrism and Latin America." *Nepantla* 1 (3): 533–580.
Quiroz, Alfonso. 2013. *Historia de la corrupción en el Perú*. Lima: Instituto de Estudios Peruanos e Instituto de Defensa Legal.
Radcliffe, Sarah. 1990. "Ethnicity, Patriarchy, and Incorporation into the Nation: Female Migrants as Domestic Servants in Peru." *Environment and Planning D* 8 (4): 379–393.
Radcliffe, Sarah, and Sallie Westwood. 1996. *Remaking the Nation: Place, Identity and Politics in Latin America*. New York: Routledge.
Raffaeta, Roberta, and Cameron Duff. 2013. "Putting Belonging into Place: Place Experience and Sense of Belonging among Ecuadorian Migrants in an Italian Alpine Region." *City and Society* 25 (3): 328–347.
Rahier, Jean Muteba. "Introduction: Mestizaje, Mulataje, Mestiçagem in Latin American Ideologies of National Identities." *Journal of Latin American and Caribbean Anthropology* 8 (1): 40–50.
Ralph, David, and Lynn Staeheli. 2011. "Home and Migration: Mobilities, Belongings and Identities." *Geography Compass* 5 (7): 517–530.
Ramírez-Arcos, Fernando. 2013. "Cuestionamientos a la geografía a partir del cruising entre hombres en Bogotá." *Revista latino americana de geografía e gênero* 4 (2): 134–147.
Reding, Andrew. 2010. "Sexual Orientation and Human Rights in the Americas." In *The Politics of Sexuality in Latin America*, edited by Javier Corrales and Mario Pecheny, 290–302. Pittsburgh: University of Pittsburgh Press.
Reygada, Luis. 2010. "The Construction of Latin American Inequality." In *Indelible Inequalities in Latin America: Insights from History, Politics, and Culture*, edited by P. Gootenberg and L. Reygada, 23–52. Durham, NC: Duke University Press.
Rios, Victor. 2011. *Punished: Policing the Lives of Black and Latino Boys*. New York: NYU Press.
Romero, Mary. 1992. *Maid in the USA*. New York: Routledge.
Rottenbacher de Rojas, Jan Marc. 2015. "Trato discriminatorio hacia empleadas domésticas y segregación socioespacial en balnearios de Lima." *Revista de psicología* 33 (2): 242–275.
Rottenbacher de Rojas, Jan Marc, Laura Amaya López, Karen Genna Miyahira, and Maribel Pulache Páez. 2009. "Percepción de inseguridad ciudadana y su relación con la ideología política en una muestra de habitantes de la ciudad de Lima." *Revista española de investigación criminológica* 4 (7).
Ruiz, Melvyn Arce. 2012. "Gustavo Rodríguez: "Es una exageración decir que mi libro habla sobre el boom gastronómico en el Perú.""

Rumbaut, Ruben. 2009. "Pigments of Our Imagination: On the Racialization and Racial Identities of 'Hispanics' and 'Latinos.'" In *How the U.S. Racializes Latinos: White Hegemony and Its Consequences*, edited by J. Cobas, J. Duany, and J. Feagin, 15–36. Boulder, CO: Paradigm Publishers.

Russo Garrido, Anahi. 2009. "El Ambiente According to Her: Gender, Class, Mexicanidad and the Cosmopolitan in Queer Mexico City." *NWSA Journal* 21 (3): 24–45.

Ruz, Robert. 2003. "Queer Theory and Peruvian Narrative of the 1990s: The Mass Cultural Phenomenon of Jaime Bayly." *Journal of Latin American Cultural Studies* 12 (1): 19–36.

Sabogal, Elena. 2005. "Viviendo en la sombra: The Immigration of Peruvian Professionals to South Florida." *Latino Studies* 3:113–131.

———. 2012. "Denaturalized Identities: Class-Based Perceptions of Self and Others among Latin American Immigrants in South Florida." *Latino Studies* 10 (4): 546–565.

Sabogal, Elena, and Lorena Núñez. 2010. "Sin papeles: Middle- and Working-Class Peruvians in Santiago and South Florida." *Latin American Perspectives* 37 (5): 88–105.

Sagar, Aparajita. 1997. "Homes and Postcoloniality." *Diaspora: A Journal of Transnational Studies* 6 (2): 237–251.

Said, Edward. 1978. *Orientalism*. New York: Pantheon.

Saldivar-Hull, Sonia. 2000. *Feminism on the Border: Chicana Gender Politics and Literature*. Berkeley: University of California Press.

Sanmartino, Gloria. 2010. "Peruvian Restaurants in Buenos Aires (1999–2009): From Discrimination to Adoption." *Anthropology of Food* 7: 1–35.

Santa Ana, Otto. 2013. *Juan in a Hundred: The Representation of Latinos on Network News*. Austin: University of Texas Press.

Santos, Martín. 2014. "La discriminación racial, étnica y social en el Perú: Balance crítico de la evidencia empírica reciente." *Debates en sociología* 39:5–37.

Sassen, Saskia. 1998. "The De Facto Transnationalizing of Immigration Policy." In *Challenge to the Nation-State: Immigration in Western Europe and the United States*, edited by C. Joppke, 49–85. Oxford: Oxford University Press.

Schunck, Reinhard, Katharina Reiss, and Oliver Razum. 2015. "Pathways between Perceived Discrimination and Health among Immigrants: Evidence from a Large National Panel Survey in Germany." *Ethnicity and Health* 20 (5): 493–510.

Seidman, S. 2009. *The Social Construction of Sexuality*. New York: W. W. Norton and Company.

Seligmann, Linda. 2004. *Peruvian Street Lives: Culture, Power, and Economy among Market Women of Cuzco*. Chicago: University of Chicago Press.

Serrano-Amaya, José Fernando. 2014. "Chiaroscuro: The Uses of 'Homophobia' and Homophobic Violence in Armed Conflicts and Political Transitions." PhD diss., University of Sydney, Australia.

Severson, Nicolette, Miguel Muñoz-Laboy, and Rebecca Kaufman. 2014. "'At Times, I Feel Like I'm Sinning': The Paradoxical Role of Non-lesbian, Gay, Bisexual and

Transgender-Affirming Religion in the Lives of Behaviourally Bisexual Latino Men." *Culture, Health, and Sexuality* 16 (2): 136–148.

Shakow, Mirian. 2014. *Along the Bolivian Highway: Social Mobility and Political Culture in a New Middle Class.* Philadelphia: University of Pennsylvania Press.

Sibalis, M. 2004. "Urban Space and Homosexuality: The Example of the Marais, Paris Gay Ghetto." *Urban Studies* 41 (9): 1739–1758.

Sigad, Laura, and Rivka A. Eisikovits. 2009. "Migration, Motherhood, Marriage: Cross-Cultural Adaptation of North American Immigrant Mothers in Israel." *International Migration* 47 (1): 63–99.

Silverman, Helaine. 2015. "Branding Peru: Cultural Heritage and Popular Culture in the Marketing Strategy of PromPerú." In *Encounters with Popular Pasts: Cultural Heritage and Popular Culture*, edited by Mike Robinson and Helaine Silverman, 131–148. New York: Springer.

Skeldon, Ronald. 2006. "Interlinkages between Internal and International Migration and Development in the Asian Region." *Population, Space, Place* 12:15–30.

Skornia, Anna Katharina. 2015. *Entangled Inequalities in Transnational Care Chains: Practices across Borders of Peru and Italy.* New York: Columbia University Press.

Skrbis, Zlatko, Gavin Kendall, and Ian Woodward. 2004. "Locating Cosmopolitanism: Between Humanist Ideal and Grounded Social Category." *Theory, Culture, and Society* 21 (4): 115–136.

Sokoloff, Natalie. 2008. "The Intersectional Paradigm and Alternative Visions to Stopping Domestic Violence: What Poor Women, Women of Color, and Immigrant Women Are Teaching Us about Violence in the Family." *International Journal of Sociology of the Family* 34 (2): 153–185.

Sollund, Ragnhild Aslaug. 2012. "The Essence of Food and Gender and the Embodiment of Migration." In *Transnational Migration, Gender and Rights*, edited by Liam Leonard and Ragnhild Aslaug Sollund, 77–98. Bingley, UK: Emerald Group Publishing Limited.

Spitta, Silvia. 2007. "Lima the Horrible: The Cultural Politics of Theft." *PMLA* 122 (1): 294–300.

Spivak, Gayatri Chakravorty. 1988. "Can the Subaltern Speak?" In *Marxism and the Interpretation of Culture*, edited by C. Nelson and L. Grossberg, 271–313. Basingstoke: Macmillan Education.

Stepputat, Finn. 2005. "Violence, Sovereignty, and Citizenship in Postcolonial Peru." In *Sovereign Bodies: Citizens, Migrants, and States in the Postcolonial World*, edited by Thomas Blom Hansen and Finn Stepputat, 61–81. Princeton, NJ: Princeton University Press.

Stern, Steve J. 1999. "The Tricks of Time: Colonial Legacies and Historical Sensibilities in Latin America." In *Colonial Legacies*, edited by Jeremy Adelman, 135–150. New York: Routledge.

Sulmont, David. 2005. "Encuesta nacional sobre exclusión y discriminación social." http://alertacontraelracismo.pe/wp-content/uploads/2013/01/Encuesta-nacional-sobre-exclusi%C3%B3n-y-discriminaci%C3%B3n-social-David-Sulmont.pdf.

Sussman, Nan. 2010. *Return Migration and Identity: A Global Phenomenon, a Hong Kong Case*. Hong Kong: University of Hong Kong Press.
Takenaka, Ayumi. 1997. "Towards Nikkeiism: Japanese (Nikkei)–Peruvian Migrants as a New Ethnic Minority." In *Beyond Boundaries: Selected Papers on Refugees and Immigrants*, edited by D. Baxter and R. Krulfeld, 5:82–98. Arlington, VT: American Anthropological Association.
———. 2009. "How Ethnic Minorities Experience Social Mobility in Japan: An Ethnographic Study of Peruvian Migrants." In *Social Class in Contemporary Japan*, edited by Hiroshi Ishida and David Slater, 221–238. London: Routledge.
———. 2014. "The Rise and Fall of Diasporic Bonds in Japanese-Peruvian 'Return' Migration." *International Migration* 52 (6): 100–112.
Takenaka, Ayumi, and Karen A. Pren. 2010. "Leaving to Get Ahead: Assessing the Relationship between Mobility and Inequality in Peruvian Migration." *Latin American Perspectives* 37 (5): 29–49.
Takenaka, Ayumi, Karsten Paerregaard, and Ulla Berg. 2010. "Peruvian Migration in a Global Context." *Latin American Perspectives* 37 (5): 3–11.
Tamagno, Carla. 2003. "'You Must Win Their Affection . . .': Migrants' Cultural and Social Practices between Peru and Italy." In *Work and Migration: Life and Livelihoods in a Globalizing World*, edited by Karen Fog Olwig and Ninna Nyberg Sorensen, 106–125. New York: Routledge.
Tapias, Maria. 2015. *Embodied Protests: Emotions and Women's Health in Bolivia*. Urbana: University of Illinois Press.
Teerling, Janine. 2011. "The Development of New 'Third-Cultural Spaces of Belonging': British-Born Cypriot 'Return' Migrants in Cyprus." *Journal of Ethnic and Migration Studies* 37 (7): 1079–1099.
Teo, Sin Yih. 2011. "'The Moon Back Home Is Brighter'? Return Migration and the Cultural Politics of Belonging." *Journal of Ethnic and Migration Studies* 37 (5): 805–820.
Theidon, Kimberly. 2013. *Intimate Enemies: Violence and Reconciliation in Peru*. Philadelphia: University of Pennsylvania Press.
Timberlake, Jeffrey, and Rhys H. Williams. 2012. "Stereotypes of U.S. Immigrants from Four Global Regions." *Social Science Quarterly* 93 (4): 867–889.
Torresan, Angela. 2007. "How Privileged Are They? Middle-Class Brazilian Immigrants in Lisbon." In *Going First Class? New Approaches to Privileged Travel and Movement*, edited by Vered Amit, 103–125. New York: Berghahn Books.
Tsuda, Takeyuki. 2003. *Strangers in the Ethnic Homeland: Japanese Brazilian Return Migration in Transnational Perspective*. New York: Columbia University Press.
Tummala-Narra, P. 2004. "Mothering in a Foreign Land." *American Journal of Psychoanalysis* 64 (2): 167–182.
Twine, France Winddance, and Bradley Gardener. 2013. *Geographies of Privilege*. New York: Routledge.
UNFPA. 2012. *Implicancias de la migración laboral femenina peruana en las mujeres migrantes y sus familias*. Lima: UNFPA, CISEPA.

Upadhya, Carol. 2013. "Return of the Global Indian: Software Professionals and the Worldling of Bangalore." In *Return: Nationalizing Transnational Mobility in Asia*, edited by Xiang Biao, Brenda Yeoh, and Mika Toyota, 141–161. Durham, NC: Duke University Press.

U.S. Census Bureau. 2011. "The Hispanic Population." http://www.census.gov/prod/cen2010/briefs/c2010br-04.pdf.

Valentine, G. 1999. "Eating In: Home, Consumption and Identity." *Sociological Review* 47:491–524.

Valentine, G., and T. Skelton. 2003. "Finding Oneself, Losing Oneself: The Lesbian and Gay 'Scene' as a Paradoxical Space." *International Journal of Urban and Regional Research* 27:849–866.

Valentino, N., T. Brader, and A. Jardina. 2013. "Immigration Opposition among US Whites: General Ethnocentrism or Media Priming of Attitudes about Latinos?" *Political Psychology* 34 (2): 149–166.

Vásquez del Aguila, Ernesto. 2012. "'God Forgives the Sin but Not the Scandal': Coming Out in a Transnational Context—between Sexual Freedom and Cultural Isolation." *Sexualities* 15 (2): 207–224.

———. 2015. *Being a Man in a Transnational World: The Masculinity and Sexuality of Migration*. New York: Routledge.

Veronis, Luisa. 2007. "Strategic Spatial Essentialism: Latin Americans' Real and Imagined Geographies of Belonging in Toronto." *Social & Cultural Geography* 8 (3): 455–473.

———. 2010. "Immigrant Participation in the Transnational Era: Latin Americans' Experiences with Collective Organising in Toronto." *International Migration and Integration* 11:173–192.

Vertovec, Steven. 2001. "Transnationalism and Identity." *Journal of Ethnic and Migration Studies* 27 (4): 573–582.

Vogel, Erika. 2014. "Predestined Migrations: Undocumented Peruvians in South Korean Churches." *City & Society* 26 (3): 331–351.

Wade, Peter. 1997. *Race and Ethnicity in Latin America*. London: Pluto Press.

Washington Blade. 2016. "Police Use Water Cannons against Peruvian LGBT activists." February 15, http://www.washingtonblade.com/2016/02/15/police-use-water-cannons-against-peruvian-lgbt-activists/.

Weismantel, Mary. 2001. *Cholas and Pishtacos: Stories of Race and Sex in the Andes*. Chicago: University of Chicago Press.

Werbner, Pnina. 1999. "Global Pathways: Working-Class Cosmopolitans and the Creation of Transnational Ethnic Worlds." *Social Anthropology* 7 (1): 17–35.

Wesely, Jennifer, and Emily Gaarder. 2004. "The Gendered 'Nature' of the Urban Outdoors: Women Negotiating Fear of Violence." *Gender & Society* 18 (5): 645–663.

Weston, Kath. 1998. "Get Thee to a Big City: Sexual Imaginary and the Great Gay Migration." *GLQ: A Journal of Lesbian and Gay Studies* 2 (3): 253–277.

Williams-Forson, Psyche. 2014. "'I Haven't Eaten If I Don't Have My Soup and Fufu': Cultural Preservation through Food and Foodways among Ghanaian Migrants in the United States." *Africa Today* 61 (1): 68–87.

Wolf, Eric. 1982. *Europe and the People without History*. Berkeley: University of California Press.
Wyman, Mark. 2005. "Emigrants Returning: The Evolution of a Tradition." In *Emigrant Homecomings: The Return Movement of Emigrants, 1600–2000*, edited by M. Harper. Manchester: Manchester University Press.
Yan, Miu Chung, Ching Man Lam, and Sean Lauer. 2015. "Return Migrant or Diaspora: An Exploratory Study of New-Generation Chinese-Canadian Youth Working in Hong Kong." *International Migration Review* 15:179–196.
Yepez del Castillo, Isabel, and Gioconda Herrera. 2007. *Nuevas migraciones latinoamericanas a Europa*. Quito: FLACSO.
Yuval-Davis, Nira. 1997. *Gender and Nation*. Thousand Oaks, CA: Sage.
———. 2006. "Intersectionality and Feminist Politics." *European Journal of Women's Studies* 13 (3): 193–209.
Zavella, Patricia. 2011. *I'm Neither Here nor There: Mexicans' Quotidian Struggles with Migration and Poverty*. Durham, NC: Duke University Press.
Zhang, Li. 2010. *In Search of Paradise: Middle-Class Living in a Chinese Metropolis*. Ithaca, NY: Cornell University Press.
Zong, Jie, and Jeanne Batalova. 2016. "South American Immigrants in the United States." Migration Policy Institute. 16 March, http://www.migrationpolicy.org/print/15574#.VyH5wtctY4o.

INDEX

Page numbers in italics refer to illustrations.

accent. *See* foreign language skills and accents
acculturation, 74
Acurio, Gastón, 145–146, 151–152, 183n6
Afro-Peruvians, 36, 38. *See also* racialization and racial hierarchies
Ahmed, Sara, 58–59
aji amarillo, 143–144, 181n2
ají de gallina, 142
Aldo (research participant), 43, 85, 94, 100, 148
Alicia (research participant), 34, 97–98, 111, 144, 165
Amalia (research participant), 129–130, 132–133, 139, 150
American Chica (Arana), 54
American Psychiatric Association (APA), 180n2
Amit, Vered, 6
Ana María (research participant): child-rearing and, 56–57; gender roles and, 68, 76, 80–81, 83–85, 90; racial hierarchies and, 56–57; security concerns and, 94–95
Anthias, Floya, 13
anthropology: middle- and upper-class migrants as focus of, 5; native anthropologists and, 14–15
antidiscrimination laws and ordinances, 37, 125–129, *126*
Anzaldúa, Gloria, 12, 173n3
apartheid, 35–36
Appiah, Kwame Anthony, 58

Arana, Marie, 40, 54
Argentina: gated communities in, 99; LGBTQ people in, 125; Peruvian migrants in, 18, 19, 22, 174n11, 175n13; same-sex unions in, 180n3
Arturo (research participant), 153, 163
Asia beaches, 53–54
asylum seekers, 73
autonomy: impact of migration on gender roles and, 68, 74–79, 80–85, 90, 108–109; professional opportunities for women as migrants and, 85–89, 90
Ayllón, Eva, 159

Babb, Florence, 149
Bachelet, Michelle, 178n13
Bárbara (research participant), 52, 111, 135
Barranco (Lima), 79
Bayly, Jaime, 122–123
Bell, C. Scott, 21
belonging: constructions and meanings of, 3–10, 17; cosmopolitanism and, 57–58, 67; intersectionality and, 171–172; LGBTQ Peruvians and, 119, 137, 139–141; vs. mobility, 6–10; multiculturalism and, 22; racial-gender-class hierarchies and, 35, 65–66, 171; return migration and, 27, 140, 166–167. *See also* exclusion and exclusionary cosmopolitanism; home
Berg, Ulla: on access to citizenship rights, 41, 107–108; on *cholos*, 64, 66; on domestic servants, 80; on security concerns, 93; on technology, 10

Berta (research participant), 111
bisexual Peruvians. See LGBTQ Peruvians
Boehm, Deborah, 75
Boesten, Jelke, 37, 113, 114
Bonnerjee, Jayani, 9, 22
Brah, Avtar, 4
Brain, Kelsey, 144
Bravo, Christian, 145–146
Brazil, 24, 99, 125, 173n4, 175n14, 180n3
Bruce, Carlos, 123
Bueno-Hansen, Pascha, 37, 114

Cabanillas, Mercedes, 121
Cacho, Lisa Marie, 141
Cadena, Marisol de la, 168
cafés, as research sites, 14, 27–29, 47, 68, 133, 163
Canada: eldercare workers in, 80; immigration and, 21, 22–23; multiculturalism in, 20, 22, 62–63, 130. See also transnational Peruvians in Toronto, Canada
Canépa, Gisela, 147
career and professional life, 85–89, 90
carework, 80
Carlos (research participant), 56
catcalls. See street harassment
"Catcall your mother" (campaign ad), 109
Catholicism and Catholic Church, 73–74, 122, 137–138
Catia (research participant), 154
causa rellena, 142, 161
ceviche, 142, 147, 156–157, 157–158, 160, 161–162
Chabela (research participant), 1, 91, 101–102, 145, 165
Chaudhuri, Mayurakshi, 13
children: domestic servants and, 81–83; racial hierarchies and, 56–57; return migration and, 72, 81–82; security concerns and, 91–92, 95–96, 99–106, 115–116
Chile: migration to Canada and, 22; Peruvian food in, 153; Peruvian migrants in, 18, 19, 130, 131, 174n11, 175n13; same-sex unions in, 180n3
China, 176n4
Choleando (documentary), 38
cholification, 62
cholos, 1–2, 62–64, 66, 167
Chullo (Inca Kola commercial), 149
Cipriani, Juan Luis, 122, 138

citizenship, 57–58, 139–141, 147–150. See also dual citizenship
civil unions, 123
class and class hierarchies: belonging and, 65–66; exclusion and, 6, 171; exclusionary cosmopolitanism and, 166–169; homophobia and, 125; impact on international migrants of, 15–18, 42–43; internal migration and, 17; Peruvian food and, 146; power and, 5–6, 17–18; prejudices and, 50–54; short-term return visits and, 43, 44, 50, 59, 84–85, 107–108, 113, 170
Clínica Anglo-Americana (Lima), 127
Club Regatas (Lima), 29–30, 82, 108
Coca-Cola, 148–149
Cocinero en su tinta (Rodríguez), 163
Collins, Patricia Hill, 12
Colombia, 24, 125, 175n14, 180n3
coloniality of power, 168
El Comercio (newspaper), 37–38, 145, 163, 180n7
"Con mis hijos no te metas" campaign, 122
Contreras, Ricardo, 74–75
corruption, 93–94
cosmopolitanism, 57–59, 61. See also exclusion and exclusionary cosmopolitanism
Crenshaw, Kimberlé, 12
Cuba, 24
Cuevas, Elder, 147
cultural food colonialism, 181–182n5

danger, perceptions of, 92–95, 98–99, 105–107
Dario (research participant), 48, 51–52
Davíd (research participant), 104, 131, 139
Davis, Kathy, 7, 50
Decena, Carlos Ulises, 131
Delfín, Victor, 126, 127
Delgado, Jesus, 151
De ollas y sueños (documentary), 146, 151, 163
Dinzey-Flores, Zaire Zenit, 99
discrimination: antidiscrimination laws and ordinances, 37, 125–129, 126; *cholos* and, 62–64, 66; domestic servants and, 53–54, 55, 169–170; foreign language skills and accents, 49–50, 86, 177n7; intersectionality and, 13–14; Latinos and, 20, 21, 43–44, 167, 170, 172; LGBTQ

people and, 123–129, 140–141; racial-gender-class hierarchies and, 6; women and, 37–38, 53–54
domestic servants: discrimination and, 53–54, 55, 169–170; middle- and upper-class family dynamics in Peru and, 68–70, 75–77, 79–80, 81–85; migrants as, 80; return migrants and, 69–70; sexual harassment and, 113; as status marker, 79–80
Dominican Republic, 131
Dreby, Joanna, 74
dual citizenship, 10, 73, 95–96, 141

Ecuador, 175n14, 180n3
Eduarda (research participant), 134–135
Egypt, 120
El Salvador, 22
emotions and emotional attachments, 4, 9–10, 11
Empleada Audaz (Audacious Maid) campaign, 53–54
Encuentro de Liderazgos Políticos LGBTI de América Latina y El Caribe (Meeting of LGBTI Political Leadership of Latin America and the Caribbean), 124
Encuentro Feminista Latinoamericano y del Caribe (Feminist Latin American and Caribbean Meeting), 124
entrepeneurship, 84–85, 147–149. *See also* career and professional life
Eugenia (research participant), 78, 85
Everlast, 109
exclusion and exclusionary cosmopolitanism: definition and concept of, 57–59, 166–168; food and, 143, 181–182n5; homophobia and, 119; intersectionality and, 13–14; power and, 171–172; racial-gender-class hierarchies and, 6, 56–57, 59–67, 166–169; return migration and, 169–170. *See also* discrimination
exclusionary incorporation, 119, 140
exoticization: Peruvian food and, 146, 150–152, 157–158, 159–163; transnational Peruvians and, 25, 45–46, 54

Facebook, 8, 10, 136
family: homophobia and discrimination in, 122–123, 129–130, 132–137; middle- and upper-class family dynamics in Peru and, 68–70, 75–80; return migration and, 1, 72–73, 78–79. *See also* domestic servants; gender roles; short-term return visits
Farahani, Fataneh, 48
fear. *See* danger, perceptions of
Federico (research participant), 49–50
Ferguson, Priscilla Parkhurst, 156
Fernando (research participant): accent and, 50; gender roles and, 76–77; on multi-culturalism, 62; professional opportunities and, 89; security concerns and, 100, 104–105, 113
food. *See* Peruvian food
foreign language skills and accents, 8, 49–50, 86, 177n7
Fouron, Georges, 177n8
France, 80, 132
Francke, Marfil, 12
friendships, 39, 59–61, 65–66
Fujimori presidency (1990–2000), 23–24, 119–120
Fuller, Norma, 179n2

Gabriela (research participant), 62–64, 66
Galarza, Francisco, 37–38
Gandolfo, Daniella, 92, 107, 110–111, 112–113
Garcia, Maria Elena, 146, 151
García presidency (1985–1990), 23
gated communities, 29, 96, 98–99, 105–106
gender hierarchies: belonging and, 65–66; exclusion and, 166–169, 171; Peruvian food and, 146; power and, 17–18. *See also* women
gender roles, 7–8, 68, 74–79, 80–85, 90, 108–109. *See also* women
gente decente (decent people), 16–17, 107. *See also* class and class hierarchies
gente del pueblo (village people), 16–17
Germany: crime rates in Munich and, 93; exclusionary incorporation in, 119; homophobia in, 120; *Kindergeld* (allowance for children) in, 179n4; migrants in, 24; Peruvian restaurants in, 157–163, 157–158. *See also* transnational Peruvians in Germany
Ghana, 143
Giuffre, Patti, 182–183n6
Glick-Schiller, Nina, 58–59

Gmelch, George, 10–11
Golash-Boza, Tanya, 38
González Cruz, Rodolfo, 122
Greene, Shane, 62
Griffith, David, 74–75
Gruner-Domic, Sandra, 58, 65
Guardian (newspaper), 180n7
Guatemala, 22
Gutsche, Astrid, 183n6
Guyana, 175n14

Harris, Deborah, 182–183n6
Hartman, Todd, 21
Heldke, Lisa, 181–182n5
Hernán (research participant), 63–64, 66, 67, 94
heteronormativity, 118–123. *See also* gender roles; homophobia
Hiebert, Daniel, 58, 61
Hilda (research participant), 102–103
home: constructions and meanings of, 4–5, 9–10; food and, 142–145, 157; romanticized visions of, 11; short-term return visits and, 14, 89. *See also* return migration
homonegativity, 137–139
homophobia: citizenship and, 139–141; intersectionality and, 13–14; migrant communities and, 129–132, 139; in Peru, 119–129, 140–141; resistance to, 123–128, 126; return migration and, 118, 132–139, 140–141
homosexuality. *See* LGBTQ Peruvians
hooks, bell, 12
household chores. *See* domestic servants; gender roles
Household Workers' Labor Union of the Lima Region (SINTTRAHOL), 113, 184n1

illegality. *See* undocumented migrants
Inca Kola, 143–144, 148–149
India, 79–80, 110, 116–117
indigenous populations, internal migration and, 18, 35, 39–42, 177n7
insecurity. *See* security concerns
insider/outsider binaries, 4
internal migration: in China, 176n4; in Peru, 17, 18, 35, 39–42, 177n7
international migration, 18–19, 39–40, 70–71. *See also* transnational Peruvians

intersectionality, 12–13, 19–21, 171–172
interviews, 14–15, 26, 27–30, 142
Inti Raymi festival, 25, 154–156, *155*, *158*
Irving, Andrew, 58
Italy, 18, 19, 80, 175n13
Iván (research participant), 46–48, 53, 55, 60–61
Izquierdo, Teresa, 182–183n6

Jamaica, 85
Japan, 18, 19, 173n4, 174n11
Jerolmack, Colin, 29
Jimena (research participant), 114–115
Jordan, María José, 183n6
Juan (research participant), 49
Julián (research participant), 53, 86, 87–89, 94

Kanai, J. Miguel, 125
Kant, Immanuel, 57–58
Kaufman, Rebecca, 138
Khan, Shamus Rahman, 29, 59, 139
kidnappings, 96, 101, 102–103, 104–106, 127–128
King, Richard, 177n5
The Kiss (Delfín), 126, 127
"Kisses against Homophobia" demonstration, 123–124
Kogan, Liuba, 5, 37–38
Kuczynski, Pedro Pablo, 113–114

La Molina (Lima), 40, 96–97, 98, 168
language barriers, 49–50, 86, 177n7
Latino masculinities, 12–13, 46–47, 175–176n18
Latinos: discrimination and stereotyping of, 20, 21, 43–44, 167, 170, 172, 177n7; food and, 143; transnational Peruvians identified as, 43–48, 54, 167, 170; as undocumented migrants, 141; use of term, 21
Laurier, Eric, 168
Law of Incentive to Return Migration (2013), 19
LGBTQ Peruvians: activism and, 123–128, 126; belonging and, 119, 137, 139–141; discrimination and, 123–129, 140–141; political violence and, 119–120. *See also* homophobia
Liliana (research participant), 51, 77–78, 79, 85, 87

Lima: Club Regatas in, 29–30, 82, 108; crime and security concerns in, 93, 96–97, 99, 104; exclusionary cosmopolitanism in, 168; gastronomic boom in, 146–147, 152; homophobia and resistance to homophobia in, 118–119, 121–123, 124–129, 126–127, 139, 140–141; internal migration and, 40–41; Markham College in, 104; Mistura food festival in, 157–158. *See also* return migration
lomo saltado, 142, 160
longitudinal research, 26
Lucy (research participant), 45–47, 54, 67, 135–136

Mahler, Sarah, 13
Málaga, Natalia, 109
Manolo (research participant): class and racial hierarchies and, 53, 55, 59–60, 170; security concerns and, 92–93, 95–96, 99
Marca Perú, 145–146, 147–148, 152, 163
Marco (research participant): class and racial hierarchies and, 1, 55–56; identification as Latino of, 167–168; security concerns and, 91, 101–102, 109
María (research participant), 111, 154, 156–159
María José (research participant), 45, 73–74, 106–107
Marina (research participant): homophobia and, 133; Peruvian food and, 150; racial hierarchies and, 34, 44–45, 64, 67; security concerns and, 111–112
Marisela (research participant), 143–144
Markham College (Lima), 104
Martínez, Virgilio, 152, 182n6
masculinity, 74, 146
Mexican American studies, 172
Mexico and Mexican migrants, 21–22, 74–75, 125. *See also* Latinos
MHOL (Movimiento Homosexual de Lima), 124–125, 135
middle class, definition of, 16–17. *See also* class and class hierarchies
migrant associations, 24–25, 39
Miraflores (Lima): as middle- and upper-class neighborhood, 40, 118, 133, 168; Park of Love in, 126–127, 127, 139–140; security concerns in, 94, 97, 110, 112–113

Mistura food festival, 157–158
mobility: vs. belonging, 6–10. *See also* return migration; transnational Peruvians
Mohanty, Chandra Talpade, 176n1
Moore, Henrietta, 141
Moraga, Cherríe, 12
Movimiento Homosexual de Lima (MHOL), 124–125, 135
Movimiento Misionero Mundial (Global Missionary Movement), 122
Movimiento Revolucionario Túpac Amaru (MRTA), 37, 120, 175n16
multiculturalism, 20, 22–23, 62–63, 130
multi-sited fieldwork, 26
Muñoz, Braulio, 62
Muñoz-Laboy, Miguel, 138

Namibia, 120
National Citizen Security System, 93–94
nation-branding projects, 142–143, 145–151, 160
native anthropologists, 14–15
Nazi Germany, 120
Nencel, Lorraine, 7, 50
Newman, Benjamin, 21
newspaper delivery, 16, 88
newspapers. *See El Comercio* (newspaper); *La República* (newspaper)
"Ni una menos" (march), 113–114
No se lo digas a nadie (Bayly), 122–123
nostalgia, 8, 11–12, 142–145, 157, 164
NoTengoMiedo (IAmNotAfraid) campaign, 128

Ocampo, Anthony, 134
Olivia (research participant), 49, 79, 112, 134, 169
Olwig, Karen Fog, 15
online survey: on food, 142, 144–145; on homophobia, 121, 136; participants in, 26–27, 177n10; on return migration, 71–72
Opus Dei, 122
Osterling, Rafael, 152
othering, 26, 176n1. *See also* exoticization

Paerregaard, Karsten, 19, 75, 153
papas a la huancaína, 142, 147, 156, 162
parenting. *See* children
Park of Love (Lima), 126–127, 127, 139

participant observation, 26, 27–30
Partridge, Damani, 119
Patil, Vrushali, 13
Patricia (research participant), 50–51
Paulson, Susan, 149
people of color, 55. *See also* Afro-Peruvians; indigenous populations
"Perpetual Peace" (Kant), 57–58
Peru: class hierarchies in, 16–17; homophobia in, 119–129, 140–141; internal migration and, 18; internal migration in, 17, 18, 35, 39–42, 177n7; international migration and, 17–18, 39–40, 70–71; political violence in, 23–24, 92, 100–101, 130; racism in, 168–169, 171; *seguridad ciudadana* in, 93–94, 94; sexual violence in, 109–110, 113–114
Peru, Nebraska (Marca Perú spot), 145–146, 147–148, 163
Peruanos en el Extranjero (Facebook page), 8
Peruvian food: exclusionary cosmopolitanism and, 143, 181–182n5; gastronomic boom and, 142–143, 145–153; middle- and upper-class status and/social hierarchies and, 142–143; Peruvianness and, 8–9, 143, 145–151, 157–158, 163–164, 165–166; restaurants and, 156–163, 157–158; as source of comfort and nostalgia, 142–145, 157, 164
Peruvian Gastronomy Society (Apega), 146–147
Peruvianness: constructions and meanings of, 4–5, 7–8; food and, 8–9, 143, 145–151, 156–157, 163–164, 165–166
The Peruvian Notebooks (Muñoz), 62
Phadke, Shilpa, 110, 116–117
Philippines, 143
Philo, Chris, 168
Piero (research participant), 94, 103–104, 105
Pizarro, Claudio, 159
political violence, 23–24, 92, 100–101, 130. *See also* Shining Path (Sendero Luminoso)
Pontifical Catholic University, 122
positionality. *See* research methods
power: cosmopolitanism and, 58–59; intersectionality and, 12–15; nation-branding projects and, 147; racial-gender-class hierarchies and, 3, 5–6, 9, 17–18, 65–67, 166–172; research methods and, 26–30. *See also* autonomy; class and class hierarchies; racialization and racial hierarchies
Pren, Karen, 108
Pride Parade, 124
privilege, 59, 166–172. *See also* class and class hierarchies; power
Probyn, Elspeth, 9
public transportation: in Germany, 96; law on street sexual harassment and, 109–110; return migrants and, 92, 93, 99, 101–102, 107, 112, 117
Puerto Rico, 99

Quechua (language), 177n7
Quijano, Aníbal, 168

racialization and racial hierarchies: belonging and, 35, 65–66, 171; children and, 56–57; *cholos* and, 1–2, 62–64, 66, 167; exclusion and, 171; exclusionary cosmopolitanism and, 56–57, 59–67, 166–169; impact on international migrants of, 35, 42–48, 54–56; indigenous internal migrants and, 35, 39–42; as part of everyday life in Peru, 34, 35–38; power and, 17–18; regionalization of race and, 36–37, 51–52; return migrants and, 1; short-term return visits and, 34, 52–53, 55, 61. *See also cholos*
refugees, 73
religion. *See* Catholicism and Catholic Church
remittances, 10, 19, 75, 174n11, 176b2
La República (newspaper), 114, 178n17, 184n1
research methods: cafés as research sites and, 14, 27–29, 47, 68, 133, 163; interviews and, 14–15, 26, 27–30, 142; online survey and, 26–27, 71–72, 121, 136, 142, 144–145, 177n10; participant observation and, 26, 27–30; power and, 26–30
restaurants: Peruvian food and, 156–163, 157–158; as research sites, 14. *See also* cafés, as research sites
return migration: belonging and, 27, 140, 166–167; domestic servants and, 69–70;

exclusionary cosmopolitanism and, 169–170; family and, 1, 78–79; fluidity of migration and, 89–90; homophobia and, 118, 132–139, 140–141; intersectionality and, 13–14; Law of Incentive to Return Migration and, 19; middle- and upper-class family dynamics in Peru and, 78–79; Peruvian food and, 145, 150; professional opportunities for women and, 86–87; racial hierarchies and, 1; reasons for, 71–73; scholarship on, 70–71; security concerns and, 91–92, 101–103, 106–109, 115–116, 169; street and sexual harassment and, 169; trajectories and experience of, 10–12. *See also* short-term return visits

Reygada, Luis, 36
Risas y salsas (television show), 36
Rodrigo (research participant), 137–139
Rodríguez, Gustavo, 163
Ronaldo (research participant), 118, 125, 128–129, 134, 136–137, 141
Rottenbacher de Rojas, Jan Marc, 98–99
RPP Noticias, 180n7
Rumbaut, Ruben, 43

Sabogal, Elena, 88
safety. *See* security concerns
Said, Edward, 176n1
same-sex unions and marriage, 123, 138
Sandra (research participant), 78–79, 80–82
San Isidro (Lima), 40, 81, 97, 168
Sara (research participant), 87
Schiaffino, Pedro Miguel, 146, 152
security concerns: children and, 91–92, 95–96, 99–106, 115–116; middle- and upper-class neighborhoods and, 97–99; perceptions of danger and, 92–95, 98–99, 105–107; return migration and, 72–73, 91–92, 101–103, 106–109, 115–116, 169; street and sexual harassment and, 108–115, 116–117, 169
seguridad ciudadana (citizen security), 93–94, 94
Sendero Luminoso (Shining Path), 23–24, 37, 114, 119–120
serenazgo (municipal security officer), 126–128
Severson, Nicolette, 138
sexual harassment and sexual violence, 108–115, 116–117, 127–128, 169, 175n17
sexuality and sexual identities, 73–74. *See also* LGBTQ Peruvians
Shining Path (Sendero Luminoso), 23–24, 37, 114, 119–120
short-term return visits: class hierarchies and, 43, 44, 50, 59, 84–85, 107–108, 113, 170; extended family and, 116; fluidity of migration and, 10, 11; homophobia and, 130–131, 132, 170; racial hierarchies and, 34, 52–53, 55, 61; research participants and, 61; security concerns and, 72, 92–93, 94, 95–96, 99–100, 106–107, 111, 116; sense of home and, 14, 89
Skeldon, Robert, 177n5
Skornia, Anna Katharina, 107
social capital, 52–53, 134
social hierarchies. *See* class and class hierarchies
social media, 10, 14, 71, 89, 108, 115–116. *See also* Facebook; YouTube
South Africa, 35–36
Spain: homophobia in, 120; Peruvian food in, 153; Peruvian migrants in, 18, 19, 20, 174n11, 175n13
Spanish (language), 8. *See also* foreign language skills and accents
Spivak, Gayatri Chakravorty, 176n1
street harassment, 108–115, 116–117, 169
Surco: discrimination in, 128; as middle- and upper-class neighborhood, 40, 97; return migrants in, 1, 91, 102, 145

Takenaka, Ayumi, 108, 183n8
Tania (research participant), 86–87
Tapias, Maria, 10
Tatiana (research participant): gender roles and, 80–81, 82–83, 85; racial hierarchies and, 52–53; security concerns and, 103, 105
technology, 10. *See also* social media
television shows, 36
Teresa (research participant), 132–133
Theidon, Kimberly, 114
Toledo, Alejandro, 62
Toronto, Canada: crime rates and, 93. *See also* transnational Peruvians in Toronto, Canada

214 INDEX

Torresan, Angela, 15
transnational Peruvians: common themes in, 1–6; exclusionary cosmopolitanism and, 59–67; identification as Latino of, 43–48, 54, 167, 170, 177n7; on internal migration, 41–42; popular destinations of, 18, 19–20; on racism in Peru, 34, 51–56, 63–64, 66. *See also* research methods; return migration
transnational Peruvians in Germany: barriers to professional integration and, 86, 87; class hierarchies and, 59–60; discrimination and, 48–49; gender roles and family dynamics and, 77–78; intersectionality and, 19–21; Inti Raymi festival and, 25, 154–156, 155, 158; Peruvian cultural associations in, 24–26; Peruvian food and, 154–162, 157–158; racial hierarchies and, 55, 59–60; security concerns and, 92–93, 95–96, 99, 112
transnational Peruvians in the United States: class hierarchies and, 16, 42, 60; foreign language skills and accents and, 49–50; gender roles and family dynamics and, 82–83; homophobia and, 134; identification as Latino of, 43–48; intersectionality and, 19–21; Peruvian food and, 143–144; professional opportunities for, 88; racial hierarchies and, 55–56; remittances and, 174n11; security concerns and, 103, 105
transnational Peruvians in Toronto, Canada: *cholos* and, 62–64; class hierarchies and, 16, 60; discrimination and, 50; gender roles and family dynamics and, 83–85; homophobia and, 129–132, 139; intersectionality and, 19–21; Peruvian food and, 144, 148, 150, 153, 163, 165; professional opportunities for, 87–89; security concerns and, 94–95, 97–98, 100, 103–105, 113; weather and, 129–130
transportation. *See* public transportation
trenzas de dominación, 12
Truth and Reconciliation Commission, 37, 114, 120, 175n17
Tsuda, Takeyuki, 173n4

Turkey and Turkish migrants, 24, 25, 49

Uganda, 120
undocumented migrants, 21–22, 73, 141
United States: crime rates in, 93; eldercare workers in, 80; Latinos in, 12–13, 20, 21, 43–44, 141, 143; Mexican American studies in, 172; migrants in, 18, 21–22; Peruvian food in, 151–152; Peruvian migrants in, 175n13–14; racism in, 171; women in culinary industry in, 182n6
Upadhya, Carol, 11
upper class. *See* class and class hierarchies
Uruguay, 22, 180n3

Vásquez del Aguila, Ernesto, 125, 130
Velasco presidency (1968–1975), 23
violence. *See* political violence; sexual harassment and sexual violence; street harassment

Weismantel, Mary, 36
Werbner, Pnina, 58
women: access to education and labor markets and, 73–74; acculturation and, 74; discrimination and, 37–38, 53–54; as domestic servants, 53–54, 69, 79–80, 169–170; homophobia and, 124; impact of migration on gender roles and, 68, 74–79, 80–85, 90, 108–109; impact of migration on professional lives of, 85–89, 90; middle- and upper-class family dynamics in Peru and, 68–70, 75–79, 81–83, 90; Peruvian cuisine and, 182–183n6; racialization and, 37; sexuality and, 73–74; street and sexual harassment and, 108–115, 116–117, 169
World Health Organization (WHO), 180n2

Yamada, Gustavo, 37–38
You Know You Are Peruvian When (video), 7–8
YouTube, 7–8, 109

Zavella, Patricia, 173n2

M. CRISTINA ALCALDE is an associate professor of gender and women's studies at the University of Kentucky. She is the author of *The Woman in the Violence: Gender, Poverty, and Resistance in Peru*.

The University of Illinois Press
is a founding member of the
Association of American University Presses.

University of Illinois Press
1325 South Oak Street
Champaign, IL 61820-6903
www.press.uillinois.edu